marketing campaigns for both Undergraduate and Masters programmes. With specialist expertise in assistive technologies, she is co-ordinator for Supporting Learners with Specific Learning Difficulties (SpLD) across the Business School.

PROFESSIONAL AND BUSINESS COMMUNICATION

Personal Strategies for the Post-Digital World

Third Edition

Peter Hartley
Helena Knapton
Susie Marriott

LONDON AND NEW YORK

Designed cover image: metamorworks

Third edition published 2023
by Routledge
4 Park Square, Milton Park, Abingdon, Oxon, OX14 4RN

and by Routledge
605 Third Avenue, New York, NY 10158

Routledge is an imprint of the Taylor & Francis Group, an informa business

First edition published by Routledge 2001
Second edition published by Routledge 2015

British Library Cataloguing-in-Publication Data
A catalogue record for this book is available from the British Library

ISBN: 978-1-032-28586-3 (hbk)
ISBN: 978-1-032-26800-2 (pbk)
ISBN: 978-1-003-29755-0 (ebk)

DOI: 10.4324/9781003297550

Typeset in Perpetua
by Deanta Global Publishing Services, Chennai, India

Access the Support Material: www.routledge.co.uk/9781032268002

CONTENTS

Contents

ACKNOWLEDGMENTS

Thanks to previous co-authors: Clive Bruckmann (first edition) and Peter Chatterton (2nd edition). Clive sadly passed away before the second edition was planned; we wish Peter well in his retirement and look forward to his memoirs.

Thanks to Dawne Irving-Bell for assembling the current team. And thanks to all her colleagues in the Centre for Learning and Teaching at Edge Hill University for their support and expertise over the years.

Thanks to all the staff at Routledge for their support, expertise, and patience.

Thanks to all our former and current colleagues and students, too numerous to mention, who have inspired us and asked all the awkward questions which we have tried to answer in this book.

This book is dedicated to the next generations of future communicators: especially Jasmine, Jenson, Jackson, Eddie, Alexander, Gregor, Phoebe, Finlay, and Sophia.

INTRODUCTION

Introduction

Communication is complex and always affected by the social context so we *cannot* offer a definitive approach which will always work (beware any books or courses which do offer this!). We can offer you approaches and techniques which have been shown to increase your chances of success.

Throughout this book, we invite you to apply our ideas to your own situation. An obvious exercise here is to consider how many of the principles we offer apply to your organisation, and to what extent. For example, what evidence do you have that your senior management are committed to fostering communication? If not, then what effect does this have on the rest of the organisation?

We analyse how people communicate within business and professional organisations and how this communication is changing.

This book aims to help you reflect upon and improve the way you communicate in professional and business settings.

We are confident it will help if you identify with at least one of the following descriptions.

Are you:

- an undergraduate or postgraduate student aiming for a career in business or a professional context?
- an undergraduate or postgraduate student with ambitions to work for yourself and/or assemble a portfolio career?
- working in an organisation in the early stages of your career?
- someone who has been working in organisations for some years and wants to refresh your ideas on "good communication"?
- managing a team in an organisation?
- wondering how new technology is reshaping communication in organisations like yours and thinking about how you need to respond?

DOI: 10.4324/9781003297550-1

We have also developed a website to give you:

- updated comments and suggestions for each chapter.
- further links and sources.

Technology is changing so fast that no book can be completely up-to-date.

Make sure you check the website when you are following up specific ideas.

Do we need another book on professional and business communication?

Yes.

For six reasons:

1 The legacy of the pandemic.

As well as the devastation and personal loss many of us experienced, the pandemic forced us *all* to change our professional and working practices. The long-term effects of these changes are not yet clear. We identify significant changes and discuss developments which have yet to be fully resolved. For example, many organisations have now embraced virtual or hybrid working and abandoned traditional offices; others have insisted that their staff return to the workplace; others have moved to flexible arrangements with different degrees of staff choice (see Chapter 5).

2 Ever-increasing pace of change.

Even before the pandemic forced "overnight change", we experienced increasing pace of change in the social and economic climate and in the use of computer technology. Analysing detailed economic changes is beyond the scope of this book but we highlight relevant aspects of the general economic/social context – this obviously influences organisational communication.

3 Further development of new computer technology.

We emphasise the potential of new technology. As this book was going through final editing and production, we saw major developments in applications supported by artificial intelligence (AI), *including* the main office software we all use everyday (see the website for updates). Other claims regarding a new phase of computer applications – "the Metaverse" – mean that we must *all* develop a more sophisticated understanding of computer technology and its applications.

There are also significant differences in different parts of the world. For example, which country is widely acknowledged as the 'world leader in high-tech mobile money'? See our answer on the website.

4 The need to review and revise basic principles.

You can find fundamental principles in virtually every textbook on communication – but do these need refining or updating in the light of new technology?

For example, how do you define an "audience"? Nowadays anything you say in public or at a meeting could be on the internet in a matter of minutes thanks to social media and smartphones. You have always had to assume that you are talking to multiple audiences, as there will be sub-groups in any audience, but now you also have to consider that some of these will not even be in the room.

As speaker or workshop leader, this gives you both challenges and opportunities. For example, you can use the "back-channel" or chat function to increase dialogue between presenter and audience. Only a few years ago, many organisations invested in special handsets – "clickers" – so that the audience could respond to questions and see results onscreen. Now you only need software available to anyone with a suitable laptop, tablet, or smartphone.

5 Information and communication overload.

The notion of information overload is not new but the growth of new communication channels has made this problem much more serious. How can we manage this, both for ourselves and for the people we work with?

6 Online media are not the "answer to everything".

We did consider moving this text to online media. In the end, we decided on a combination of book plus online support. This combination offers some advantages in terms of flexibility and access, although we may not be able to say that with quite the same conviction in a few years.

Our aims

We offer you suggestions and techniques to improve the way you communicate.

Communication is complex and always affected by the social context so we *cannot* offer a definitive approach which will always work (beware any books or courses which do offer this!). We can offer you approaches and techniques which have been shown to increase your chances of success.

We analyse how people communicate within business and professional organisations and how this communication is changing. Previous editions of this book had a sharper focus on commercial 'business' organisations – we have broadened the scope of this book for a couple of reasons:

- our main ideas and principles apply equally to non-commercial and voluntary sectors, and to small, medium and large enterprises (SMEs).
- organisations have tended to converge in the way they operate, especially when it comes to new technology. For example, Microsoft 365 is now used by corporations and businesses of all types and sizes, by educational institutions at all levels (all staff and students), and by individual professionals.

We focus on communication by individuals and groups within and across the organisation and do not say much about external communication (advertising, public relations etc.). But all the principles we discuss can be applied to both internal and external communication. For example:

- we emphasise the importance of understanding how different audiences may have very different perspectives on the same message.
- we highlight the importance of plain/clear language.
- we underline the significance of careful planning and a clear strategy in formal communication.

Why do we need to 'rethink' communication?

The world has changed dramatically since the last version of this book (Hartley and Chatterton, 2015). Apart from unforeseen catastrophes such as the pandemic, the global economic crisis, and the war in Ukraine, advances in technology have brought fundamental changes in the ways we live and work.

Consider the following headlines – all paraphrased from radio and news broadcasts over a couple of days in late 2022. None of these would have made immediate sense to readers of our previous editions:

- Facebook and the true meaning of "meta".
- Cryptocurrency firm going green.
- Nano ink solar cells allow tech to charge in any light.
- Smart glasses allow deaf people to "see" conversations with subtitles.
- Meet the metaverse: creating real value in a virtual world.

All these stories have important implications for business and professional communication and activity. How many did you recognise? See the website for further details.

Among the most important trends are:

Developments in computing power and applications

Developments in areas like machine learning and artificial intelligence (AI) mean that we can no longer regard computers just as "fast number crunchers" or just as devices to support ever-expanding communication networks. They are developing new capacities and potential with implications for all of us, as illustrated by the recent book which explains 'how computers have become creative writers' (Sharples and Pérez y Pérez, 2022)

The continuing growth of mobile computing

Industrial experts in 2012 forecasted that internet traffic would "grow four-fold over the next four years" fuelled by the growth of mobile computing. This rate of growth has accelerated – see the statistics in Chapter 5.

The rise of social media

Many organisations now take social media very seriously as they recognise opportunities for new relationships with their customers and their staff. For example, consider recent trends in television advertising, especially around major holidays – the focus is no longer to sell products but to persuade the audience to go to the relevant website where the "real" promotion of the product is located.

Growing sales of televisions with built-in internet forces further changes. This is an example of the 'internet of things' – internet connections are built into devices to enable data communications and new facilities. And we now have the "internet of bodies" promoted as a major growth area for the next decade (see Chapter 5).

The growth of social media has also seen a corresponding growth in people's willingness to share much of their lives online. Does this mean that we have to modify our approach to personal relationships?

But not everything has changed

While we have experienced dramatic change, we must also remember important principles which have *not* changed. We can explain this by revisiting two examples from our first edition in 2000:

- in a business speech, Gerald Ratner described some of his company's cheaper jewellery products as "crap", suggesting that others would not last as long as a supermarket sandwich. He did not anticipate reports in the national press the following day. The immediate effect on sales was actually *positive* – customers looked for cheap bargains – but the publicity created an image which the company could not counteract when the economy dipped. People did not

want to buy from a store with a reputation for "cheap rubbish". Sales slumped and the company never recovered.
the irony was that Ratner had used these remarks before in speeches, *and* been quoted in the financial press. But this time his comments made the front pages of popular newspapers. As he later reflected: "Because of one ill-judged joke, 25,000 people lost their jobs" (quoted in Tibballs, 1999, page 192).
in the next few years, the phrase "'doing a Ratner" became a popular description of a senior executive making ill-judged comments with damaging consequences. Ratner did manage to "rise again" through a new company – you can find him on YouTube discussing his experience.

- the British railway company claimed that many trains were having trouble with the "type of snow" falling at the time (1991). This was technically true – weather conditions were very unusual. But this became a newspaper headline – "British Rail blames the wrong type of snow". This phrase stuck in the media and public consciousness. The company should have realised that this sort of explanation would not be taken seriously by a public already critical of the railways' poor punctuality and reliability.
Moving onto the present day – this phrase is still used and recognised in the UK as the classic example of a lame excuse.

These examples show the long-lasting impact of careless communication. They still work as examples of important communication problems. And they illustrate important principles which are independent of technological change, for example:

- if your message can be captured or summarised in a memorable phrase. This may "stick" for a very long time.
- messages are simplified and generalised as they are passed on. Ratner made his "crap" comment about *one* of his brands but *all* his brands suffered the same fate by association.
- messages are always interpreted in context, as illustrated by the changing reactions to Ratner's description and the general dismissal of the "wrong snow" explanation.

If these events happened today, the overall impact and damage to reputation would be similarly memorable. But it would happen much quicker – initially through social media. Ratner's quotes and messages would be on the internet while he was talking, never mind the next day. And he would not have been able to repeat his remarks and go unnoticed. The same would happen with the railway example. We would doubtless be able to enjoy online videos of both Ratner and the railway spokesperson as they unwittingly placed foot in mouth.

Recent examples illustrate the power and speed of new media. In his book and TED talk, Jon Ronson provides case studies of individuals who sent (what they thought were) private messages which were shared and went viral. Their messages were widely condemned for their insensitivity, resulting in loss of jobs, careers, and personal reputation, most of which could not be "rescued" (Ronson, 2015). A recent example was widely publicised as we were revising this chapter: after a TV interview described as "robust", the presenter used a swear word to describe the politician in an "off-air remark". This clip appeared on YouTube and the presenter was suspended (Youngs, 2022).

We said in previous editions that the boundaries between internal and external communication are sometimes difficult to draw. This is even more complex today. For example, we have all taught in higher education institutions for many years. We are now very conscious that *anything* we say and/or do in the classroom could be available for public inspection at any time, thanks to the mobile phone. We know examples of serious misuse, including some staff being bullied online by students. While new media offer major advantages, they also offer new opportunities for negative and abusive behaviour.

We also said in 2000 that the most important external communicators in any company are the employees, as they determine the company image in their interactions with customers. This is still true.

We are *not* concentrating on "corporate communication", where managers take responsibility for strategic planning, managing company identity, and public relations. This perspective tends to concentrate on communications management. We shall refer to these issues but we are concentrating on communication as a process in which *all* employees participate.

Communication working well?

If good communication is important and can offer tangible benefits, then why can we find so many examples where it does not seem to work effectively? Why do so many organisations seem to ignore longstanding research into leading companies with reputations for effective communication?

Back in 2000, we found research consistently highlighting factors listed below (e.g. Tourish, 1997):

Are these factors still the key ones?

More recent research offers similar recipes but would highlight the significance of new technology to both enable and influence the impact of communication. And a key development is the degree of interactivity available. Social media allow a much greater degree of two-way/multiple-way communication and this presents challenges and opportunities for organisations.

Table 0.1 Factors in effective organizational communication

Factor	Explanation	Our comment
Management commitment	Senior management must commit to the importance of communication and act accordingly. Other levels of management must share this commitment. All managers must act in ways which *confirm* their communication. Communication training is given high priority and is well supported.	This is still a very important factor.
Two-way communication	There must be an effective balance between downward and upward communication. Surveys of employee opinion must lead to action plans and visible results.	The focus on action is still critical here.
Face-to-face communication	Wherever possible, communication is delivered face-to-face to allow for immediate feedback and discussion.	This is now more complex because of the growth of virtual interactions, as we discuss later.
Messages are well-structured to meet the audience needs	Management recognise what information employees need to know and make sure that they receive it in the most appropriate form.	Again, this factor is still critical. And we now have many more channels available.
New technology is used to speed up communication.	Many companies have made an enormous investment in new technology which enables them to spread messages very quickly across dispersed sites and offices.	The technology landscape is now more complex as we see in Chapter 5.

Throughout this book, we invite you to apply our ideas to your own situation. An obvious exercise here is to consider how many of the principles above apply to your organisation, and to what extent. For example, what evidence do you have that your senior management are committed to fostering communication? If not, then what effect does this have on the rest of the organisation?

Organisations may ignore communication because it is time-consuming and sometimes difficult, especially when the organisation is going through a bad time. Again, an example from 2000 is still depressingly topical. A major British retail chain responded to a significant drop in profits by dramatic cost-cutting and management redundancies. Staff were quoted as “furious” at the “insensitive manner” in which this was done; the process was described by one as “barbaric”. Assuming this press coverage was fair comment, what effect did this have on the long-term development of relationships and communication in that company? What if the press coverage was not representative of staff feelings? Does the company have effective internal communication which could counteract the public criticism?

In the late summer and autumn of 2022, UK media focused on the aftermath of the death of Queen Elizabeth II and the accession of King Charles III. One sub-story that received attention was the fate of staff employed from Charles' previous title and position. They received emails about likely redundancies during a thanksgiving service for the late Queen, while many were preparing for the Queen's funeral. A typical UK media headline was "'King Charles' staff left heartbroken after they're axed during church service for the Queen" (from *The Sun*). The timing of this announcement was described as "heartless".

Although communication is important, we must always recognise that it is not a universal cure. We cannot turn a message about redundancy into good news by changing the words or tone. But organisations *should* respect their employees and treat them fairly and honestly – communication can either support or destroy these obligations.

Improving communication – using evidence and research

In this book, we show how communication can "work" not just by analysing what happens when people communicate within organisations but also by suggesting techniques and strategies which can make communication more effective. This makes two important assumptions, that:

- we know enough about what happens in different types of organisations.
- techniques and strategies which work in one situation can be applied equally well in others.

Unfortunately, we can question *both* assumptions.

We try wherever possible to back up claims with research evidence, but there is not enough research on everyday events in organisations. Some important processes are under-researched. For example, do we know enough about the organisational politics which can affect organisational change and development? This has important implications for communication (Buchanan and Badham, 2020) – the success or failure of a proposal at a business meeting may depend more on political manoeuvring than on the clarity of the proposal!

There are also problems with the balance of research in some areas. For example, Steve Duck suggested that researchers have been less willing to look at the *negative* side of (personal) relationships. We need to know much more about the impact of events such as deception, hurtful messages, gossip, boring communication, and so on (Duck, 2010). There is now much more research on this but there are still important gaps and limitations. On a broader scale, we can find much more research on large organisations in western cultures than on, say, small businesses in Asian cultures. These imbalances make it difficult to generalise. Problems of generalisation also apply to techniques and strategies.

Because of these limitations, you should approach *all* the recommendations in this book as *hypotheses* – as generalisations to be *tested* and not as absolute or binding truths. Even findings which are based on fairly substantial evidence are *never* 100% reliable. For another longstanding example, John Kirkman researched the reactions of scientists to papers which were rewritten using the plain language principles which we summarise and review later in this book. The scientists clearly preferred the rewritten examples, feeling that they were "more interesting" and also that the author had a "better-organised mind". Although this positive reaction was strong, it was not universal – nearly 70% agreed that the rewritten examples were better and 75% agreed that the author was better organized. (Turk and Kirkman, 1989, page 17ff). In other words, a small but significant minority did *not* agree with the changes.

Deciding what is appropriate language is not just a simple technical problem – all sorts of social issues and pressures may be relevant. We know one consultant who produced a beautifully written plain language report for a major national organisation. He was asked to revise it to make it look "more complicated" and "academic" so it would "impress" the government department who commissioned it. These issues of context and audience will recur regularly as we look at different types and levels of communication.

Consider your context and situation carefully before you apply techniques or concepts from this (or from any other) text on communication. You should also try to check the most recent research – many topics we cover in this book are both controversial and subject to social change. For a simple example, suppose you are chairing a meeting and one of your colleagues takes out their smartphone to respond to a text. Is this appropriate behaviour in this context? A survey of American business professionals we came across in 2015 found very different reactions, depending on age and gender. Men were much more likely to judge it as "OK" than women; older professionals were more likely to see this behaviour as "rude" or "unprofessional". Have social norms changed on this?

Apart from changes in expectations and behaviour over time (which we expect will become more frequent), there is a final very good reason for treating all our statements and suggestions as hypotheses to be tested in your context. Superficial appearances which organisations present may be misleading –

> *the world of business isn't always what it pretends to be. Things aren't as rational, well-organised and well-oiled as we're told they are.*
>
> (Vermeulen, 2010)

You can say the same for *all* organisational sectors. We may assume that others are behaving openly, sensibly, fairly, and honestly – but these are assumptions that we need to check. Discrimination of various sorts can easily be found in many workplaces. For example, Buchanan and Badham described "sex-role stereotyping, the systematic underestimation of women, and the resultant hostility" as "widespread" behaviour in organisations (Buchanan and Badham, 2008, page 151). How much change has there been?

Sheryl Sandberg, CEO of Facebook, often asks the audience at her talks whether they have been called "too aggressive" at work:

> *I've never seen more than 5% of men raise their hands. Every woman I know, particularly the senior ones, has been called aggressive at work.*
>
> (quote from an interview in *The Guardian* Weekend, 5/4/14)

Sandberg's bestselling book – *Lean In* – offered suggestions to women on how to overcome such structural biases in the workplace (Sandberg, 2013, 2014). At the campaigning website – http://leanin.org – you can find the report of "the largest study on the state of women in corporate America". The 2022 edition:

> focuses on how the pandemic has changed what women want from their companies, including the growing importance of opportunity, flexibility, employee well-being, and diversity, equity, and inclusion.

There is evidence of positive change but we cannot afford to be complacent (as in debates in the UK over "everyday sexism" – Bates, 2014) or any other area of social discrimination.

What does communication involve?

As we see in Chapter 1, communication can be defined in rather different ways. For example, we can define it as:

> *shared meaning created among two or more people through verbal and nonverbal transaction*
>
> (Daniels and Spiker, 1994, page 27)

This emphasises sharing ideas and/or information. Ideally, at the end of the process, all parties involved share the same ideas and information. What are the important factors which will either assist or detract from achieving this goal? We emphasise some important factors which are often neglected in practice, including for example:

Assumptions and expectations

Throughout the book, we aim to identify biases which can distort our thinking and "myths" about communication and behaviour in the workplace. Fortunately, there is a growing literature on these topics (e.g. Carvill and MacRae, 2023) which we should all put on our future reading list.

Purpose and strategy

The "art" of communication is finding the most effective means of sharing ideas and information. We need to study how people choose and develop strategies and tactics for sharing ideas and information. Implicit in this is the idea of a communicative purpose or objective, such as informing or persuading. Many problems in communication arise from unclear or inappropriate purposes or strategies.

We also need to consider how these purposes are expressed. For example, objectives may be found in the organisation's mission statement. Is a mission statement the best way of expressing objectives in a way that the employees will accept and understand? Again there are longstanding issues here. Some organisations have explicitly rejected mission statements. One British Vice-Chancellor suggested that

> *although universities should be run in a business-like way... there are some business techniques that we should tear up into shreds. Mission statements, for instance, are an abject waste of time. We were just as effective before we had one.*
>
> (*Times Higher*, July 24th 1998)

Eden and Ackermann (2013) found similar concerns with mission/vision statements in the business world:

> the last two decades have seen managers being bombarded with vision statements and mission statements and the requirement for vision and mission statements, with many of these statements being regarded as a joke by them and others in the organisation as they provide little in the way of guidance.

Alongside concerns that many mission statements are rather idealised statements which could apply to virtually every organization and that others are hopelessly unrealistic, they found that

> a careful analysis of statements of purpose (mission and vision statements)—particularly those more detailed versions—demonstrates incoherency, emanating from unrecognised conflict between aspirations, opaque reasoning, and incompatibility of goals statements—where some are aspirational and others' statements of what currently exist.

As with any specific example of communication, we need to 'look behind' the words on the page to uncover the underlying reality. Think about your own organisation:

- does it have a mission or vision statement?
- what is it and what does it really mean?
- does it make a difference?
- who is it aimed at?

We may be less than impressed with some organisational mission statements but we must not underestimate the importance of shared values across the organisation (Ingram and Choi, 2022). New technology can offer opportunities here – enabling organisations to gain contributions and commitment through a more interactive and collaborative process.

Social and cultural background

Cultural and social differences affect the way we interpret what communication means. Some degree of common background is essential for exchanging messages. Sometimes, practical problems crop up because the communicators fail to establish this common background.

Codes

A code is a coherent set of symbols plus the rules you need to structure a message. Our language is the most important code we use but gestures, illustrations, and mathematics are all codes that have important roles in communication.

Situation and relationships

Situation is the context in which a message is sent and received, with both physical and relational aspects. For example, communication in a lecture room is influenced both by the layout of the room and by the relationship between the lecturer and the students.

We always interpret communication in terms of the relationship we have with the other person. In many organisations, status relationships are particularly important. For example, consider the message: "Please bring me the Smith file". Imagine the different ways this could be delivered through intonation (and perhaps without the "please"?) The meaning of a message depends on the relationship between the people involved.

Reviewing these and other factors, this book aims to highlight different reactions and potential ambiguities which affect our communication.

How this book is organised

The structure of this book reflects how we think professional and business communication is best understood and how you can improve it.

Chapter 1 suggests you start by NOT thinking about communication itself – communication is always a means to an end. If you do not have some idea about where you are heading in personal and professional terms then you are unlikely to choose the most effective communication methods and approach. So, we start by considering more general goals and objectives. You need to understand your own approach to communication and how you can best develop your capacity and understanding.

Then you need to develop a more detailed appreciation of what communication means and what it involves. This is what Chapters 2 and 3 are about. As well as looking at how we can define communication (and the practical implications of that), we investigate the factors which comprise communication in more detail and suggest overall principles which we feel are critical aspects of communication for people working in modern organisations.

Communication always takes place in a specific organisational context. Chapters 4 and 5 explore what this means in organisations by looking at different forms and levels of social context, and in ways that technology has developed.

The dominant form of communication in many organisations is written, whether it ends up as a paper or online message or as the text in an oral presentation. That is the focus of Chapters 6–9. As well as looking at practice and research on the advantages of plain language, we look at how effective design can influence how documents are understood. We also look at how documents can be best organised and look at the range of documents which are now used in most organisations.

Communicating face-to-face (whether in person or online) is often as important, if not more important than, written communication, and that is the focus of Chapters 10–14. After defining the major interpersonal skills, we look at how these can be used in a range of contexts, including formal presentations. We look at group dynamics and team development and suggest ways to improve formal and informal meetings, both face-to-face and online.

Chapter 15 raises issues of organisational change as they apply to all forms and types of communication.

Chapter 16 concludes the book by offering suggestions on how you can use our ideas to support your own personal and professional development in communication.

And finally

We make numerous references to websites and web resources. As many of these change frequently, we have only included web references in this print copy where we are confident that the website will have a reasonably long shelf life. All weblinks quoted in this book were checked at the end of January 2023.

On the website, you will find further notes and updated and expanded links/websites wherever we have found new materials. We look forward to meeting you there to carry on our discussion.

References

Bates, L. (2014) *Everyday Sexism*. London: Simon & Schuster.

Buchanan, D.A. and Badham, R.J. (2008) *Power, Politics and Organizational Change: Winning the turf game*, 2nd edition. London: Sage.

Buchanan, D.A. and Badham, R.J. (2020) *Power, Politics and Organizational Change*, 3rd edition. London: Sage.

Carville, M. and MacRae, I. (2023) *Myths of Social Media: Dispel the Misconceptions and Master Social Media*. London: KoganPage.

Daniels, T.D. and Spiker, B.K. (1994) *Perspectives On Organisational Communication*, 3rd edition. Madison, WI: W.C.B. Brown and Benchmark.

Duck, S. (2010) *Human Relationships*, 4th edition. London: Sage.

Eden, C. and Ackermann, F. (2013) Problem structuring: On the nature of, and reaching agreement about, goals. *EURO Journal on Decision Processes*. Springer-Verlag Berlin Heidelberg and EURO – The Association of European Operational Research Societies. http://link.springer.com/article/10.1007%2Fs40070-013-0005-6/fulltext.html.

Hartley, P. and Chatterton, P. (2015) *Business Communication: Rethinking Your Professional Practice for the Post-digital Age*. London: Routledge.

Ingram, P. and Choi, Y. (2022) What does your company really stand for? *Harvard Business Review*, November–December, pages 41–47.

Ronson, J. (2015) *So You've Been Publicly Shamed*. London: Picador.

Sandberg, S. (2013) *Lean In: Women, Work, and the Will to Lead*. London: W H Allen.

Sandberg, S. (2014) *Lean In: The Graduate Edition*. London: W H Allen.

Sharples, M. and Pérez y Pérez, R. (2022) *Story Machines: How Computers Have Become Creative Writers*. London: Routledge.

Tibballs, G. (1999) *Business Blunders*. London: Robinson.

Tourish, D. (1997) Transforming internal corporate communications: The power of symbolic gestures and barriers to change. *Corporate Communications: An International Journal*, 2(3), pages 109–116.

Turk, C. and Kirkman, J. (1989) *Effective Writing: Improving Scientific, Technical and Business Communication*, 2nd edition. London: E and FN Spon. Close.

Vermulen, F. (2010) *Business Exposed: The Naked Truth about What Really Goes on in the World of Business*. Harlow: Pearson.

Youngs, I. (2022) Channel 4's Krishnan Guru-Murthy suspended for insulting minister. *BBC News*. https://www.bbc.co.uk/news/entertainment-arts-63331322.

PART 1

How we understand and analyse the ways we communicate in organisations

CHAPTER 1

Developing your communication

Deciding where to start

Introduction

You want to improve your communication – where do you start?

We suggest you do *not* start by focusing on specific details of communication itself. To make a significant change, you need to decide on your overall career and personal goals. Then we suggest you work on your professional development in ways which will enhance your communication. We suggest you should:

- become self-sufficient in your learning and personal development.
- adopt a self-critical approach to your own and your organisation's behaviour.
- be proactive – search for systematic research to analyse human behaviour and communication.
- avoid the many myths about organisational life/behaviour which are available online and across the media. We aim to "explode" as many of these myths as we can in this book.
- self-monitor, i.e. understand (and manage) how you behave and present yourself. Pay special attention to your digital identity.
- review and expand the range of communication tools you use.

We cannot give you all the answers to effective communication because (as we illustrate in every chapter) the world is changing too fast and we cannot know the specific circumstances of your organisation. For example, different responses to online working and office work following the pandemic had very different longer-term effects on different organisations.

Our aim is to provide useful ideas and techniques you can use as the springboard to personal change.

Firstly, you need to step back and reflect upon your overall aims and priorities.

This chapter suggests three starting points – three distinct but interrelated aspects of communication and learning:

DOI: 10.4324/9781003297550-3

- reviewing your personal objectives and goals.
- adopting learning strategies to improve your communications, including learning from others.
- reviewing (and deciding on) the tools and enhanced skills you need to support your continual professional development.

We suggest you consider these topics in the order presented here but this does not mean you should do them in a rigid sequence. Throughout this book, we emphasise the advantages of continuous review/reflection/revision, and the need to be both open and flexible. Your plan should be a starting point and not a straitjacket.

OBJECTIVES

This chapter will:

- suggest how to review your current approaches and perspectives as the first step to improving your communication.
- suggest some tools and opportunities to consider as you review your learning approach and compile your personal development plan.

Reviewing your objectives and goals

Virtually every book on Business Communication/Skills emphasises the importance of goals and objectives. But different authors use these terms differently and also focus on different levels (e.g. compare our approach with other leading business texts such as the series by Bovee and Thill (2022)).

One common approach is to identify characteristics of goals/objectives which help us achieve them – SMART goals – which are:

- Specific (so we have clear targets to aim for).
- Measurable (so we know when we have achieved them).
- Achievable (within the resources and constraints we have).
- Relevant (so we are aiming for something meaningful).
- Time-defined (so we know when to stop).

Of course, you need to break down goals into their component parts. We recommend ideas from John Kay (2011). He distinguishes between high-level objectives, intermediate goals, and basic actions, where:

> *High-level goals are typically loose and unquantifiable – though this does not mean it is not evident whether or not they are being achieved.*

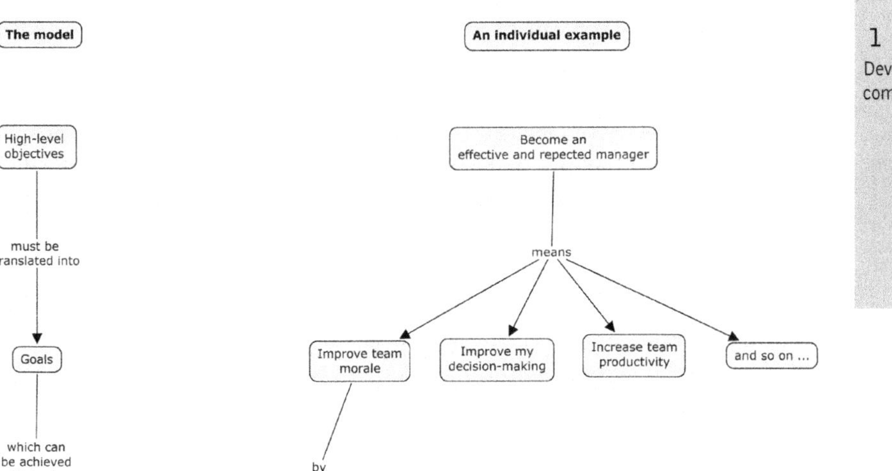

Figure 1.1 Objectives, goals, and activities

You can translate this hierarchy into personal individual terms – see our example in Figure 1.1. If your high-level objective is "being an effective manager" then this must be broken down into goals which relate to both productivity and social relationships (where it is useful to use the SMART criteria) and then specific actions.

There are two other important points to highlight from Kay's analysis:

- problems are often best solved indirectly or "obliquely" as we live in unpredictable and fast-changing environments.
- objectives, goals, and actions must be constantly reviewed to ensure that they retain their importance and relevance. Becoming an effective manager is not something which can be defined just once as it will change. See the website for further discussion.

Figure 1.1 also introduces our approach to concept mapping.

We use and recommend this approach to our own students because it can help you make sense of an area by defining and linking concepts. Maps drawn in this way can be read by others so it can kick off useful dialogue. Concepts are shown in boxes which are linked to make propositions, as in –

high-level objectives ...
must be translated into ...
goals ...
which can be achieved through ...
activities.

This illustrates how you can "read" this map (and other maps we have included in the book).

The overall structure of a concept map depends on what you want to demonstrate – here we have included two maps side by side – the abstract approach on the left hand of the page and practical illustrations on the right. All the diagrams we use in this book are available to download either as image files or in their original format (using Cmap software available from https://www.ihmc.us/cmaptools/). On this website, you will also find links to tutorials and examples so that you can use this software effectively. It is both very useful and very easy to learn. And you can find a map online explaining why one of us uses this technique (Hartley, 2022).

Returning to goals and objectives, can we accept Figure 1.1 and move on?

You may like to consider this question for a few moments.

There is one major problem with this analysis so far – it does not include any analysis of the starting point or the broader social context in which you operate.

For example, in Figure 1.1, the activities of regular team meetings and weekly progress summaries seem to support the goals. But they could be counter-productive. If deep-seated personal conflicts already exist between group members, then regular meetings may offer more opportunities to "fight". Conflict may need to be resolved or at least weakened *before* meetings can become amicable and productive.

As a result, we created Figure 1.2 – this includes several review loops, including:

- reviewing the present situation in relation to the original goals.
- defining the gap between what is happening now and what you would like to see happen.
- suggesting activities which will "plug this gap".

Reflecting on the future of work

Consider general social economic and political trends which may directly affect your longer-term future. For example, one leading UK researcher on the future of work, Professor Lynda Gratton, suggested five major forces changing the way we work and three recommended shifts to deal with these. (Gratton, 2014) The forces are: technology; globalisation; demography and longevity; society; and energy resources. The three shifts are summarised in Table 1.1.

In subsequent publications, Gratton has discussed different permutations of work based on different combinations of place and time supported by technology (Gratton, 2021) and offered a four-step process for redesigning work:

- "understand what matters".
- "reimagine the future".

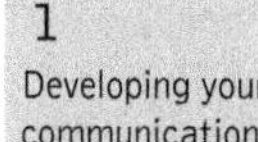

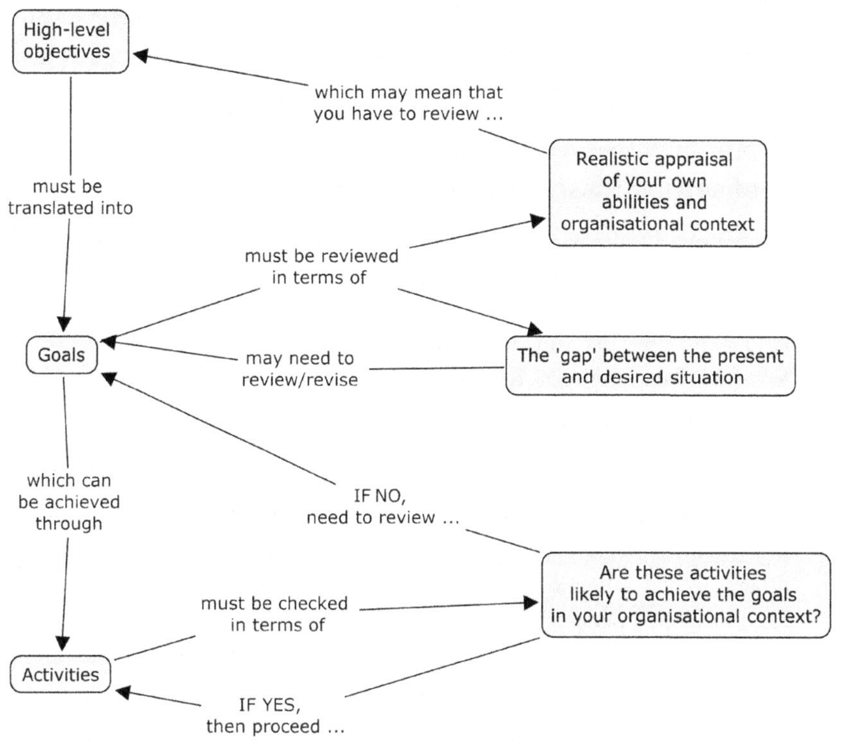

Figure 1.2 Revised model of objectives, goals, and activities

Table 1.1 Recommended responses to the future of work

You need to shift from	You need to shift to	Because (rationale)
"shallow generalist"	"serial master"	There will be fewer jobs requiring very general skills. You will need in-depth knowledge and skills in a number of areas. These areas will change over time.
"isolated competitor"	"innovative connector"	You will need to develop networks of colleagues who can provide support and expertise when you need it.
"voracious consumer"	"impassioned producer"	You will have the opportunity to engage with more meaningful work and find a better work/life balance.

- "model and test ideas".
- "act on your ideas".(Gratton, 2022, pages 16/17)

As with many of the approaches suggested in this book, this is not recommended as a rigid sequence, but organisations should cover all this ground. Grattan has provided a workbook and other resources to support this process (www.hsm

-advisort.com) and has also written about broader implications of current social changes such as the longer working life (Scott and Grattan, 2020).

Our recommendations in this book reflect these trends and other suggestions on the likely stages or shifts in the workplace.

Ways of setting those long-term improvement goals

There is no one best way of doing this. Here are some suggestions to get you started:

1. Find approaches that suit your lifestyle and personality.
   We introduce ways of reviewing important personality characteristics below.
2. Select evidence-based techniques.
   For example, based on research, Wilson (2011) recommends private reflective writing over a period of days as a very powerful technique for working through difficult experiences. Some forms of writing have more impact than others. When reflecting on unpleasant or very negative experiences, you need to adopt a perspective which gives you "some distance from the event" and which enables you to "analyse why the event occurred" (page 57) – a "step-back-and-ask-why strategy" (page 58).
3. Avoid self-help recipes which simply reflect the style or perspective of the author.
   Numerous books and online sites offer the promise of immediate and dramatic change. While some *are* strongly based on research evidence (e.g. Beattie, 2011; Wiseman, 2012; Burkeman, 2011) many simply offer "'remedies' (which) make people feel good but don't cure what ails them" (Wilson, 2011, page 42).
4. Consider a programme which gives you responsibility but also offers tools and social support.
   See some suggestions and further discussion on the website.

BOX 1.1 PRACTICAL TIPS ON GOAL-SETTING

Be realistic

Be realistic about your goals; recognise that you will need practice, time, and repetition.

Prioritise your goals

Prioritise goals that will be of most use to you and work on these first before moving on to the others. To get started, it is a good idea to focus on just one goal.

Phrase your goals to be achievable and practical

Use our model (Figure 1.2) or a similar approach to avoid very open-ended goals. Select more focused goals.

Plan "small steps"

Once you have identified an achievable goal, create "small steps" – regular, practical, and achievable activities that you can undertake to reach the goal.

Adopting learning strategies to improve your communications: review, plan, and improve

An underpinning principle for this book is that "communication can always be improved". This might appear obvious but is often neglected in practice. We suggest a "review, plan, and improve" philosophy based on "continuous improvement" approaches used in many organisations. Reviewing the impact of your own behaviour on others (including the influence of your own assumptions and possible prejudices/stereotypes) is key to this, as is seeking out feedback to help inform your strategies and plans.

This sort of approach is not new and you may think we have simply repeated existing wisdom. However, two aspects are often neglected:

Do *not* regard review, plan and improve as separate or discrete stages

We advocate *continuous* review – keeping alert at all times for feedback which suggests that all is well or not so you can respond flexibly and immediately.

For example, as experienced teachers/lecturers we always try to gauge the atmosphere in the teaching room. In one session, one of us noticed an especially "flat" atmosphere in a lecture room:

> *Rather than battle on, I stopped and asked the group if everything was ok. I then discovered that this was the fifth time they had been "introduced" to this topic. None of my previous colleagues had noticed.*

We must update our approaches to reflect the opportunities and challenges of the post-pandemic and digital world. For example, see below on the concept of "digital identity" that people acquire as they engage with digital media (e.g. social networks) and how such digital identities influence communications, in both positive and negative senses.

With these caveats in mind, you can use the "review, plan, and improve" cycle in your daily practice.

Self-review

Reviewing your own skills is harder than it first appears. This is perhaps not surprising as our education systems typically see assessment and feedback as something "done" to students, rather than students being in the driving seat of self-assessment and review (happily this is changing).

Moving into the workplace, there may be CPD (continuing professional development) programmes and appraisals as well as opportunities for feedback from supervisors, managers, and colleagues, However, these often do not address communications skills or follow the philosophy of regular small improvements. Performance review which relies on the "annual appraisal interview" is very far from the process we are proposing.

The capability of "self-review" is one that all professionals should develop. There are a number of ways of doing this – see the website for further suggestions – but consider the objectives in Table 1.2 as a starter for ten. Think of a recent situation you have been in and rate how well you did against each objective.

Table 1.2 Reviewing your objectives

Objective	**Rate your skill**
There is a clear purpose to my communication	1 2 3 4 5
I have taken steps to understand my target audience and listen to their perspectives	1 2 3 4 5
I understand the specific social, cultural, historical, and technological context to the communication	1 2 3 4 5
I have evaluated several options for achieving my purpose and selected the one most likely to succeed	1 2 3 4 5
I've tried to ensure that there is consistency between what I say, my behaviour, and my body language – as well as no ambiguity	1 2 3 4 5
Where feasible, I've looked for non-verbal clues to see how my communication has been understood and interpreted	1 2 3 4 5
I have taken steps to get feedback to see how well the target audience has understood the communication and how they interpreted its meaning	1 2 3 4 5
I have followed through on promised actions	1 2 3 4 5
I keep up-to-date with new forms of digital communications and have spent time using them in order to assess their value	1 2 3 4 5

In a perfect world, you will have rated yourself as 5 on all these characteristics. If you have, then we respectfully suggest that you are fooling yourself. Ask a friend or colleague to rate you on the same basis and compare your results. You are much more likely to end up with a variety of scores and this gives you some ideas for priorities and immediate action.

Personality analysis

We are not always good at making judgements on how others see us. Our behaviour and body language give off all sorts of clues to our personalities and we may not be fully aware of the impressions we are presenting to others (see Chapter 10).

Many psychological studies show that we often misjudge our own personality and capabilities. For example, are you a good multi-tasker? Judging by their behaviour, many people seem to think so. But recent research suggests that very few of us can effectively multi-task. Most of us would be more effective if we deliberately focused on one thing at a time.

Think about your fundamental personality characteristics. Large organisations often employ a range of personality tests in their staff recruitment and continual professional development (CPD) programmes. Many tests are now available online and it is possible to use these to help in the analysis of your personality and your team abilities. However, we suggest a word of caution. Ideally, tests should be overseen by a skilled psychologist, particularly in the analysis and interpretation of results.

Test results are best used within a context of "review, plan, and improve", though sometimes they are used in less positive contexts, e.g. for staff screening. There are also complex issues in terms of how people respond to and act on the results. For instance, our response to tests can be influenced by the "authority" of the tester. There is the risk that we only hear what we want to hear. We can also take the results too literally – becoming "dependent" upon the personality traits revealed by the test and abandoning attempts to improve areas of "weakness".

Bearing these health warnings in mind, there is value in considering broad aspects of your personality without professional support. But always "check" your results with close friends and colleagues. We suggest three specific areas to pursue:

1. Overall personality measures

One particularly important dimension is introversion-extraversion where:

> *introverts and extroverts differ in the level of outside stimulation that they need to function well*
>
> *(Cain, 2012, page 10)*

This leads to differences in behaviours such as preferred work practices and decision-making.

Susan Cain argues that:

> *many of the most important institutions of contemporary life are designed for those who enjoy group projects and high levels of stimulation*
>
> *(op cit, page 6)*

In other words, our school and workplaces explicitly favour extravert personalities. As a consequence, they lose valuable contributions from more introverted people who have to adapt to be successful. She also emphasises the importance of recognising your own tendencies and working to accommodate these (Cain et al., 2016).

2. Mindset

Carol Dweck popularised this term. Her studies focused on differences between the fixed mindset – "believing that your qualities are carved in stone" – and the growth mindset – "based on the belief that your basic qualities are things you can cultivate through your efforts" (Dweck, 2008, pages 6 and 7). Her studies show the potentially damaging impact of fixed mindset. She offers tools and techniques to support change to the growth mindset:

> *seeing things in a new way. When people ... change to a growth mindset, they change from a judge-and-be-judged framework to a learn-and-help-learn framework.*
>
> *(page 244)*

James Reed and Paul Stoltz (2011) claim to have found the mindset which top employers really want. They list "Top 20" mindset qualities – the top six being honesty, trustworthiness, commitment, adaptability, accountability, and flexibility.

3. Team roles

Various inventories claim to establish how you operate in teams – one of the most well-known is the Belbin test, discussed in detail in Chapter 14.

Feedback from colleagues

Feedback from colleagues – *if* it is candid, open and honest – can help you review your communication capabilities. While formal organisational appraisals can provide useful feedback, in practice they are often infrequent and only provided by a few colleagues. Many organisations now prefer "360-degree feedback" which aims to provide useful feedback from a range of colleagues. However, all these processes are "done to you" rather than proactively seeking out feedback.

One advantage of more proactive approaches is that feedback can be timed when you need it. For instance, you could ask colleagues/friends to identify examples of when you are good and not so good at communications – as they happen. There are caveats though – for instance, any feedback you receive must be interpreted in context. Will they be open and balanced in their comments? As feedback, your colleagues may tell you what you want to hear, so you must stress that you would *really* like candid and honest feedback.

This discussion assumes you are ready and able to accept feedback. Useful advice on this comes from Heen and Stone (2014). They suggest six steps to becoming better at taking feedback on board (explanation and our comments in the parentheses):

- "know your tendencies" (you may have a particular pattern in the way you receive comments which will get in the way of considering them fully, e.g. going on the defensive and arguing back).
- "disentangle the 'what' from the 'who'" (consider both the content of feedback and the relationship you have with the "giver").
- "unpack the feedback" (make sure you really understand what they are saying – clarify any general, possibly vague, comments).
- "ask for just one thing" (feedback on specific areas can be really useful).
- "engage in small experiments" (make small changes and see if they work in the desired direction).

Spontaneous or unrequested feedback from colleagues can also be useful but this may be clouded with self-interest. Their motivation might be more to do with boosting their own self-worth or political/personal agendas.

Your digital identity

Nowadays, anyone can create their own identity on the internet which may be far removed from their real identity – fraudsters regularly take advantage of this. This criminal activity has significant implications for *everyone*: do you know who you are dealing with online?

And how are you perceived online?

People make assumptions about who you are based on the clues and trails you leave online, e.g. your profiles on social networks, your postings on social media, what you say in discussion groups, what's been published about you on websites etc. All these help others to build a picture of your personality, traits, preferences, and attributes – in other words, your digital identity.

But there will be other information online that you have no control over. And there are two unfortunate consequences here:

- information that builds up about you is created in an unplanned, haphazard way, and sometimes without any control from you.
- it is often very difficult (and sometimes impossible) to get rid of unwanted information about you, e.g. on social networks.

So, your digital identity – how others perceive you online – is not completely under your control and there are serious consequences/implications for your professional life. For example, employers and job recruiters will actively research your digital identity and base decisions on what they find.

You can influence your digital identity and the first step is to review what this currently is by searching for all online references to yourself. Check social networks such as Facebook and LinkedIn etc. as well as websites, discussion groups etc. Remember to look for images, audio, and video as well as text. Then, review the postings as if it were another person.

Box 1.2 gives some practical suggestions on this.

Perhaps the most important (and safest) overall principle is to treat *every* digital communication – including *every* email and *every* Facebook entry – as potentially a public message. Are you happy to make this information known to the world at large?

If you are in any doubt about the importance of being careful, look at the case studies in the book we have already mentioned by Jon Ronson (2015) – a joke in poor taste can destroy your professional career if it goes viral.

BOX 1.2 MANAGING YOUR DIGITAL IDENTITY: PRACTICAL SUGGESTIONS

- develop your social media strategy by thinking of yourself as a "brand".
- what are your key attributes that you want to convey?
- choose social media.
- which social media apps/blogs suit your "brand"?
- claim your IDs
- claim your unique ID at sites even if you don't use it.
- in choosing an ID, make sure it aligns with your "brand".
- have separate private and professional accounts.
- look out for changes in privacy/copyright settings/terms of service/preference settings. Social media sites can change their privacy settings from time to time and are not always good at proclaiming this. Bear in mind copyright terms, e.g. Google Docs claim certain rights to use *anything* in your online documents.

- be selective in choosing "friends".
- don't automatically accept all "friend/colleague" requests.
- follow netiquette.
- be vigilant for fraudsters, scammers, and bullies.
- engage on a regular basis.
- always respond to feedback/messages unless they are obviously spam or malicious.
- keep others informed of your progress, news, and ideas.
- use the network to share your professional news and ideas, while avoiding blatant self-promotion.

Developing your digital literacy

Higher education in many countries is now working hard to develop the concept of digital literacies, equipping graduates with digital skills, though there is still some variation in their definitions and very different interpretations by employers on graduate digital skills. Some employers still talk in limited terms (being able to use word-processing and/or spreadsheets etc.). Others demonstrate more sophisticated understanding – wanting their graduates to apply key management/professional skills in the selection, adoption and application of new technologies. Some go even further – wanting graduates to have the skills to "influence" colleagues in the strategic/operational adoption of new technologies. So-called "digital influence" has been identified as a key skill for managers in the next few years.

Our model of digital literacy below reflects this position and suggests that we need to give graduates far more than expertise with a few mainstream software packages to prepare for employment.

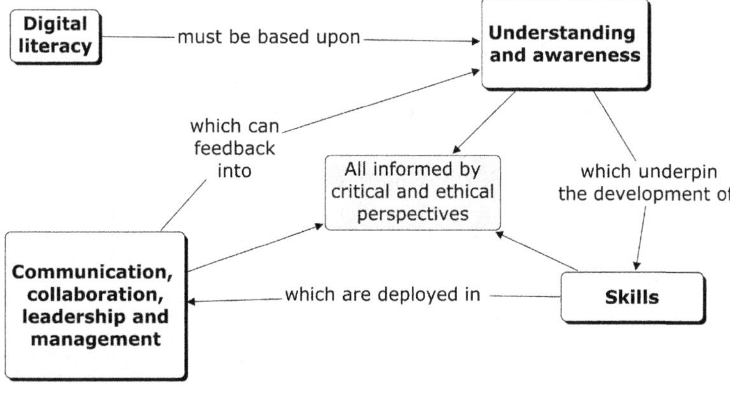

Figure 1.3 Overall model of digital literacy

You can see that this model emphasises that we need to develop an overall understanding of technology to underpin our skill development. Then we must apply this both to our own development *and* working with colleagues and the broader organisation. And all of this must be self-critical and ethical. Figure 1.4 offers a more detailed version. How far do you "tick all the boxes"? How would you assess your digital literacy against this recipe?

There are other models of digital literacy and this term is debated/contested. Perhaps the best known across UK Higher Education comes from Jisc (2014) which suggests seven elements:

- media literacy.
- communications and collaboration.
- career and identity management.
- ICT literacy.
- learning skills.
- digital scholarship.
- information literacy.

This model is obviously tailored for the educational institutions that Jisc serves but certainly all of these elements are both valuable and useful.

For a good example of research which explores these arguments, see work by Ibrar Bhatt on adult learners coming to terms with the technical and academic demands of their college environment (Bhatt, 2012). He illustrates how specific learners

> *successfully make the link between their own everyday digital literacy practices and the requirements of their course.*
>
> *(op cit, page 289)*

If we add "and/or organisation" to this last sentence then this is something we *all* have to do.

Choosing appropriate communication tools

We now have many tools (possibly too many?) we can use to communicate! This can be a good thing as we can pick the tool that best suits the specific situation, but it can mean we don't fully explore the strengths and weaknesses of each tool. We highlight useful tools in later chapters. For the moment, consider the range of tools you are currently using and ask yourself whether this range is the most effective for your development. Box 1.3 shows how even a very simple task like taking notes can now be done in a variety of ways using different mixes of technology.

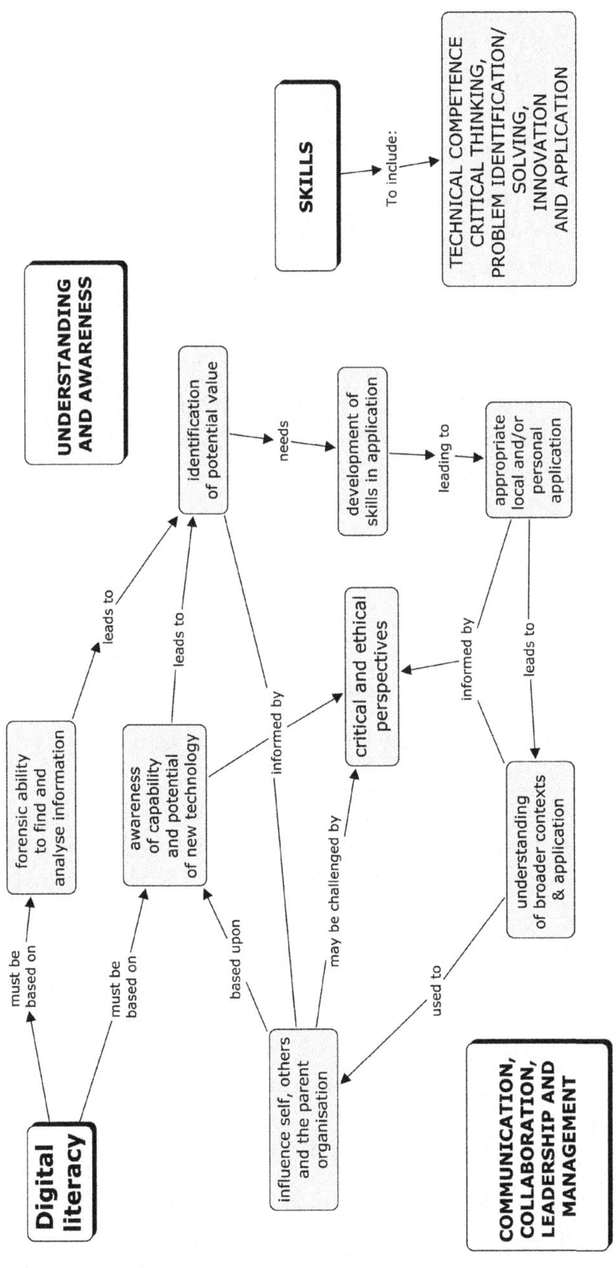

Figure 1.4 Detailed model of digital literacy

BOX 1.3 HOW DO YOU TAKE NOTES?

Every manager and every professional in organisations has to take notes in meetings, presentations, interviews etc.

What is your preferred technology?

The following list suggests possibilities and we return to some of these in later chapters. The most effective method will depend on your working style, your budget, and your organisational context. The most important thing is that you use an approach and tools which make the best use of your time. It is worth experimenting with different methods until you find the best ones for you:

- pen and paper, using a dedicated notebook (and perhaps a favourite pen?).
- pen and paper using a planning/diary system like Filofax.
- pen and paper plus software, as in the Moleskine system.
- speech recognition technology, either individually in Microsoft Word or using a tool on the web such as Otter.ai or the speech recognition functions in software such as Microsoft Teams.
- handwriting recognition directly onto tablet such as iPad.
- notetaking application on smartphone/laptop/tablet (e.g. Evernote) which can synchronise notes across devices.
- Concept mapping (e.g. Cmap on PC or Mac – or on the web, or on iPad).
- Sketchnoting or other visual method.

New learning paradigms using digital communications

A few years ago, a Motor Company HR executive told us that:

> *the half-life of an engineering degree is getting shorter and shorter – graduates therefore need to regularly update their skills, knowledge and capabilities on an on-going basis via lifelong learning and continuing professional development (CPD) approaches.*

The emergence of the internet and low-cost computing which is helping to change the CPD paradigm from one of teaching (something "done" to the learner) to concepts such as self-directed learning and assessment. Organisations are changing their CPD approaches and techniques, particularly in how they are using digital technologies to support their CPD strategies.

Using this technology re communication

The main implication of this explosion in technology is that we should be taking full advantage of it to support our own professional development in communication. For example, we can write our own development plan using free/open source software or commercial software, much of which is modestly priced.

We return to this topic in Chapter 16 and there is also more information on the website.

SUMMARY OF KEY POINTS

- review your more general goals and objectives as a starting point for reviewing your communication.
- self-review is a key capability that all professionals should develop.
- feedback from colleagues and co-workers can be especially valuable but make sure that it is helpful and focused.
- you need to review and manage your digital identity as best you can. Find the tools and new technologies which can best support your professional development – choose the ones which suit your context and give you the necessary support.

References

Beattie, G. (2011) *Get the Edge: How Simple Changes will Transform Your Life*. London: Headline.

Bhatt, I. (2012) Digital literacy practices and their layered multiplicity. *Educational Media International* 49(4): 289–301.

Bovee, C.L. and Thill, J.V. (2022) *Business Communication Today*, 15th edition. London: Pearson.

Burkeman, O. (2011) *Help! How to Become Slightly Happier and Get a Bit More Done*. Edinburgh: Canongate.

Cain, S. (2012) *Quiet: The Power of Introverts in a World That Can't Stop Talking*. London: Penguin.

Cain, S. with Mone, G. and Moroz, E. (2016) *Quiet Power: Growing Up as an Introvert in a World That Can't Stop Talking*. London: Penguin.

Dweck, C.S. (2008) *Mindset. The New Psychology of Success*. New York: Ballantine.

Gratton, L. (2014) *The Shift: The Future of Work is Already Here*. London: Williams Collins.

Gratton, L. (2021) How to do hybrid right. *Harvard Business Review*, May–June, 2021, pages 66–74.

Gratton, L. (2022) *Redesigning Work: How to Transform Your Organisation and Make Hybrid Work for Everyone*. London: Penguin.

Hartley, P. (2022) Concept mapping using Cmap. *National Teaching Repository*. Poster. https://doi.org/10.25416/NTR.21379242.v1.

Heen, S. and Stone, D. (2014) *Thanks for the Feedback: The Science and Art of Receiving Feedback Well*. London: Portfolio Penguin/Viking.

Jisc. (2014) *Developing Digital Literacies*. https://www.jisc.ac.uk/guides/developing-digital-literacies.

Kay, J. (2011) *Obliquity. Why Our Goals are Best Achieved Indirectly*. London: Profile Books.

Reed, J. and Stolz, P.G. (2011) *Put Your Mindset to Work: The One Asset You Really Need to Win and Keep the Job You Love*. London: Portfolio Penguin.

Ronson, J. (2015) *So You've Been Publicly Shamed*.

Scott, A.J. and Gratton, L. (2021) *The New Long Life: A framework for flourishing in a changing world*. London: Bloomsbury.

Wilson, T.D. (2011) *Redirect. The Surprising New Science of Psychological Change*. London: Allen Lane.

Wiseman, R. (2012) *Rip it Up: The Radically New Approach to Changing Your Life*. London: Macmillan.

CHAPTER 2

How should we analyse communication?

Introduction

Many popular guides to "improving your communication" (*and* some management training courses) do not spend enough time considering what is *meant* by "communication". We neglect this at our peril. Our understanding of what communication "is" influences how we act and how we analyse situations. It is important, both practically and theoretically, to work out what communication involves.

So this chapter looks at how we define communication and how we can best understand the way communication "works".

We argue that you need to examine communication from two contrasting perspectives – analysing the process and interpreting the meanings. You *always* need to integrate these perspectives to decide what is happening.

We conclude with some basic principles which inform the rest of this book.

OBJECTIVES

This chapter will:

- show how our personal definitions of communication influence how we act.
- review popular models of communication and explain why we recommend a more complex approach.
- introduce our approach and suggest basic principles.

Communication and action

Deciding what we mean by communication is not just an academic exercise. As human beings, we *act* on the basis of our perceptions and beliefs. So if we have a particular view of human communication then we will *act* on that view. If we have a faulty view, then our behaviour may cause problems. An example of how managers act upon their perceptions and cause problems will make this point clearer.

DOI: 10.4324/9781003297550-4

Consider Fred Davis, recently promoted telecommunications manager, who is responsible for implementing a new communication system (phone/voicemail/email) in a large organisation.

We used this case in previous editions of this book, as originally described by Finn (1999), based on experiences with organisations implementing new technology. We are using it again to highlight the fact that some issues and problems are almost timeless – in today's world, Fred would (hopefully) consider different technologies but this would not resolve his difficulties. The problem here is not the technology – it is Fred's approach. He would suffer much the same problems whatever technology he decided upon.

Back to the actual case – Fred was not having a good time:

- senior management were unhappy with the new system.
- 700 complaints were received in its first week.
- less than half the employees turned up for training sessions.
- some units within the organisation cancelled the system and opted for different solutions.

What made it especially frustrating for Fred was that he could not see where he had gone wrong. The changeover went smoothly from a technical perspective, and the system could achieve everything management requested – but *only* if people used it properly.

What was Fred's problem?

His main problem was failure to manage, based upon his *perception* of his role – how to act and communicate as a manager. He sees himself as an expert and a "doer". He makes decisions on his expert knowledge and then concentrates on making those decisions happen. During the planning and installation, he arranged everything in precise detail. What he did *not* do was communicate in any meaningful way with prospective users of the new system. He did *not* make sure that the users knew:

- exactly what was happening.
- why it was happening.
- how they could benefit from the new system.

The new system could have worked *if* he had built a consensus within the organisation to support his plans. Of course, such communication would have slowed him down. But a system which is not used cannot be effective. In terms of the approach which we advocate, he failed on both counts – he did not consider the *process* of communication and he did not think about the *meanings* which others in the organisations could read into his actions.

Unless managers like Fred reconsider their role very quickly, their careers will come to an abrupt end.

In the same way that we all have views about how to manage, which may be more or less effective, we also have views on how to communicate. In other words, we have an *implicit* view or theory of communication.

Compare Fred's approach with the strategy used by the developers of the Post-It note. This originated because scientists at 3M had developed a glue which was not very sticky. Rather than throw their hard work away, the originator took time to investigate possible uses for a "temporary" glue. He developed some trial products and gave them to colleagues to try. They clamoured for more so he developed a business plan which showed demand for the product. A new and very successful product line was launched.

Different views of communication

Different views of communication have very real practical consequences, so what are the main differences? Philip Clampitt (2016) suggests managers typically use one of three different approaches to communication: the "arrow", the "circuit", and the "dance".

Arrow managers believe that communication operates one way, as in firing an arrow. If your aim is good then you will hit the target. If you have a clear message then you will communicate. On the positive side, arrow managers spend time working out their ideas, making sure that their messages and instructions are as specific as possible. However, it can be very dangerous to see your listeners as passive processors of information. It is also very difficult to construct messages which are unambiguous.

In contrast, circuit managers concentrate on communication as a two-way process, emphasising the importance of feedback. They emphasise "good listening" and trust in relationships. Clampitt argues that this also has weaknesses. Circuit managers can overemphasise agreement and fail to recognise real differences in views. Circuit managers may assume that disagreement is caused by poor communication and that more communication will almost automatically lead to agreement. More communication is necessary but it needs to focus on *how and why* we have different opinions and values.

Clampitt concludes (and we agree) that the metaphor of dance is the most appropriate way of describing communication. He highlights similarities between communication and dance, including:

- both have multiple purposes.
  You can dance to entertain others, to impress your partner, to express yourself, and so on. In the same way, you can communicate for different reasons – to inform, to persuade, to impress etc.
- both involve the co-ordination of meanings.

Co-ordination is an obvious feature of dance – you have to know what your partner is going to do next! When we communicate we also have to recognise how other people see the situation, recognise what they are doing, and respond accordingly.
- both are governed by rules.
  Rules apply to different types of dance: e.g. what steps to use, how these steps are organised. Similarly, different rules apply to different communication situations. Most importantly for both dance and communication, rules can change over time and be negotiated by the participants.

This analysis has very important practical implications – these different views of communication influence how we behave. In similar situations, these different types of managers will respond very differently. And this is why it is important to think very clearly about how we define communication and what that definition involves. How we think about communication *always* influences what we do.

Analysing communication

We suggest that you think about communication by putting together two different perspectives and working out if this is creating any gaps in understanding between the parties involved:

- define the process: examine major components of the communication process and the sequence of events which is taking place.
- interpret the meanings: investigate the social and cultural context, and the historical background, to see how the participants *interpret* what is going on.

Once you can identify any differences in perceptions, you can develop your communication hypotheses and an appropriate action plan – as in Figure 2.1.

These two perspectives – process and meaning – are a simplified version of communication theory. You can find much more complicated accounts from scholars which you may wish to follow up – details on the website. But we want to home in on what we think is one of the most fundamental distinctions which causes practical difficulties – between an approach which assumes the importance of "the message" and an approach which focuses on "meaning". In the rest of this chapter, we shall explain these different perspectives and show how you can put them together to arrive at a clearer picture of what communication involves.

Communication as process

Many management texts use a model of communication first popularised in the 1950s – developed from work on telecommunications systems. It shows how

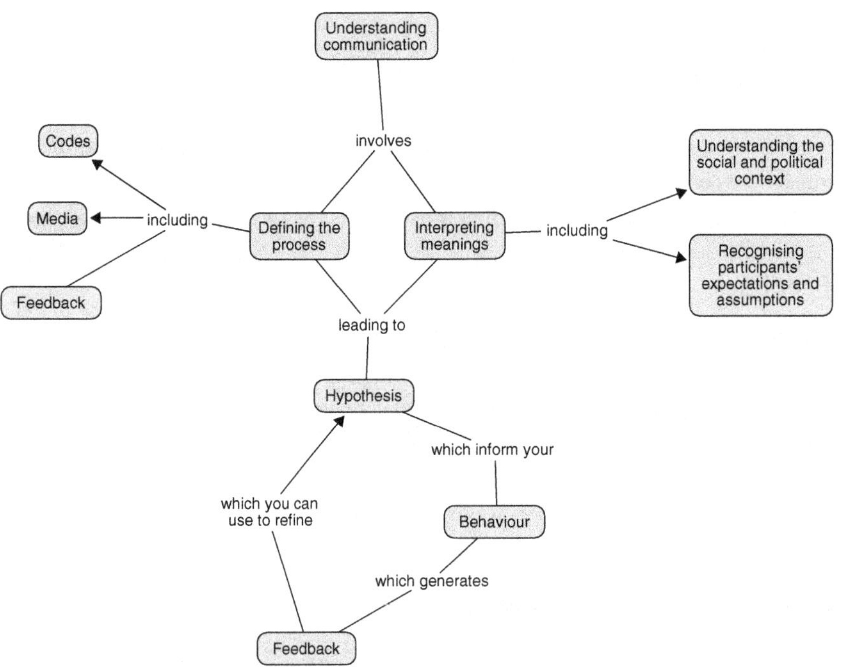

Figure 2.1 An integrated approach to analysing communication

information is transmitted from source to destination and analyses what can affect the quality of the information during this process. The model became very influential with researchers in human communication who saw communication as essentially a one-way process – information passing from Sender to Receiver. The most important early development added a feedback loop. Various authors have added slightly different emphases but this basic model is still very common. For example, Bovee and Thill (2014) talk about different meanings which people can take from the same message and offer an eight-step process model which includes the following main concepts:

Codes

A code is a set of symbols plus the rules to create a message. For example, a language code consists essentially of a list of words, and a set of rules for preparing a text. These rules are the grammar or syntax of the language.

Encoding and decoding

Encoding means using a code to structure a message in a particular way. Decoding is the reverse – we use our knowledge of the code to work out what the message means.

Media/channel

This is the physical system which carries the message from sender to receiver. Some texts use "channel" for this concept and there is often confusion as to what constitutes a medium or a channel. Bovee and Thill use both concepts to distinguish between the "*form* a message takes (such as a Twitter update) and the channel as the system used to deliver the message (such as the Internet)" (op cit, page 49).

Feedback

Feedback refers to any signals which are received by the sender.

One concept which you can see in some process models is "noise" – usually defined as any random input which distorts, or which interferes with the transmission or reception of a message. This was a very important component of early models of communication systems when we were trying to understand electronic communication. We have reservations about using this concept in human communication on the grounds that factors like loss of concentration are not really random.

Limitations of the process approach

The process approach has been fiercely criticised. We would highlight three criticisms which have very real practical implications:

- it does not take sufficient account of social or historical factors.
- It seems to assume that the meaning of an event is "given", as opposed to being "negotiated" between the participants.
- it does not take account of business realities – it suggests one sender and one receiver whereas most business communication involves "multiple senders and multiple receivers".

(Waller and Polonsky, 1998)

One response to these criticisms is to create a more complex model (as Waller and Polonsky did). But more complex models still imply that there is *one central message* which we can define unambiguously. This approach is not sufficient – we also need to emphasise the social and cultural background and look at how meaning is developed and negotiated through interaction – we need to interpret the meanings.

Interpreting the meanings

In order to fully understand how people communicate, we need to understand not just the immediate background but the much broader social context and history of their relationship. Not only do we have to examine how people *come to agree* on what is happening, but we also have to look at how they *feel* about events. The following examples illustrate some of this complexity.

The case of the confused trainees

A colleague was invited to run residential training events for managers in a large manufacturing organisation. He came back from the first event very dispirited, complaining he could not understand the reactions from the managers, who were supposed to be very committed to personal development. There seemed to be at least three different reactions:

- some managers looked really interested and spent the weekend frantically scribbling notes.
- some managers seemed overanxious and did not seem to be concentrating on the events.
- some managers seemed to see the event as a "bit of a holiday".

At the next event, he asked the managers *why* they had come and found that *none* had been told why – their "commitment" was a senior management *assumption*. As a result, they had "worked out" the meaning based on their own experience. Three different meanings emerged:

- one group thought it was a test which would influence their next promotion/regrading – they were the "scribblers", trying to impress the trainer.
- another group were worried that they were there because of problems with their performance. They were not participating – too busy working out where/how they had failed.
- the third group saw the event as reward for good behaviour which need not be taken seriously.

Our colleague was only able to communicate with these groups *after* these expectations and assumptions had been revealed and discussed. Training could not begin until the participants had *negotiated* the meaning of the event.

War in the training room

Another colleague was invited by the head of a local college to run a staff workshop on effective communication. The head insisted that staff had requested this event. But, arriving at the training room, our colleague's first impression was of unease and tension. He delivered a session which usually received very positive feedback but was unable to achieve any real dialogue with the staff who attended.

At the coffee break, he started to talk to one of the more friendly participants and eventually discovered what was going on:

- staff had *definitely not* requested the event! They were involved in a longstanding and bitter dispute with the head over staffing and workload.

- this event was seen as the head asserting his authority.
- the head was seen by staff as dogmatic, authoritarian, and insensitive.

Our colleague later discovered that the head felt that the staff were lazy and incompetent. He had inadvertently put himself in the firing line. The training session was a complete waste of time – it only intensified the conflict. Our colleague retired hurt.

In both these cases, communication depended upon a complicated history. People had developed shared meanings over time which meant that communication was based on *very different* assumptions and expectations. Potential consequences in both situations were further misunderstanding and possible conflict.

If we look at the way people develop shared meanings, then we can also look at the way people express those meanings. In the last decade, organisational researchers have become very interested in the way people in organisations tell stories, tell jokes, and use metaphors to describe what is going on in their organisation. These stories and metaphors can provide very useful insights into the way people typically behave and communicate in that organisation. Storytelling has now become a useful technique for uncovering organisational dynamics as well as being recommended to managers as a useful if not essential skill (Denning, 2011):

> *stories can be used to create change, build culture, disseminate learning, and capture knowledge.*
>
> (Hutchens, 2009)

And so to basic principles

Principle 1: You can improve (but not guarantee) your chances of "success" in communication if you have clear purpose(s) and select appropriate strategies.

Your chances of effective communication can be improved if you can decide what you really want to achieve and then selecting the best strategy to make this happen. But this cannot guarantee success and there is no "one best way" which will work all the time.

One of our starting points is the fact that humans are *always* interpreting the meaning of events on the basis of the information available. Whatever our message it will have *some* effect on our audience and we should at least be clear in our own minds what outcome we wish to achieve. If we are unclear then our audience will be more so.

We can also cause difficulties in two ways – by having vague or inconsistent objectives and/or by choosing an inappropriate strategy.

Principle 2: Always question your assumptions.

We have ample evidence to support Hans Rosling's assertion that

> *you (and almost everyone I have ever met) do not see the world as it really is.*
> (Rosling, 2018, page 17)

Rosling's book demonstrates how we are all susceptible to biases in our thinking and misperceptions and suggests ways of countering these. A similar argument is presented by Bobby Duffy:

> *Our misperceptions are often biased in particular directions.*
> (Duffy, 2018, page 18)

The good news is that we can become aware of these biases and overcome them – but only if we spend some time questioning and checking our assumptions. Try the self-test in Rosling's book as a starter (op cit, page 3ff).

Principle 3: Communication always means more than "the message".

To communicate effectively, you need to anticipate how "messages" will be interpreted in context. And there is never "just one message". No matter how simple the situation, you can always think of a number of different messages which can be exchanged. You need to consider the meanings which will be "taken" from your behaviour. Ambiguity is an inherent feature of both language and nonverbal communication.

Ambiguity can be worse if some forms of digital communications are used as there can be less opportunity to interpret meaning through signals which we take for granted in face-to-face communication, e.g. voice tone, body language etc. Hence it is important to ensure clarity and use of plain language when using digital forms like email or social media platforms.

And this also suggests some very simple approaches we can use to support this principle:

- recognise that ambiguity is an inevitable feature of human communication.
- look for feedback and check understanding.
- accept that others' interpretations are legitimate.
- realise that discussion is essential to arrive at clear, shared meaning.
- recognise that some forms of digital communication provide limited opportunities for effective discussion and interpreting messages through non-verbal cues.

Do these approaches characterise everyday interactions in your organisation?

Principle 4: Communication is always based in a specific social, cultural, and technological context.

We need to recognise the constraints which influence communication because of the social, historical, and technological contexts in which it occurs, and respond accordingly. We will criticise attempts to provide guidelines or techniques for communication which ignore the context. For example, many management texts endorse the values of assertiveness without referring to the research which shows that assertive behaviour may be seen as aggressive or inappropriate in certain cultural settings or by certain individuals.

This principle is very important in a situation of change. Management who wish to introduce new processes or procedures should be sensitive to the meaning of the existing patterns of behaviour.

Principle 5: Communication and action must "match".

Your verbal and nonverbal communication must express the same meaning if you are to be believed. If your body language contradicts what you say then the other person will have to choose which channel to believe. Early research suggested that the nonverbal channel would always be believed and many popular handbooks simply repeat this conclusion. We now know that it is more complicated but we do know that we are very sensitive to this sort of ambiguity. If your speech and body language do not agree then this will almost certainly be noticed and interpreted by your audience.

Linked to this idea is the oft-quoted statement that "you cannot not communicate". In other words, failing to act can be seen as meaningful. For example, how do staff feel about the Chief Executive who always stresses the importance of communication in public meetings and media interviews but who never contributes anything to the staff blogs or newsletter?

And this suggests how to follow this principle – act in the way that you say that you do. Of course, there may be some issues of interpretation and these should be sorted out as soon as possible. The management team who announce an "open door" policy to employees should clarify what they mean with some examples or through discussion. It is very easy to set up expectations with a snappy slogan which makes claims which are obviously over-optimistic when you consider their likely interpretation by the audience.

The use of email and social media in organisations makes this even more important – it is so easy for anything that is digitally distributed to reach large audiences instantaneously and for large groups to discuss what you have said and done (or not done) – even if they were not part of your intended audience. It is best to assume that *anything/everything* that you say or send electronically can reach people who you did not intend to communicate with.

Principle 6: Communication can always be improved.

Although we accept that some people are inherently more skilled in their communication, we can all improve our skills with the right coaching or preparation.

As we said in the previous chapter, if you believe that communication can be improved then you will devote time to at least some of the following activities:

- reviewing the impact of your own behaviour on others.
- requesting feedback from others.
- developing strategies or plans to improve your communication.
- developing your digital literacy, including the ability to choose the appropriate means of traditional or digital communications for a specific context and audience.
- developing your skills in self-review.
- trying new techniques and reviewing their effectiveness.

Principle 7: Communication is a fundamental management responsibility (which we must all share).

If management do not accept responsibility for the quantity and quality of communication (both traditional and digital) in the organisation, then who will? Management must take responsibility – but this does not absolve us all from our responsibility to behave effectively and ethically.

This principle can be translated into practice in various ways. For example, we can ask how far the behaviour of managers at all levels throughout the organisation reflects concern for and commitment to communication.

This has been a longstanding concern for organisation theorists. Our first edition referred to Werner David's (1995) five fundamental steps:

- making a senior manager formally responsible for "linking every employee into the communication network" (page 4).
- systematic training in communication.
- building the organisation's communication network to use all the available media, ensuring it is especially sensitive to information which indicates the need for change.
- continually monitoring the network to make sure it works effectively.
- costing communication so that its effectiveness can be measured.

As with all general strategies, there are possible pitfalls. For example, the notion of making one senior manager "responsible" could lead to other managers "leaving it to him or her" rather than taking equal responsibility. Costing is difficult to organise and monitor. Furthermore, these ideas were developed in 1995, before the advent of social media and mobile devices. We now work in a world where business and technology are tightly integrated, allowing individuals to communicate in a multitude of ways with large audiences – both within the boundaries of "corporate" systems and externally with the world at large. This places an even greater need for management to take responsibility and balance open communications with communication protocols that address corporate needs relating to e.g. confidentiality, intellectual property, privacy, data protection, and other compliance agendas. At the very least, the fundamental steps listed above need to be enlarged with, for example, systematic staff training in digital literacies and the development of communications protocols for staff. Although we have reservations about some aspects of David's approach, we wholeheartedly agree with the overall concept – management in every organisation should have an explicit strategy which is regularly reviewed.

Principle 8: New media can and should enhance communication.

We now have a wider choice of communication media than at any time in history. These media can make a profound and positive impact if they are carefully introduced and maintained.

We discuss various aspects of new media throughout the book, including:

- use of social media, such as blogs, wikis, social networks etc. For example, tools such as Twitter can support teams in sharing ideas and information, building knowledge-bases and task management.
- the potential of all these technologies and media to support cost-efficient (or "lean") ways of working and new business relationships e.g. global teams.
- application of real-time conferencing (e.g. audio/video/web-conferencing) to enable meetings which might otherwise be too expensive to sustain.

All of these examples depend upon management strategy – they must invest to provide the facilities and then commit to sustain its appropriate use.

We do not have to look far to find examples of computer failures and their repercussions. But we can learn from the mistakes of the past and devise effective ways of using new technology to augment human aptitudes. The same is true of communication in general. Reflecting on some of the problems and pitfalls of human communication in organisations can show us how to avoid them, providing we are prepared to take responsibility.

Principle 9: Digital literacy should be a core part of staff professional development.

Digital communications are now so integral to business operations and working practices that "digital literacy" must be considered a prerequisite for staff development.

Professional development in organisations has to place more emphasis on:

- self-directed awareness and learning about new technologies – particularly awareness of the capability and potential of new technology.
- forensic ability in finding, analysing, using, and managing information.
- effective practices of digital communication, e.g. collaboration and participation in networks, sharing, facilitation, mentoring, coaching, critiquing, group learning etc.
- effective practices of critical reading, creative production, persuasion, argument, expressing, and sharing ideas.
- knowing how to choose and apply technologies to cost-effective business practices, e.g. project management, product innovation, sales and marketing, finance, lean working, teamworking – with an understanding of broader contexts.
- ability to influence colleagues and the organisation to adopt appropriate communication technologies.

Principle 10: The ability to influence has become a key communication skill in modern organisations.

Most current working practices are predicated on teamworking with the days of the isolated lone-worker long gone. To be an effective teamworker requires specific communications skill to influence others towards achieving goals.

SUMMARY OF KEY POINTS

- our understanding of communication influences the way we behave.
- some managers define communication as a linear process which may or may not incorporate feedback. This definition is not sufficient and can be misleading in many situations.
- you can analyse human communication from at least two different perspectives – the process perspective and the interpretive perspective.
- the process perspective emphasises the way messages are constructed and delivered, and the various factors which influence how those messages are received.
- the interpretive perspective emphasises the meaning which we perceive in situations. This meaning is often the result of complicated historical and cultural processes.
- we need to consider *both* process and interpretive perspectives when we examine specific examples of business communication. And we need to define both the intended and the received meanings.

References

Bovee, C. and Thill, J. (2014) *Business Communication Today*. London: Pearson.

Clampitt, P.G. (2016) *Communicating for Managerial Effectiveness*, 5th edition. Thousand Oaks, CA: Sage.

David, W. (1995) *Managing Company-Wide Communication*. London: Chapman and Hall.

Denning, S. (2011) *The Leader's Guide to Storytelling: Mastering the Art and Discipline of Business Narrative*, 2nd edition. San Francisco, CA: Jossey Bass.

Duffy, B. (2018) *The Perils of Perception*. London: Atlantic Books.

Finn, T.A. (1999) A case of telecommunications (mis)management. *Management Communication Quarterly* 12(4): 575–579.

Hutchens, D. (2009) Applications of narrative and storytelling as an organizational discipline. http://www.davidhutchens.com/Biz%20Writing/articles/organizationalst.html.

Rosling, H. (2018) *Factfulness: Ten Reasons We're Wrong about the World – And Why Things Are Better Than You Think*. London: Sceptre.

Waller, D.S. and Polonsky, M.J. (1998) Multiple senders and receivers: A business communication model. *Corporate Communications* 3(3): 83–91.

CHAPTER 3

What does communication mean?

Introduction

You cannot transmit your mental images, ideas, and feelings directly to another person, unless you believe in telepathic communication. We have to translate or encode our thoughts so that others can receive and interpret what we think.

Encoding is the focus of this chapter – we need to understand the variety of codes we use in everyday communication. For example, we use both verbal and nonverbal codes every time we talk and we need to consider how much scope there is for ambiguity and interpretation. If we can anticipate how other people will interpret what we say and do, then we can make our communication more effective. And we now have a growing range of new media which we can use to reinforce, extend, or replace our face-to-face contact.

Of course, we also need to bear in mind the implications of the last chapter – communication is not just the transmission and reception of information. No matter how carefully we feel we have "encoded our message", we need to be aware of all the factors which can influence how other people will interpret our behaviour.

OBJECTIVES

This chapter will:

- introduce the range and variety of human communication codes.
- explain why we need to think of human language as a collection of multiple and overlapping codes.
- examine the nature and scope of nonverbal communication, and its relationship with language.
- identify practical implications for the appropriate use of language and nonverbal codes in professional business communication.

DOI: 10.4324/9781003297550-5

What are the different codes we use to communicate?

There are several ways of categorising the different codes we use when we communicate with each other. A typical example comes from Ellis and Beattie (1986) who identified "five primary systems of communication" in face-to-face interactions (page 17):

- verbal, i.e. the words, clauses, and sentences we use in speech and writing.
- prosodic, i.e. the stress and pitch patterns such as pauses and intonation which we use in speech and which are "linguistically determined" – we use them to punctuate the speech and make its meaning clear. Ellis and Beattie use the simple phrase, "old men and women" as an example. Leave a silent pause after "men" when you say this sentence, and it changes the meaning.
- paralinguistic, i.e. all the pauses, "ums", "ahs", and other sounds which are not "real" words.
- kinesic, i.e. all the ways we move our bodies during communication, including posture, gestures, and so on.
- standing features, i.e. more static nonverbal features such as appearance, orientation (the angle at which you stand to the other person), or distance.

There are important issues with this (and with all other systems of) classification:

- does this mean that the different systems "work" in different ways?
- do we somehow interpret or process them differently?
- do the different systems have different functions?

These issues have important practical implications. For example, what do you attend to when you are meeting someone for the first time? Do you concentrate on what they are saying or on some aspect of their nonverbal behaviour? How would you give them some clues that you liked them – what signals would you use?

As we see in the rest of this chapter, these questions are not always easy to answer. For example, based on more recent research, Beattie suggested that gesture is one code with particular characteristics. In an important recent book, Nick Enfield offers an analysis of language which is compatible with the notion of "communication as dance" from the last chapter:

> *Language is our most important tool for achieving social coordination, and using language is itself a coordination game.*
>
> (Eindhorn, 2022, page 27)

We return to these issues later. We start by examining the distinction between verbal and nonverbal codes while emphasising that the most important issue is how they *work together* to create a particular meaning.

Understanding human language

We follow Michael Clyne's suggestion (1994) that language has four main functions:

1. our most important medium of human communication.
2. a means of identification. We use language to express our membership of social groups, which may be national, ethnic, social, religious etc.
3. a means of intellectual development. The way that children develop their language skills is very strongly related to the way they experience their surrounding environment. In adulthood, we use language to develop new ways of thinking and new concepts.
4. an instrument of action. Much of what we say is directly linked to what we do. When we promise or apologise, we are not simply passing on information.

This book concentrates on function (1), but we must not forget the practical implications of the other functions. For example, people who concentrate on function (2) often have very strong views on what language use is appropriate in each situation. Function (4) causes difficulties if we do not recognise the action implications of what we say. This may be especially important in cross-cultural encounters.

Language and social identity

You can see the importance of language as a symbol of broader social identities in the following examples:

- U.S.English is the campaign in the USA which aims to make English the "official language of the United States" (www.usenglish.org).
- the Académie Française attempts to protect the French language from "foreign" words and expressions (https://www.academie-francaise.fr).

These movements (and other similar ones) often claim that some varieties of language are *inherently* inferior. They try to define one version of language as the ideal or standard. They face serious challenges on both these counts. All languages grow and develop. Any attempt to "police" a language which does not recognise these processes is unlikely to succeed.

Codes within language

Language does not just deliver information – it can convey various levels of meaning depending on the situation. In even a simple conversation, there may be several different codes which we can recognise:

A: "I'm getting an error message – could be a driver problem".

B: "OK, Bones, what are you going to do about it? They're all supposed to have the 3.5 upgrade".
A: "Obviously, you need to try it on the other two machines first".

In this brief conversation between two people trying to get a computer programme to work, we see various codes at work:

- technical jargon, as in "driver problem."
- the joke based on a Star Trek character (as this comes from the first Trek generation, this might be a clue to the age of the characters).
- the private joke over who does what – "obviously you" do this. (You can imagine different ways of saying this – it could be a "put-down" rather than a joke.)

All of these depend upon their relationship. B would have adopted a very different tone with a relative stranger or a new boss.

This illustrates Kurt Danziger's view that *all* communication simultaneously works on two levels:

- presentation of information (he calls this "representation").
- presentation of a particular relationship which is implied in what is said and how it is expressed (he calls this "presentation").

(Danziger, 1976)

He shows how certain individuals are very conscious of this distinction and may manipulate what they say to entrap the other person. His examples include sales representatives and interrogators! This is *not* the same as the distinction between verbal and nonverbal codes as we usually express a relationship *both* verbally and nonverbally. One very important practical implication here is that we need to review both *what* we communicate and *how* we do it. We need to establish the appropriate relationship.

Language variety

We need to introduce three main concepts: register, dialect, and accent. All of these have important practical implications – for example, people have expectations about the "correct" register for particular occasions and make judgements about the people they meet on the basis of their dialect and accent.

Register

Different groups use different subsets of their language to suit their purposes. So we can identify the characteristics of different subsets or registers. For example, one early study of scientific reports found common features which were very rare in everyday conversation, such as compound nouns, passives, conditionals, and so on.

Without going too far into linguistic technicalities, you can recognise main features of different registers. The important implication is that certain registers are accepted as the norm in certain situations even if they are not very "efficient" (see the discussion of Plain English in Chapter 7). If you select the wrong register, you can easily create the wrong impression.

Dialect

A dialect is a language variety which is characteristic of a region or a socioeconomic group. In the UK, for example, there are a wide variety of regional dialects such as Cockney (London), Scouse (Liverpool), and Doric (North-East Scotland).

Over the years in the UK, there has been considerable pressure to achieve "Standard English". Despite growing acceptance of regional dialects, many people still consider some dialects "better" than others. This is also true in other parts of the world with other languages – we cannot look at the way language is used without investigating the *opinions* people have about language variety. We can illustrate the problems this may cause by looking at the impact of different accents.

Accent

Accent is often confused with dialect because a non-standard accent is often associated with a non-standard dialect. Accent refers to the distinctive pronunciation which characterises a group or a geographical area. In an area like the UK, accents tend to be regional.

Research confirms that certain accents are more highly regarded than others, and some organisations are deliberately selecting staff to deal with customers based on these perceptions. This preference for certain accents varies from country to country and group to group. Of course, many people deliberately cultivate an accent as a means of reinforcing group or cultural identity.

The great danger in our attitude to people with an accent that differs from our own is that we stereotype them with attributes that have little or nothing to do with ways of speaking. For example, we may consider people less well (or better) educated merely because they speak with a different accent. Of course, people may also discriminate against a particular accent to discriminate on racial or class grounds.

Structural features of language

Every language has certain structural features which has implications for how we communicate in (and how we learn) that language. For example, if I tell you "it rained last night" then you have no way of knowing from this whether I know this because I was there, or because I heard the weather forecast or from some other source. If I was speaking to you in the Hopi language then my source would be clear from what I said. Their language specifies context as well as the event or information.

Among the most interesting features of the English language are:

Expanding and developing vocabulary

Many English words in dictionaries are virtually extinct as far as everyday use is concerned. Does it matter if we no longer use terms such as "velleity", "aposiopesis", or the "myoclonic jerk" (Bryson, 1990, page 60)? The British media regularly debate which new words should be recognised in the next edition of the Oxford English Dictionary.

The important principle for our purposes is that new expressions appear all the time in various ways:

- we borrow words from other languages, such as "ketchup" from China.
- we put new meanings into old words. An obvious example here is "gay".
- we add or subtract parts from old words, usually by abbreviating them. Sometimes, we can take a longstanding word (such as political) and add to it to create a new expression. According to Bill Bryson, the word "apolitical" appeared in 1952 (ibid, page 76).
- we create new words, usually by making some analogy. We now talk of politicians talking in "sound-bites" (short snatches of political rhetoric) – a phrase first popularised during the 1988 American elections.

Multiple meanings for words

An example here would be "set" with 58 uses as a noun, 126 uses as a verb, and ten uses as an adjective. Many other words have multiple meanings – we have to work out what they mean from the context.

Variety in pronunciation

The English language has more sounds than many others, a particular problem for language learners, especially when they find that many spellings and pronunciations do not match (e.g. how would you pronounce "chough"?) There are changes in pronunciation which seem to reflect changing fashion and the obvious variations in dialect. These variations can be quite dramatic.

Variety in spelling

According to linguistics expert David Crystal,

> *English spelling is difficult but is not as chaotic as is often claimed.*
>
> (Crystal, 2013, p.6)

He explains how several historical changes to English spelling – understanding these provides important clues to accurate spelling and explains many seeming inconsistencies.

Flexible syntax

UK English has rules of grammar but no formal ruling body to enforce them (see Box 2.2 for related issues). Although some rules are more "powerful" than others, they may all change over time.

The important practical implication is that we cannot simply rely on a dictionary to choose effective language for a given situation. We need to assess both situation and context. For example, how do we know when a word or expression has become sufficiently accepted so it can be used, especially in more formal situations? This depends on the audience. For example, are they familiar with expressions which arise from popular culture? In a business document, would you use any of the following phrases which we found in British daily papers – "trial by Tik Tok"; "road rage'; "spin doctor"; "trend towards retro"; and "prosecution of spam king"? Or do you have an audience which is openly hostile to "trendy catchphrases" or to Americanisms? There is also the question of business jargon. We have several guides to jargon which has gone "past its sell-by date" and is best avoided (e.g. Taggart, 2011).

Speaking vs writing

There is a longstanding academic debate about the differences between spoken and written language. The following table gives some common distinctions.

This comparison uses analysis from the Linguistics Society of America (e.g. see Baron, 2008). But how far are these differences affected by context? And

Table 3.1 Spoken vs written language

Characteristic	Spoken language	Written language
universality	everyone can speak, if they are physically able	some problems of literacy systematically exclude certain individuals and groups
complexity	tends to be less complex using simpler sentences	often uses complex sentences and expressions
rate of change	more likely to change and at a faster rate	less change, likely to change much slower
formality	likely to use many colloquial terms	likely to use more official terms and avoid slang

what about new media which seem to muddy the distinction between spoken and written language?

Is online language written or spoken?

Text messages are written messages but often read more like a conversation. Naomi Baron concludes that instant messaging is more like speech than text in terms of overall characteristics, but she found some interesting gender differences to complicate the issue, e.g. that females tended to use a style more similar to their writing style.

This debate has important practical significance when we consider the impressions we make on each other. We return to this issue in Chapter 9.

Nonverbal codes

When the media talk about nonverbal communication or body language, they often focus on what is known as kinesics. Signals studied under this heading include facial expression, eye contact, gesture, and body posture.

Much of this communication is unconscious. The face in particular signals a wide range of emotions and there seems to be a range of "basic emotions" which are very similar across many cultures. Several classic studies suggested six fundamental emotional states: happiness, surprise, fear, sadness, anger, and disgust/contempt. (Ekman, 1992) Many training courses and resources use these categories to help you interpret emotions "correctly". However, this was challenged by recent research by Rachael Jack and colleagues at the University of Glasgow (Jack et al., 2014). Their research suggests four "biologically basic emotions" and a hierarchy which has developed over time to signal other emotional states. For example, they suggest that fear/surprise is one basic category. These two emotions can be confused by viewers as they start from the same bodily movement – raised eyelids – but then are distinguished by different following movements. The same applies to anger/disgust – starting from the nose wrinkle.

These researchers continue to explore how individual facial movements combine to signal different emotions, and how they are perceived. We do not yet fully understand how this works:

> *the specific facial signals that drive (i.e. explain) these perceptions are unknown.*
>
> (Liu et al., 2022)

The important practical consequence of this is that we may need to re-examine some training methods to give more sophisticated insight into how we judge emotional states. And it is worth questioning your own assumptions about the meaning of nonverbal signals.

There is an enormous amount of research on different nonverbal signals. This has focused on how different signals are used and what they usually mean. For example, eye contact signals interest and helps to control social interaction. Body posture often signals the attitude towards the interaction, whether it be tense, relaxed, interested, or bored. Gestures are often used for submission. Sometimes gestures become ritualised, as in an army salute. Body posture can also become ritualised as in bowing, kneeling etc.

For the rest of this chapter, we shall highlight important practical aspects of nonverbal codes.

Nonverbal codes may contradict the verbal

Often body language contradicts a spoken message – we say that the sender does not "mean what he says" and is insincere. This raises another fundamental question which we return to later – how far can you become skilled at reading body language?

Nonverbal messages *may be* very important

Many popular books about nonverbal communication (NVC) make strong claims about the "power" of NVC. This is a longstanding issue. For example, Judi James (1995) suggested that certain research did "discover exactly what it is that contributes to the total message" (page 9), as follows:

- verbal – 7%.
- tone of voice – 38%.
- visual – 55%.

These statistics come from the 1960s and are typically used to support claims like:

- "most of the messages in any interaction with another person (face to face) are revealed through body signals or 'bodytalk'" (Borg, 2013, page 61).
- "eye contact can account for as much as 55 per cent of information transmission in a given conversation" (Dutton, 2011, page 72).
- "we as human beings pay more than 90% attention to body language and tone of the voice more than the actual words" (Harappa Education, 2020).

Unfortunately, this does *not* reflect how NVC really works in everyday practice – we explain why in Chapter 10. Also see the website for further analysis.

Even though subsequent research paints a much more complicated picture, this finding is still regularly repeated, often without any attempt to suggest reservations.

Do *not* rely upon these statistics, which are actually difficult to interpret. Research has shown that nonverbal signals *can* be very important, but they may not be so dominant in every situation. We must *always* consider the relationship between words and nonverbal cues.

Nonverbal communication cannot be avoided

You cannot avoid sending nonverbal signals. In the UK, avoiding eye contact usually signals that you do not wish to communicate. Eye contact, a smile, or a handshake all signal varying degrees of willingness to communicate.

Much nonverbal communication is culture-bound

Some nonverbal behaviour appears universal but the expression of less intense emotions and general social feelings is much more culture-bound. For example, in many situations in British and American culture, failure to "look a person in the eye" is interpreted as shiftiness. But in many African and Hispanic cultures averting the eyes is a mark of respect for a person of higher status. Similarly, the American "OK" hand sign has an obscene or vulgar meaning in other countries as diverse as Brazil and Greece.

As a result, we now have "dictionaries" of nonverbal signs and guides to "correct" nonverbal expression in a range of cultures. There are obvious problems with all these generalisations, including whether they apply equally across the culture. There are also problem of deciding which rules are current, which are changing, and which are really important. For example, in the 1990s, we came across the recommendation that, in England, "men's shirts should not have pockets" – which meant that one of us had to buy a new wardrobe! We can only guess what this guidance would have made of current trends towards open-necked shirts by many managers and executives.

But how can we make sense of these differences? McDaniel (1997) argued that nonverbal behaviour reflects or represents dominant cultural themes. He used the example of Japanese culture where there are several clear themes, including social balance and harmony, strong group and collective loyalty, formality, humility, and hierarchy. He showed how Japanese nonverbal behaviour at the time both illustrated and reinforced these cultural themes. For example, the Japanese tended to avoid direct eye contact except "unless a superior wants to admonish a subordinate" (page 259). Thus, the typical behaviour reflected the norm of humility – this norm was only broken to reinforce another cultural theme, hierarchy.

As McDaniel acknowledges, this form of analysis is easier in cultures with very strong themes such as Japan. It is more difficult in more diverse cultures. And we have the problem of measuring cultural themes.

The meaning of nonverbal behaviour depends on the context

Even within one culture, we cannot expect particular nonverbal signals to mean the same thing in different situations. For example, Mark Knapp and Judith Hall (2010) reviewed research on nonverbal signals associated with dominance. A non-smiling face is seen as dominant but does this mean that dominant people smile less? Some studies have found that dominant members of a group smile more! They suggest that people who are *trying to achieve* dominance use a different set of nonverbal signals from those who have already achieved high status.

You can improve your interpretation of nonverbal communication

It is possible to improve your skill in interpreting body language. One key principle here is to look for "leakage" where the other person tries to control their expression in certain parts of their body but the true emotion "leaks out" elsewhere. I may feel very angry and put on a poker face but you may be able to spot anger in my gestures, or the way my foot is furiously tapping, or some other "leak" which I cannot control. Linked to this is the notion of "micro-expressions" – small and very quick changes of facial expression or bodily movements which are claimed to reveal the "true" emotion that you are feeling.

How nonverbal signals can communicate (or not) in everyday work situations

One point we will repeat as it is so important – you should interpret communication in a holistic way – interpret the *total* picture before you, looking at all the verbal and nonverbal codes together. However, there are situations where a specific nonverbal code can have particular significance.

Paralinguistics can provide very useful clues

In work situations, paralinguistic messages can be the most important. When someone says "everything is going well", hesitancy in the voice may show that everything is *not* going well.

The reverse can also happen. You may have a good proposal to put forward to management. If your behaviour is badly affected by nerves, then the proposal may come over as uncertain and hesitant. As a result, you may not be taken seriously. If you have an important verbal message to put across, you need to ensure that paralinguistic messages support, and do not detract from it.

Appearance

Dress also has a cultural dimension and can sometimes be a source of discord or discrimination. Certain groups signal their affiliation through clothes. Examples are the turbans of Sikhs and the yarmulkes of certain Jewish groups. In addition, minority groups may have their own dress codes which clash with prescribed codes. As dress can be a source of miscommunication and friction in organisations, management should develop a sensible policy which should be reviewed regularly as attitudes and fashions change over time.

What our clothes say about us

What we wear has symbolic influence on the way we are perceived – for example, it can affect perceptions of students for lecturers and vice versa. At work, the way we dress is often a mixture of tradition and organisational culture. Historically, men in business organisations always wore a suit and tie – business wear continues to be dominated by this approach. The shift to a more casual approach has generated online tips for how to dress appropriately, such as:

> *the dressed down version of business professional, which means you can keep the suit but lose the tie, wear dress pants with a blazer, or wear a wider variety of more casual clothes, such as chinos, sweaters and cardigans.*
>
> (Van Tongeren, 2020)

The online move due to Covid has extended the discussion about what level of casual dress is acceptable at work (Shaw, 2022). Where the casual business look is acceptable, personal preferences come into play. For example, at a recent planning day held away from the office, one colleague was still in a suit and tie, whereas another ditched the tie, wore jeans but was still wearing his trademark waistcoat. Another was wearing an unironed T-shirt and chinos. Certain fields have very specific rules about business dress; in the City some firms not only require staff to wear a suit and tie but where suits should be bought, to reflect the status of the organisation.

Work by Maran et al. (2020) has shown that leaders can influence their impact on their organisations by having the "right" mix of formality and informality in what they wear. CEOs of major organisations dressed in ways that carried symbolic associations with characteristics such as leadership, charisma, and aptitude, and therefore influence. Their research used drawings of middle-aged men in different styles of dress reflecting the fact that other considerations are at play for women in leadership, revealing the increased levels of complexity for women when choosing what to wear at work (Brescoll, 2016).

New members of staff may receive guidelines – a business dress code – reflecting expectations that are appropriate for the organisation and culture. This is particularly obvious where a uniform is required, such as airline staff, or in a profession such as law or health. In the UK, where an organisation uses a dress code, Government guidance (2018) requires it to go beyond having codes for both men and women. Reflecting the Equality Act 2010, the guidance indicates that dress codes for men and women should be equivalent, even if they are not identical. This guidance was developed following widespread media coverage and the petition resulting from Nicola Thorp's claim that she was dismissed because of refusing to wear high heels whilst working as a receptionist in London (Ridley, 2016).

Whilst the law may be clear about the expectation of equivalence for men and women in respect to their dress in the workplace, there are other, less clear factors at play. The way that women are perceived can often be related to the way they dress and the expectations of those that they work with (by both men and women) and the work by Brescoll (2016) indicates that stereotypes continue to influence the ways in which women are perceived. As a result, leadership programmes specifically aimed at women will often provide guidance on how to navigate the landscape by the choices we make, e.g. wearing clothes that reflect the role you want rather than the one that you are in; when interviewed by a woman, wear an outfit that positively mirrors *their* own dress code.

Eye contact

Barbara Shimko surveyed 38 general managers of fast-food restaurants about their employment practices and found 9% of applicants were rejected because of "inappropriate eye contact" (Shimko, 1990).

This study illustrates how people in organisations have norms and expectations about nonverbal behaviour. People who want to gain entry to a particular organisation may have to comply with these norms to get through the selection procedure. Posture may be very important here – often seen as a strong indicator of a person's attitude to the situation and audience. In high-stakes situations such as job interviews, the interviewee is unlikely to create a good impression with an "over-relaxed" posture. In superior-subordinate interactions, the subordinate who wants to impress will probably try to take up a posture that is slightly more rigid than the power-holder. Of course, there are dangers here – an over-rigid posture can signal lack of confidence.

Personal space and distance

The effect of personal space and distance in communication is complex and depends on several factors which include: the social relationship, the situation; the status relationship; and the culture. One widely-quoted formula from Edward Hall identified four distance zones for middle-class Americans (Hall, 1959).

- intimate – physical contact to 45 cm.
- casual-personal – 45 cm to 120 cm.

- social-consultative – 120 cm to 365 cm.
- public – over 365 cm.

In cultures which follow this pattern, business interactions tend to take place at the casual-personal or social-consultative levels. But expectations of the type of interaction influence the distance – if we expect an unfavourable message, we will distance ourselves from the sender. So, depending on the level of formality, we tend to alter the distance to where we feel comfortable.

One general rule is that the person with power or status controls the interaction distance, particularly in intimate and casual personal interactions. In your organisation, is it acceptable for a manager to pat someone on the back as an accompaniment to encouragement or praise? And would the reverse be resented?

Possibilities offered by new technology

We now have new ways of communicating which can augment the codes we use in face-to-face contact. And new methods/media are appearing.

Nancy Baym (2010) suggests that we use "seven key concepts" to differentiate between the new forms, as summarised in the following table

We shall look at these characteristics in more detail in later chapters. For the moment, we suggest some important implications:

- we now have techniques which allow us to make contact and reinforce relationships with relatively few limitations of time and place.
- continuous access to mobile contact brings potential issues. We must think about how much access people have to us.

Table 3.2 Key concepts for communications media

Concept	Meaning
interactivity	the forms of interaction which are supported
temporal	the timing involved – for example, asynchronous or synchronous
social cues	the range of cues available such as facial expression
storage	how do you keep the messages?
replicability	can you save and pass on the message?
reach	size of the audience you can reach
mobility	portability

- we can use asynchronous media when we want to plan our message and when we might need a fairly quick response.
- we can also keep records and store certain conversations where we need to. Of course, you must then think about how and where any records are stored.
- we need to think very carefully about the best media for particular forms of communication.

SUMMARY OF KEY POINTS

- we use a variety of codes to communicate, including verbal and nonverbal codes.
- social rules and expectations are associated with these codes, and they influence how the codes are interpreted (e.g. perceptions of accent).
- our communication will reflect our attitudes and feelings and we need to make sure that we do not send out ambiguous or misleading signals.
- although there have been exaggerated claims about the importance and meaning of nonverbal communication, we must make sure that our nonverbal signals create the appropriate relationship.
- all human codes are fuzzy and potentially ambiguous. As a result, we always need to consider their meaning in context.
- we must pay attention to the whole range of communication codes when we try to detect emotional states such as deception.
- we need to think about both the potential and drawbacks of new technological methods.

References

Baron, N.S. (2008) *Always On: Language in an Online and Mobile World.* New York: Oxford University Press.

Baym, N.K. (2010) *Personal Connections in the Digital Age.* Cambridge: Polity Press.

Borg, J. (2013) *Body Language: How to Know What's REALLY Being Said*, 3rd edition. Harlow: Pearson.

Brescoll, V.L. (2016) Leading with their hearts? How gender stereotypes of emotion lead to biased evaluations of female leaders. *The Leadership Quarterly* 27(3): 415–428, ISSN 1048-9843. https://doi.org/10.1016/j.leaqua.2016.02.005.

Bryson, B. (1990) *Mother Tongue.*

Clyne, M. (1994) *Intercultural Communication At Work: Cultural Values in Discourse.* Cambridge: Cambridge University Press.

Crystal, D. (2013) *Spell it Out: The Singular Story of English Spelling.* London: Profile Books.

Danziger, K. (1976) *Interpersonal Communication*, 1st edition. New York: Pergamon Press (Pergamon general psychology series, 53).

Dutton, K. (2011) *Flipnosis: The Art of Split-second Persuasion.* Croydon: Arrow.

Ekman, P. (1992) An argument for basic emotions. *Cognition and Emotion* 6(3–4): 169–200. https://doi.org/10.1080/02699939208411068.

Ellis, A. and Beattie, G. (1986) *The Psychology of Language and Communication*. Lawrence Erlbaum. http://www.geoffbeattie.com/books/the-psychology-of-language-and-communication-classic/.

Enfield, N.J. (2022) *Language versus Reality: Why Language is Good for Lawyers and Bad for Scientists*. Cambridge, MA: MIT.

Gov.uk. (2018) Government guidance on dress codes. https://assets.publishing.service.gov.uk/government/uploads/system/uploads/attachment_data/file/709535/dress-code-guidance-may2018-2.pdf.

Hall, E.T. (1959) *The Silent Language*. New York: Doubleday.

Harappa. (2020) *Understanding Body Language in Nonverbal Communication*. https://harappa.education/harappa-diaries/body-language-in-communication/.

Jack, R.E., Garrod, O.G.B. and Schyns, P.G. (2014) Dynamic facial expressions of emotion transmit an evolving hierarchy of signals over time. *Current Biology* 24(2): 187–192.

James, J. (1995) *Body Talk: The Skills of Positive Image*. London: Industrial Society.

Knapp, M.L. and Hall, J.A. (2010) *Nonverbal Behaviour in Human Interaction*, 9th edition. Fort Worth: Harcourt Brace.

Liu, M et al., (2022) Facial expressions elicit multiplexed perceptions of emotion categories and dimensions, *Current Biology* 32, 200–209

Maran, T., Liegl, S., Moder, S., Kraus, S. and Furtner, M. (2020) Clothes make the leader! How leaders can use attire to impact followers' perceptions of charisma and approval. https://doi.org/10.1016/j.jbusres.2020.11.026.

McDaniel, E.R. (1997) Non-verbal communication: A reflection of cultural themes. In Samovar, L.A. and Porter, R.E. (eds) *Intercultural Communication: A Reader*, 8th edition. Belmont, CA: Wandsworth.

Ridley, L. (2016) London Receptionist Nicola Thorp 'Sent Home From Work For Not Wearing Heels.' Huffington Post, at https://www.huffingtonpost.co.uk/entry/high-heels-receptionist-sent-home-pwc-nicola-thorp_uk_573324b4e4b0e6da49a72f9f

Shaw, D. (2022) CEO secrets: What's a modern boss to wear. *BBC*. https://www.bbc.co.uk/news/business-62992989.

Shimko, B.W. (1990) New breed workers need new yardsticks. *Business Horizons*, November/December, pages 34–36.

Taggart, C. (2011) *Pushing the Envelope: Making Sense Out of Business Jargon*. London: Michael O'Mara Books.

Van Tongeren, R. (2020) Business casual for men: Dress code guide (+Outfit examples) from restart your style. https://restartyourstyle.com/business-casual-.

CHAPTER 4

Communication context 1: organisational culture and structure

Introduction

This chapter introduces two interdependent characteristics of organisations which have profound implications for the ways we communicate: culture and structure. We introduce these separately while offering examples which suggest how they interact and influence our communication. In Chapter 5, we attempt to define what we call the "new technology landscape" and show how that also interacts to create the overall context for communication in all organisations.

Notions of organisational culture have been prominent in management literature since the 1980s. One impact of the pandemic was to revitalise the need to investigate and influence organisational culture, especially given debates and differences over virtual and homeworking. One well-publicised example is Google's redesign of their base office in London and their work on "inclusive meeting rooms for hybrid working" (BBC Business News, 2022). Other organisations have radically downsized their office space to support increased homeworking while facing challenges on how to inculcate and maintain effective business cultures.

Organisational structures have also seen considerable change and innovation. The pandemic accelerated the trend towards "flatter" organisational structures with fewer levels in the hierarchy. And this begs the questions – do particular organisational structures encourage organisational communication? Have traditional hierarchical structures "had their day"?

OBJECTIVES

This chapter will:

- explain what we mean by organisational culture.
- explain major dimensions of organisational structure.
- discuss important relationships between these factors.

DOI: 10.4324/9781003297550-6

Organisational culture and communication

Definitions of organisational culture usually echo definitions of national culture, talking about typical or traditional ways of thinking, believing, and acting. They include the ways that ideas and behaviour patterns are shared by members of the group, and the way these are learnt and adopted by new members.

Consider how you feel when you join a new organisation. You are very keen to find out "the way they do things round here" and you probably behave cautiously to make sure that you do not offend anyone by breaking one of the "unwritten rules". What can add to the complexity of adapting to a new organisation is that there can be a variety of subcultures to negotiate. These can reflect different approaches in the various departments of an organisation or it could be that within an international business there are differing national cultures at play.

The shift to working from home, or hybrid working, has made it more difficult to identify what the dominant culture is and, for new members of staff, to find out "how they do things round here". So how can we assess the nature of an organisational culture?

Compare the two lists of components in Table 4.1 (adapted from different definitions in Senior et al., 2020, page 135).

Although they have a lot in common, there are important differences between these two lists:

- List A covers more of the ways that culture is *communicated* (myths, heroes etc.) whereas List B focuses more on underlying *principles* (e.g. how far the organisation uses teams).
- List A focuses more upon *informal* characteristics like jokes and stories, and also highlights the *historical* dimension. List B includes many *formal* organisational rules, e.g. the reward and promotions criteria. It also focuses on notions of *identity*, the degree to which employees identify with the organisation as opposed to identifying with their job or professional background.

You can use lists like this to develop a checklist to review your own organisation and compare different organisational cultures (Senior et al, 2020, page 136).

Both the above lists are long and detailed. Which aspects should we concentrate on? How do we decide what is most important? And what details should influence our interpretation?

Levels of organisational culture

Edgar Schein (2009, 2010) suggests three levels:

- "artefacts" – visible structures and processes in the organisation.

Table 4.1 Components of organisational culture

List A	List B
Brown (1995, p8 cited in Senior et al., 2020, page 135)	**Robbins and Judge (2013, cited in Senior et al. 2020, page 135)**
Ingredients of culture	**Characteristics of culture**
Artefacts	Innovation and risk taking
Language in the form of jokes, metaphors, stories, myths and legends	Attention to detail
Behaviour patterns in the form of rites, rituals, ceremonies, and celebrations	Outcome orientation
Norms of behaviour	People orientation
Heroes (past and present employees who do great things)	Team orientation
Symbols and symbolic action	Aggression
Beliefs, values, and attitudes	Stability
Ethical codes	
Basic assumptions about what is important	
History	

This includes: the language people use; stories circulating around the organisation; rituals and ceremonies; and the organisation's environment (including buildings and space allocation).

- "espoused values" – values which the organisation *claims* to follow, as expressed in the organisation website, annual report, mission statement etc.
- "basic underlying assumptions".
  The third and deepest level includes all the taken-for-granted beliefs which are the *real* source of values and actions within the organisation. These may be accepted subconsciously or unconsciously.

One obvious implication is the potential for important differences between what an organisation *says* it does and what it *actually* does. The organisation that claims to value and support its employees on its website may be extremely ruthless when it comes to hiring and firing people. Although Vishal Garg apologised for the way he fired 900 staff over Zoom, the contrast between his method and the words of apology was stark, and this was widely reported.

If an organisation operates on the assumption of "survival of the fittest" whereas the mission statement portrays a "happy family", what will employees believe? They will believe the actions and not the rhetoric. For an interesting contrast between managers on a central component of organisational culture, see Box 4.1.

BOX 4.1

The boss wants us back in the office!

The debate about how much employees can work from home has intensified since the pandemic receded and restrictions were lifted. But this is not a new argument as this example from 2013 illustrates: a leaked internal email from Yahoo to all employees proclaimed that

> *communication and collaboration will be important, so we need to be working side-by-side. That is why it is critical that we are all present in our offices.*

This created an embarrassing wave of publicity for the company. If you Google "Yahoo no work from home memo", you can read over a million results, including the full text of the memo. (e.g. at https://allthingsd.com/20130222/physically-together-heres-the-internal-yahoo-no-work-from-home-memo-which-extends-beyond-remote-workers/)

A recent "post-pandemic" example would be the typewritten note (on official notepaper) that appeared on the desks of many UK government employees from their newly-appointed boss. The note read:

> "Sorry you were out when I visited.
> I look forward to seeing you in the office very soon".

This was widely reported and commented upon, both in mass and social media. It was described as "crass and insulting" (by a union official) and as part of a "culture war" about virtual and homeworking (McGarvey and Blake, 2022).

This followed earlier reports that:

> *Civil servants must stop working from home and return to the office to ensure government buildings are at full capacity*
> (https://www.bbc.co.uk/news/uk-politics-61145692)

This very definitive ruling contrasts with the range of options for flexible working which have been offered in other organisations – see later chapters and the website for further examples.

Over the next few years we are likely to see more developments here, both in terms of organisation cultures and the technologies available to homeworkers. And we can expect to see further arguments within organisations about the appropriate location for specific job roles and the associated working conditions (as in the law firm which announced that staff could work from home if they accepted a 20% pay cut (Meierhans, 2022)).

Culture's consequences

Culture can have very clear and important practical consequences. Philip Clampitt (2017) suggests four key consequences:

- impact on economic performance and productivity.
- influence on how the organisation both analyses and solves problems.
- influence on how the company responds to change.
- the profound impact on employee motivation.

But how do workers/staff experience the culture?

Rick Delbridge (1998) worked on the production line in two factories: one Japanese-run and one British operation trying to introduce Japanese methods. He found dramatic differences between the espoused values (e.g., worker participation, open communication, etc.) and the actual practice. For example, "counselling" sessions with workers who were having difficulties turned out to be one-way communication from management to "do better"; there were also "team meetings" where only managers spoke. Although this reference is dated, similar differences in perception are still commonplace.

Major models of organisational culture

Different models have emerged from research and business consultants. We offer a couple of popular examples below (see more examples on the website).

Quinn and Cameron's Competing Values Framework (2011)

Quinn and Cameron identified two key polarities to describe culture and its impact on organisational effectiveness:

- internal focus and integration v external focus and differentiation.
- flexibility and discretion v stability and control.

This creates four dominant business cultures – Clan, Adhocracy, Hierarchy, and Market – with the following characteristics:

Clan Culture

This organisation aims to feel like a family, and communication is a key priority. It is most effective with small businesses and start-ups and allows for market growth. However, as it grows, the lack of structure makes communication more difficult. On the other hand, with remote working, this culture can work where communication is continuous, and staff have autonomy to work independently and in response to their local situation.

Adhocracy Culture

This culture celebrates innovation and adaptability, usually associated with risk-taking at the forefront of their individual industry. To be successful, this organisation needs to be tied to market growth.

Businesses set up by Elon Musk can typify this company culture and we wait to see the long-term outcomes at Twitter! This book went into its production cycle only a few weeks after Musk bought Twitter but he had already introduced major cultural and structural changes which led some commentators to question the company's long-term future. According to press reports, Musk "fired half of the workforce including top management, and is ruthlessly changing the culture to emphasize long hours and an intense pace" (Dang et al., 2022). Other reported changes included Musk's demand that staff return to the office and stopping free meals for staff. Many Twitter users abandoned the platform and alternatives like Mastodon reported significant new enrolments. See the website for our update and further comments on these developments.

Hierarchy Culture

Where the organisation is well-structured, where processes align to key objectives, this can provide a strong sense of stability. However, it can hinder change if there are few opportunities for collaboration or genuine communication between levels of the organisation. This is often found in public sector/government departments, or government-funded organisations such as schools.

Market Culture

The clear objective is usually profitability, so everything is seen in terms of (financial) costs and benefits. Individuals within the organisation exist to achieve this overarching objective. Where this works well, employees are motivated by external drivers (profitability) and are focused on achieving this.

Problems can arise if objectives create clashes with important values. A recent example was the decision by the pharmaceutical company AstraZeneca to withdraw dapagliflozin, the type 1 diabetes drug, from treating certain type 2 diabetes patients. Some charities objected that this was a decision driven by commercial factors rather than patient interest. This would reflect a market-driven culture where the focus is on much larger patient groups – more profitable than the benefits to individuals.

In other organisations, this "market" approach is used to encourage internal competition between employees. This can lead to burnout and low staff retention – apart from the senior roles where financial rewards are high (Mahase, 2022).

Culture styles (Groysberg et al., 2018)

They identified eight culture styles based upon two dimensions that apply to all organisations:

- the nature of people interactions.
- responsiveness to change.

Caring

This emphasises relationships between its members with a strong emphasis on teamwork and mutual support.

Purpose

The organisation focuses on sustainability, and global communities. Leaders emphasise the shared ideals of the organisation and its contribution to the greater good.

Learning

In this workplace, innovation, knowledge, and new ideas are welcomed and encouraged.

Enjoyment

This is characterised by fun and excitement. There will be a sense of playfulness, stimulation, and spontaneity.

Results

Achievement, target-setting, and internal competitiveness characterise the culture within a results-driven organisation.

Authority

Within this culture, the competitive element is seen in the achievement of control and dominance over others.

Safety

In an organisation with a strong culture of safety, the environment will be predictable, people will be risk-conscious and plan ahead, seeking to anticipate change in order to feel protected.

Order

This culture focuses on rules. A desire to fit in is often reflected in the hierarchical structures that develop. Employees are expected to co-operate with the traditional ways of working.

Contrasting different models of organisational culture

One common theme is that certain cultures are more (or less) suited to a particular social and economic environment.

One influential management text took this further to say that some cultures were *inherently* better than others (Peters and Waterman, 1982). They claimed that effective organisations shared specific values, including a " bias for action" and "closeness to the customer". Unfortunately for this analysis, some of the organisations they labelled as successful went on to struggle. Vermeulen (2010) suggested that only three or four of the organisations listed in 1982 had maintained excellent ratings.

This raises the question of how/whether a specific organisational culture can be maintained over the long term, especially during periods of economic and social change. A recent example is Netflix in 2022 – a very distinctive culture suddenly faced with serious and growing economic pressures – see Box 4.2.

BOX 4.2

How will the Netflix company culture develop?

Reed Hastings is Netflix co-founder and CEO; Erin Meyer is a leading business academic. Their co-authored book (Hastings and Meyer, 2020) examines the Netflix company culture from their different perspectives.

Hastings claims that the culture he initiated is both distinctive and successful:

> *a culture that valued people over process, emphasized innovation over efficiency, and had very few controls.*
>
> (page xiii)

You can find detailed descriptions of the culture on the company website (https://jobs.netflix.com/culture) and in the original internal slides which he later posted on the internet in 2009 – the Culture Deck. The slides have received a lot of attention over the years, and there are numerous commentaries online including the article on their development by Patty McCord who was involved at the time as Chief Talent Officer for Netflix (McCord, 2014).

Meyer starts the book by voicing scepticism and by highlighting aspects of the culture deck which contradict what is often regarded as good organisational practice, e.g. Netflix does *not* have a policy on holiday/vacation entitlement:

> *I loved the Netflix Culture Deck for its honesty. And I loathed it for its content.*
>
> (page xiii)

By the end of the book, she offers a positive perspective, arguing that Netflix have successfully demonstrated that:

> *you can offer a culture of freedom and responsibility, choosing speed and flexibility, and offering more freedom to your employees.*
>
> (page 269)

This book was published when the company was experiencing significant growth and economic success. For a useful summary of how the organisation developed, see Kobiruzzaman, 2022)

In 2022, circumstances changed – Netflix lost subscribers and the share value dropped. Media analysts suggested that the company would have to change to maintain its market leadership. The next few years will decide whether this unconventional culture is strong enough to survive the economic downturn. See the website for further sources/updates.

Values and organisational culture

Another important question is how far the organisation culture is related to broader social and political issues and values. One controversial proposal is that many modern organisations are taking on the values of efficiency and predictability first promoted in the American fast food industry. Box 4.3 looks at this in more detail.

BOX 4.3:

The McDonaldization thesis

George Ritzer introduced the term "McDonaldization", suggesting that many organisations have adopted four major principles which are taken to their logical extreme in fast food chains and which are increasingly adopted by online organisations (Ritzer, 2019):

- efficiency.
- accountability.
  Fast food restaurants use *exact* measures of ingredients/helpings and emphasise speedy delivery to the customer.
- predictability.
  The products in New York will be *exactly the same* as the ones in London or Paris, and they will be the exactly the same tomorrow as they were today. This predictability also applies to workers' behaviour and the scripts which service staff have to follow.
- control.
  Technology is used to control both staff and customer. One example is recent developments in the use of robots to prepare fast food (Michaels, 2022).

Although he notes some advantages, Ritzer suggests that McDonaldization can have negative and dehumanising consequences. He concludes that customers do not recognise some of the factors which make the organisation inefficient from their point of view. For example, many of these systems make the customers do a lot of the work; they may also be rather expensive; they may create a lot of waste in packaging etc. He is also very critical of their values, accusing them of double standards. Whereas those at the top of the organisation value their own freedom, they simultaneously "want to control subordinates through the imposition of rational systems" (op cit, pages 123/124). There are echoes here of debates about homeworking.

This work received very powerful reactions, not least from the organisations who are obvious targets of his criticism. See our website for further debate. For the moment, we emphasise possible conflicts between value systems which are highlighted by Ritzer's analysis.

Multiple co-existing cultures?

In the discussion so far, we have implied that a single organisation fits one culture. This is one problem with some cultural models – the assumption that the organisation is one unified whole. A number of factors argue against this:

- some cultures are stronger than others.
- employees' acceptance of the general culture can vary.
- different parts of the organisation may reflect different cultures.
- cultures can and do change.

Another possible misconception is that culture only develops in large organisations. In fact, we can observe and analyse culture in organisations of *all* sizes, including the very small.

How is organisational culture communicated and expressed?

Early research on organisational culture tended to focus on management attempts to communicate corporate values to their employees. But, of course, this may not accurately reflect what happens in the workplace. As a result, researchers have paid increasing attention to the ways in which organisational culture can be revealed in more personal communication. For example, there is research on:

- stories people tell about the organisation and about heroes in the organisation.
- slogans, catchphrases, and graffiti in the organisation.
- jokes and metaphors which people use to describe their experience of the organisation.

This research can uncover values which are accepted by the members of the organisation and also conflict which may exist between subgroups. A few examples to illustrate:

The power of metaphor

Smith and Eisenberg (1987) concluded from employee interviews that two fundamental metaphors represented the Disney approach: Disneyland was a "drama" and a "family". Employees saw themselves as "actors" putting on "costumes" to act out a "show" for their "audience" (customers). The family metaphor described management/worker relationships and attitudes. When management responded to increasing competition by adopting hard economic measures, the workers felt that this was "a breach of Disney's caring philosophy" (page 374).

Lists versus stories

Another continuing theme in the literature on organisational culture is the comparison between organisations. Browning (1992) suggested two broad types of cultures, identified by their preference for lists or stories. The "lists" organisation tends to issue written lists to staff to tell them what to do and how to do it. This reflects organisational values such as maintenance of standards and accountability. The "stories" organisation relies on face-to-face interaction and storytelling to communicate to staff. This is an organisation which values humour and performance.

Cultural differences

Much of the research to date on organisational stories has looked at Western organisations using English as the dominant language. In other cultures, members of the organisation may have different ways of expressing themselves through stories. For example, whereas stories in UK or US organisations often use images, jokes, and metaphors drawn from popular television programmes, films, and music, a study of storytelling in a Malaysian organisation found that most stories used traditional legends and historical characters (Ahmed and Hartley, 1999). The one major exception was a story in several parts which also used Power Rangers characters to comment on current management preoccupations.

Analysing your organisation's culture

A range of factors influence the culture which an organisation develops.

Practical tools and techniques you can use to analyse your organisation's culture can be found in the work of analysts we have already cited, such as Schein and Schein (2017), Senior, Swailes, and Carnall (2020) and Cameron and Quinn (2011). There are also online inventories such as OCAI (based on Cameron and Quinn). You need to consider whether you are comfortable in your organisation's culture and what this means for your communication.

Does your organisational culture inspire commitment and excellence?, as in Box 4.4.

Or does it enable negative or even immoral behaviour?

Uncovering negative information about your organisational culture can be a very difficult experience as we see in Box 4.5.

BOX 4.4

When culture goes right

In the book, *Shoot for the moon,* Richard Wiseman (2019) analyses the cultural factors which enabled the relatively young and inexperienced team – Mission Control in NASA – to successfully send the first human to the moon.

He suggests eight principles and associated techniques which were critical to their ultimate success, which we summarise in the table below with comments from our perpective.

Wiseman suggests that we can all learn from this example and apply the same techniques. As the book concludes,

> *against all the odds, they got there. You can, too.*
>
> (op cit, page 246)

Table 4.2 Cultural analysis of NASA Mission Control

Principle	Our comment
Passion	Members of the team had a strong sense of purpose and were strongly committed to what was an extremely ambitious goal given the technology of the time.
Innovation	Many original ideas came out of the project in addition to fulfilling the objective of reaching the moon.
Self-belief	Team members family believed that they could achieve the goal within the time scale although many independent observers felt it was impossible.
Learn how to fail	Not every aspect of the project was successful – astronauts died in the Apollo 1 fire. This did have the knock-on effect of making team members much more open about their mistakes.
Responsibility	There was a very strong sense of mutual responsibility.
Courage	The group had to "find the courage to stop talking and start acting" (page 242)
Preparedness	Planning was very thorough, including the contingency plans.
Flexibility	Members of the team responded flexibly to changes

BOX 4.5

When culture goes wrong

Three examples will illustrate how disastrous this can be for the organisations and individuals involved:

The previous edition of this book described the experience of Michael Woodford, following his appointment as President of the Japanese Olympus corporation. His attempts to investigate serious fraud in the company were thwarted by senior managers. Eventually, he was dismissed by the Board – pressures to conform and maintain group solidarity outweighed ethical considerations. His account of this process (Woodford, 2012) is a fascinating if depressing insight into corporate chicanery (and a very good read) – see further details and links on the website.

Yorkshire County Cricket Club was once lauded as the most successful cricket club in England and Wales, with players regularly representing England and with frequent County Championship wins (33 at the last count). However, the testimony of Azeem Rafiq to a parliamentary committee exposed endemic racism within the club – and in the sport. Moreover, it exposed a reluctance to address the issue comprehensively. The Yorkshire CC investigation into the allegations (August 2021) failed to recognise the embedded racism in the club and led to: the resignation of the chairman, Roger Hutton, and other senior figures; major sponsors withdrawing their support; and removal of the right to host England matches.

Our third example is also ongoing – the experience of a large group of sub-postmasters and sub-postmistresses who worked for the UK Post Office. They worked essentially as independent traders, often combining their post office business with other compatible enterprises, e.g. newsagent. They were convicted of fraud after shortfalls were discovered in their accounts following the installation of a new computer system from Fujitsu called Horizon in 1999. This has now been described as:

> *the most widespread miscarriage of justice in UK history.*
>
> (Peachey, April 2022)

Key facts include:

- between 2000 and 2014, the Post Office prosecuted 736 sub-postmasters and sub-postmistresses – an average of one a week.
- consequences for these individuals were life-changing and always seriously damaging, ranging from fines to jail sentences to bankruptcy and (in at least one case) to suicide.
- the shortfall in accounts is now recognised as a "glitch" in the computer software.
- prosecutions have now been squashed.
- claims for compensation and redress continue in the courts.

> *So far, nobody at the Post Office or Fujitsu has been held accountable*
>
> (Peachey, April 2022)

There is a very detailed account of this sad story on Wikipedia ("British Post Office Scandal") and also an excellent book by Nick Wallis, the journalist who first investigated the case and brought it to the attention of the British public (Wallis, 2021).

We cannot help thinking that all this could have been avoided if there had been a different culture in the Post Office (e.g. trusting employees and properly investigating the causes of errors) and a different structure (e.g. the accused staff had no easy means of communicating with others in the same position). It also happened at a time when informal contact between Post Office employees was more limited (before the explosion of social media).

How can we define organisational structure?

The most common way of representing the structure of an organisation is the organisation chart and a simple example is given in Figure 4.1. But what does this tell us? The vertical dimension shows the hierarchy and status relations; and the horizontal dimension shows the range of activities which the company is involved in. In this example of a manufacturing company, these activities include production, research and development, finance, marketing, and so on.

This diagram is *one* way of *representing* an organisation, and it can be criticised. For example, it provides an image of the organisation as a well-ordered system with clearly structured authority relations. This can be very misleading. If management see the organisation in this "clear-cut" way then they may implement policies which do not work because the organisation does *not* actually work that way.

One major issue with the standard organisation chart is what it does not tell you much about how the organisation functions. For example, what does it tell you about the main processes and systems?

Different ways of representing organisation structure are not just matters of technical detail. They represent fundamentally different approaches and different theoretical assumptions. If you review some of the classic texts on organisations, you will find very different starting points. These range from the organisation's contribution to the wider society, through approaches based upon how power and authority is organised, and on to approaches which reflect how the organisation is structured to meet the demands of its environment. One very influential management text argued that:

> *all theories of organization and management are based on implicit images or metaphors that lead us to see, understand, and manage organizations in distinctive yet partial ways.*
>
> (Morgan, 1997, page 4)

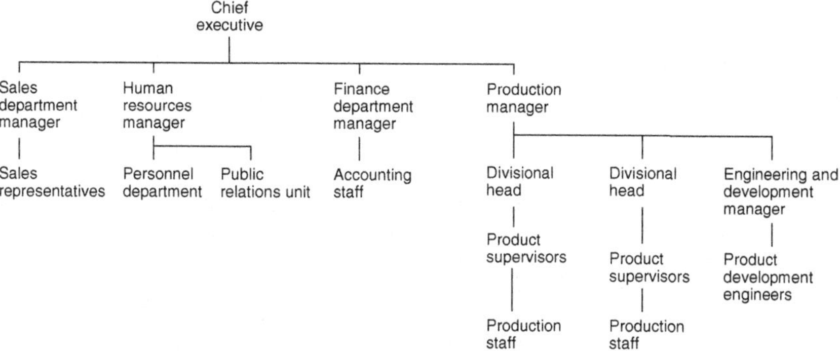

Figure 4.1 Simple organisation chart of a manufacturing company

As our main purpose is to focus on communication, we will not provide detailed analysis of different theories and metaphors. See Stanford (2022) for an excellent and detailed introduction to organisation design. She suggests five fundamental principles which you can apply to your organisation to assess the quality of its structure – that organisation design should:

1. be "driven" by "the organisation's purpose, strategy, and operating model".
2. use "systems thinking" to plan the connections between different parts of the organisation.
3. use "strong, thoughtfully used, future-oriented mindsets and methods".
4. involve "social interactions and conversations as much as formal planning".
5. be "a fundamental continuing business process, not a one-off repair job".

The examples in Box 4.5 of "culture failure" can also illustrate structural problems. For example, in the case of the Post Office, what were the lines of communication between the individual post offices and the computer support? Why did no-one consider the possibility of computer error before so many lives were ruined?

Different structural perspectives have important implications for the role of communication. We can illustrate this by offering three different ways of describing the organisation's structure:

- as a set of stakeholder groups who are connected through communication.
- as a set of managed subsystems.
- as a command hierarchy which can be realised in different ways.

Defining the stakeholders

Stakeholders are usually defined as:

> *"people who have an interest in the organisation, which may cause them to seek to influence managers' actions".*
>
> (Stewart, 1991, page 80)

Other commentators have argued that this model of business communication is much more relevant to modern organisations because they need to consider much more than simple economic motives. They must consider broader issues and implications – an obvious example is the current pressures on all organisations to improve their environmental credentials. So, communication with both suppliers and the local community must forge long-term relationships for the common good.

If you adopt this view of an organisation's structure, then you will consider communication primarily in terms of the links and quality of connections between the stakeholder groups.

Defining the organisation's subsystems

The executive group is responsible for maintaining a number of communication systems. These systems are interdependent, but they are described independently.

If you adopt this view of an organisation's structure, then you will consider communication primarily in terms of how the executive group manages and/or controls these different communication systems.

Defining the command hierarchy

We have already suggested there are different forms of hierarchy in modern organisations. One fairly typical set of definitions came from Andrews and Herschel (1996). They suggested six prominent forms of organisation, as in Table 4.3.

Stanford suggests that three important trends are making these traditional structures less popular: rapid pace of change; growth in knowledge-based work; and employee demands/aspirations for more meaningful work. Organisations are moving towards less hierarchical structures (see the discussion of self-managed teams in Chapter 14). Examples are agile, holacratic, and network structures (see Stanford, op cit, pages 83ff).

Defining structures within structures

Although broad characterisations are useful, few organisations (especially larger ones) conform entirely to a single basic structure. Large organisations often include a mix of:

- line structure.

Table 4.3 Forms of organisation

<table>
<tr><th>Structure</th><th>Important features</th></tr>
<tr><td>traditional centralised</td><td rowspan="2">Strong control from the senior management group and a very clear hierarchy</td></tr>
<tr><td>centralised structure with decentralised management</td></tr>
<tr><td>divisional form</td><td rowspan="2">Senior management devolve authority in different ways. Within a divisional structure, the organisation has a central office which co-ordinates and controls but the main work of the organisation is carried out in its divisions.</td></tr>
<tr><td>decentralised structure</td></tr>
<tr><td>matrix</td><td>A dual command structure – employees report to senior staff in terms of their specialist role</td></tr>
<tr><td>"type D"</td><td>"distributed work arrangements" mean work is distributed between the organisation "core" and peripheral units. This often involves external subcontracting and use of communication technology.</td></tr>
</table>

This is based on the idea that at each level people control and administer the work of a group in the level below them. Over the last 20 years, many organisations have restructured, reducing layers of middle management (downsizing).

- staff or functional structure.
  Here, management includes both specialist and functional managers, each one instructing workers on an aspect of their work. A version of this was advocated by one of the early management theorists, Frederick Taylor, usually associated with breaking down manual tasks into small functional tasks. He actually suggested that management should *also* operate in this way, but this was successfully resisted by the management of his day – they did not wish to lose their power base and simply applied his logic to the workers. Matrix management is probably the most common example of this form.
- committee structure.
  Clubs and professional organisations are often run by committees which try to operate on democratic principles. Decision-making is usually by majority vote, though they often try to achieve consensus. Traditional universities, for example, often operate on a system of interlocking committees, and membership of these committees is often determined by status or invitation. Increasing managerialism in higher education has weakened these structures. Most business organisations appoint committees for co-ordination and special purposes. Although committees can work well with a good chair, they are often associated with bureaucracy and inefficiency.

A further range of complexities have implications for communication:

- distinctions between employment and representative roles.
- the nature of advisory roles.
- the role of informal communication.

This raises important issues about how we define the "real" organisation structure. And we can also look at the relationship between structure and culture.

Complexities within structures: the growing organisation

Sometimes textbooks give the impression that these issues of culture and structure are only relevant to large firms. In fact, structure is just as much an issue for a small and developing company although there are obvious differences in scale. Structure becomes especially important when the company tries to grow.

Consider the case of a small service organisation set up by two partners. How many extra staff can they recruit before they need to establish a layer of management? What if they decide to open a second site? How will this be managed?

This development might also create strains in the relationship between the two partners. At the start, they may be able to share the work out equally and not worry about specialisation. But once they have a significant workforce, then they will have several additional concerns. For example, how will they deal with the complexities of employment law and welfare rights? Will they employ some advisory staff or will they ask some outside firm to handle these aspects? All of these are critical issues of organisation structure. And will they be able to retain the positive "team culture" they started with?

The "informal organisation" and "grapevine"?

Many authors distinguish the "formal" organisation from the "informal" organisation: the formal organisation is expressed in the organisation chart; the informal organisation is the network of personal relationships which co-exists.

Communication across this informal organisation is often dismissed as low quality – a mixture of leaks, rumour, and speculation. However, sometimes very accurate information (and sometimes very embarrassing to management) can reach employees through this network, which can be defined in various ways. Traditional definitions include the grapevine, the "old boy" (sic) network, and company social gatherings. Nowadays the influence and speed of social media are likely to be more important.

SUMMARY OF KEY POINTS

- you need to understand the culture (or multiple cultures) within your organisation to anticipate how colleagues and management will respond to particular messages and ways of working. There are different definitions of organisational culture which reflect different perspectives on organisational behaviour. The link between organisational culture and the organisation's overall success or effectiveness can be difficult to define.
- organisational culture can have very significant impact on both employee communications and on their well-being. The example of McDonaldization demonstrates both the power of particular principles/ideas and their probable negative effects on employees.
- the conventional organisational chart is not the most informative way of defining how an organisation actually works. You need to look more carefully at the working relationships between individuals and between groups and take account of the power dynamics within the organisation.
- you need to consider the way you define your organisation's structure and its implications for communication.

References

Ahmed, C. and Hartley, P. (1999) *Weapons of the Weak: Stories from Malaysia*. Paper at the 17th Standing Conference On Organisational Symbolism, Napier University.

Andrews, P.H. and Herschel, R.T. (1996) *Organisational Communication: Empowerment in a Technological Society*. Boston, MA: Houghton Mifflin.

BBC Business News. (2022) *Google will Spend £730m to 'Reinvigorate' its UK Offices*. https://www.bbc.co.uk/news/business-59980216.

Browning, L.D. (1992) Lists and stories as organisational communication. *Communication Theory* 2: 281–302.

Cameron, K.S. and Quinn, R.E. (2011) *Diagnosing and Changing Organizational Culture: Based on the Competing Values Framework*. San Francisco, CA: Jossey Bass.

Clampitt, P. (2017) *Communicating for Managerial Effectiveness*. 6th edition. London: Sage.

Dang, S., Dave, P. and Jin, H. (2022) After Elon Musk's ultimatum, Twitter employees start exiting. *Reuters.com*. https://www.reuters.com/technology/after-elon-musks-ultimatum-twitter-employees-start-exiting-2022-11-18/.

Delbridge, R. (1998) *Life On The Line In Contemporary Manufacturing*. Oxford: Oxford University Press.

Groysberg, B., Lee, J., Price, J. and Yo-Jud Cheng, J. (2018) The leader's guide to corporate culture: How to manage the eight critical elements of organizational life. *Harvard Business Review*, January–February, pages 44–52.

Hastings, R. and Meyer, E. (2020) *No Rules Rules: Netflix and the Culture of Reinvention*. London: WH Allen, an imprint of Ebury Publishing.

Kobiruzzaman, M.M. (2022, January 8) *Netflix Organizational Change & Structure Case Study 2022*. Newsmoor – Best Online Learning Platform. https://newsmoor.com/netflix-organizational-change-organizational-management-change-examples/.

Mahase, E. (2022) Type 1 diabetes drug was withdrawn because of "commercial conflict of interest" charity argue. *BMJ* 375: 0373. https://doi.org/10.1136/bmj.o373.

McCord, P. (2014) How Netflix reinvented HR. https://hbr.org/2014/01/how-netflix-reinvented-hr

McGarvey, E. and Blake, J. (2022) Jacob Rees-Mogg empty desk note to civil servants insulting, says union at https://www.bbc.co.uk/news/uk-61202152

Meierhans, J. (2022) Law firm says staff can work from home – For 20% less pay. https://www.bbc.co.uk/news/business-61298394.

Michaels, J. (2022) Cooking Robots: Can we automate cooking? https://robotliving.com/cooking-robots/#more-669.

Morgan, G. (1997) *Images of Organisation*, New edition. London: Sage.

Peachey, K. (2022) Post office scandal: What the horizon saga is all about. https://www.bbc.co.uk/news/business-56718036.

Peters, T.J. and Waterman, R.H. (1982) *In Search of Excellence: Lessons from America's Best Run Companies*. New York: Harper and Row.

Ritzer, G. (1996) *The McDonaldization of Society*, Revised edition. Thousand Oaks, CA: Pine Forge Press.

Schein, E.H. (2009) *The Corporate Culture Survival Guide*, Revised edition. New York: John Wiley.

Schein, E.H. (2010) *Organizational Culture and Leadership*, 4th edition. San Francisco: Jossey-Bass.

Schein, P.A. and Schein, E. (2017) *Organizational Culture and Leadership*. New York: Wiley and Sons Incorporated.

Senior, B., Swailes, S. and Carnall, C. (2020) *Organisational Change*, 4th edition. London: Prentice Hall.

Smith, R.C. and Eisenberg, E.M. (1987) Conflict at Disneyland: A root-metaphor analysis. *Communication Monographs* 54: 367–380.

Stanford, N. (2022) *Designing Organisations: Why It Matters and Ways To Do It Well*. London: Profile Books.

Stewart, R. (1991) *Managing Today and Tomorrow*. London: McMillan.

Vermulen, F. (2010) *Business Exposed: The Naked Truth about What Really Goes On in the World of Business*. Harlow: Pearson.

Wallis, N. (2021) *The Great Post Office Scandal: The Fight to Expose a Multimillion IT Disaster which Put Innocent People in Jail*. Bath: Bath Publishing Ltd.

Wiseman, R. (2019) *Shoot for the Moon: Achieve the Impossible with the Apollo Mindset*. London: Quercus.

Woodford, M. (2012) *Exposure: From President to Whistleblower at Olympus*. London: Penguin.

CHAPTER 5

Communication context 2

The new technology landscape

Introduction

Rapid advances and improvements in hardware and software have turned some very long-established ideas from computing into everyday realities which most of us can afford.

These fundamental ideas are now practical methods and procedures which we take for granted. For example, developments in portability and computing power enabled entrepreneurs, like Steve Jobs, to add more and more facilities to our devices. Can you remember when a mobile phone simply made phone calls?

These fundamental ideas also suggest ways that electronic communication will further develop:

- remote/distant operation.
- sharing resources.
- flexible messaging.
- information organised as a web of associations.
- exchange of all types of information (provided computers and networks share standard rules, usually called protocols).

The pandemic speeded up all these developments. Organisations had to change "overnight" to respond to lockdown. So we can anticipate further developments along the lines that we come back to when we attempt to "future-gaze" in Chapter 15, including:

- better ways of representing information and analysing data.
- different ways of accessing and exchanging information.
- more flexible messaging and communication.
- further integration of functions and facilities, within and between devices.

However, we cannot anticipate gradual rate of change. We are persuaded by Azeem Azhar's arguments that "we are undergoing another period of dramatic

DOI: 10.4324/9781003297550-7

transformation" (Azhar, 2021, page 3). This means exponential rather than gradual growth across a wide range of new technologies:

> *we are living in an era when technology is getting better, faster and more varied at a greater speed than ever before.*
>
> (Azhar, 2021, page 13)

We need to anticipate this rate of change by developing a "digital mindset" – determining and adopting the new applications which best suit our objectives and context.

Key phases of workplace development linked to technology

The world of work is changing and computer technology is at the heart of this change. We can illustrate that with Julia Hobshawm's characterisation of the four phases of work (Hobshawm, 2022):

Hobshawm identifies six "shifts" which characterise Phase 4:

- "Placeless, Timeless".
  Organisations have to decide how and where work will be undertaken in future.
- "Worker Beings".
  New identities for workers are emerging, e.g. as they adopt hybrid work.
- "The Productivity Puzzle".
  Workers are pressing for more meaningful and inherently satisfying work.
- "New Networks".
  New networks are enabled by technology and are changing power relationships in organisations.
- "Marzipan Management".
  Management have to change to adapt to these new realities.
- "Social Health and Well-being".
  Workplaces must "embrace…social health" (page 10).

We agree with this analysis, with one caveat: we see Phase 4 as a *transition* period of disruption and change. Organisations must decide how (or how far) they are going to incorporate techniques like hybrid working and other recent developments, such as the use of new technologies like AI (Artificial Intelligence), VR (Virtual Reality – where you enter an environment which is completely computer-generated) and AR (Augmented Reality – where a layer of computer-generated imagery is superimposed on the real world

Table 5.1 Four phases of work

Phase	Key characteristics include:	Use of technology
1. "Optimism Years" 1945–1977	"faith in corporate institutions ran high" Major investments in office spaces and buildings	Computer technology was largely restricted to "data-crunching" applications.
2. "Mezzanine Years" 1978–2006	"an intermediate phase" where office work loses some of its attractiveness and where communication technology becomes more important	The internet and social media appear and increase in their application and their acceptance (e.g. Facebook and Twitter).
3. "Co-Working Years" 2007–2019	"the beginning of the end for the office"	Smartphones and laptops enable mobile and virtual working.
4. "Nowhere Office Years" 2019ff	Much if not most office work can be done anytime and anywhere	The use of "collaboration technologies" like Zoom and Teams grows exponentially to respond to the pandemic.

around you). We highlight important developments in these technologies when we return to them later.

We anticipate Phase 5 will emerge over the next few years, characterised by different solutions to these issues across different work sectors. We have to decide how to respond to other major developments which we discuss later in this chapter – especially the calls for a "digital mindset" and the growth of "exponential technologies".

Technology roles

Many commentators identify the key change as the way that computers and communication systems have combined. Other important processes have emerged from this combination/integration:

- technology has developed new roles.
- technology is "embedded".

Changing roles

In an influential earlier book, Shoshana Zuboff identified three key processes (Zuboff, 1988).

Automating

Computers can obviously automate processes. The example of the store checkout suggests a second main function: they can *monitor and control* processes. One challenging implication of computer control is the role of the human operator. An obvious example is the self-driving car.

When computers do take charge of a process, you have to consider what happens if something goes wrong. The oft-quoted near-disaster at Three Mile Island is one illustration of what can happen when human operators do not fully understand how the system works. The operators' actions very nearly caused a major disaster. These events are still being revisited, as in the 2022 Netflix docuseries (*Meltdown: Three Mile Island*) although this may not offer the complete story (Clute, 2022).

Integrating

Computer technology can also integrate processes in new ways. Commercial examples of data integration include the ways that retailers and social media apps develop customer profiles. This enables them to send you targeted advertisements and promotions. And we are all familiar with messages from retailers like Amazon – "people who read/watched X also liked Y"; "And here is how you can access Y..."

Informating

Another critical process is what Zuboff calls "informating". This is based on the notion that computers generate a lot of additional information as a by-product of their main function. An example of how this can be used to control and monitor workers' performance would be the computerised phone system used in a call centre. Management can discover at the press of a key exactly how many calls any operator has dealt with and how long they took. The quality of service provided in a phone call can be difficult to measure, so these crude statistics may be used (perhaps unfortunately for the customer) as measures of productivity.

More recently, Zuboff has become especially interested in the "surveillance" implications of technology development and we introduce some of her concerns in Box 5.1.

BOX 5.1

Who or what is watching you?

Zuboff continued to develop her ideas about informating as she investigated the ways that companies like Google collect and use data on individuals. This data-gathering accelerated with the development of Web 2.0, and Zuboff became increasingly concerned by the ways that these companies were generating more of what she called "behavioural surplus" – "where surveillance capitalism begins". She explains this as follows:

> *"More behavioural data are rendered than required for service improvements. This surplus feeds machine intelligence - the new means of production - that fabricates predictions of user behaviour".*
>
> (Zuboff, 2019)

These predictions are now "monetised" – sold on to other businesses. The more that you as a customer use the service the more surplus is generated for the machine intelligence which can then generate more accurate predictions.

Zuboff is not optimistic:

> *It is assumed that we will accede to a future of less personal control and more powerlessness.*
>
> (op cit, page 516)

Although some of her ideas have been criticised (e.g. Gall, 2020), her work has been important in highlighting possible dangers in the practices of large tech companies who have achieved near-monopoly positions in their respective markets.

IT is embedded

Microprocessors in many domestic appliances enable functions which were not feasible before digital technology. Combining computer and communications technology means that devices can offer new functions. Manufacturers and retailers are anxious to promote the "Internet of Things" where household devices are linked through an internet connection. This also has some downsides – hackers may be able to break into your home network through the fridge or microwave!

Linking sensors to computers which can communicate offers new possibilities, including the car which diagnoses its own breakdown and contacts the breakdown service. In a previous edition of this book, we noted the opening of Amazon's store for "wearable technology". This is still a category you can search for on the Amazon website. Although the listing is dominated by smartwatches and their accessories, we note an increasing number of other devices like VR headsets. It will be interesting to see what this list contains in another five years.

After becoming accustomed to developments in the "Internet of Things", we are now seeing products and services advertised under the "Internet of the Body". In an article from the World Economic Forum, Xiao Liu defines this as:

> *collecting our physical data via devices than can be implanted, swallowed or simply worn, generating huge amounts of health-related information.*
>
> (Liu, 2020)

The obvious example of this which we are all familiar with is the fitness tracker, either as a separate device or as a built-in component of your smartwatch. A range of new devices is now appearing such as the "smart toothbrush" as well as more sophisticated sensors such as those for diabetics which integrate with smartwatches to provide detailed monitoring and support. Liu points to the advantages of this emerging technology as well as highlighting major challenges such as regulatory protections and cybersecurity. For example, a range of regulations cover "sensitive data" which your doctor will be able to access –

> *but today, all sorts of seemingly non-sensitive data can also be used to draw inferences about your health, through data analytics.*
>
> (Liu, op cit)

See Box 5.2 for an example of a major UK initiative which illustrates processes of integration using advances in sensors and data analytics. Although this example focuses on specific issues in health and social support, the underlying ideas and approaches have much wider application and potential.

BOX 5.2 BIG DATA AND OLD AGE

The UK Dementia Research Institute (DRI), a partnership between Imperial College and Surrey University, aims to "use a range of approaches - from artificial intelligence and robotics to sleep monitoring - to enable people with dementia to live safely and independently in their own homes" (Meredith, 2019). The technology includes a wide variety of sensors, from motion sensors to smart plugs to sleep mats. Sensor data is integrated with other sources such as regular health checks. This integration allows the system to spot changes in behaviour and routines which can indicate problems. The system can then initiate an appropriate response, such as alerting emergency health services. This sort of initiative would not be possible without the technological development discussed in this chapter.

Another recent example of the extension of sensor technology into our everyday lives is the introduction of "crash detection" on the Apple Watch and iPhone in 2022.

Important technology trends

An obvious way to start a discussion of technology futures is to reel off a few statistics, which invariably involve staggeringly large numbers. For instance, the US National Science Foundation predicted that five billion people would be using the internet by 2020; Eric Schmidt from Google predicted that *everyone* would be online by then.

Our trawl of internet data in September 2022 came up with the following statistics (from Statista Research Department unless otherwise credited).

You may wish to find the statistics which apply when you are reading this to see the rate of change:

- 4.9 billion internet users worldwide (5.25 billion, over 66% of the world's population, according to broadbandsearch.net)
- China is the world leader in terms of a number of users – 1.02 billion in July 2022, mostly accessing the internet through mobile phones.
- The region with the "highest internet penetration rate" is Northern Europe (98%). The global rate is 63%.
- The most common language used on the internet is English.
- Over 84% of the population in the USA are mobile internet users.
- The average daily time spent on social media worldwide is 147 minutes.
- 92% of the UK population are "recent internet users" (Office for National Statistics), including 99% of adults aged 16 to 44, and 54% aged over 75. This proportion of older users is nearly double what it was in 2013.

Of particular interest is the rise of mobile communications in developing countries – where the desktop PC seems to have been "bypassed" in favour of mobile devices. Also of interest is the uptake of the internet by children.

Technologies for the next decade

One useful set of predictions comes from the latest edition of The McKinsey Technology Trends Outlook (McKinsey, 2022, available at: https://www.mckinsey.com/capabilities/mckinsey-digital/our-insights/the-top-trends-in-tech).

These are summarised in Table 5.2 below.

Key issues and questions

As well as worrying about general factors that can derail computer applications which we highlight in Box 5.3, we suggest a number of key issues and questions which we all need to consider as we move forward.

Table 5.2 Technology Trends (adapted from McKinsey 2022)

Trend	Meaning	Our comment
"Applied AI" and "industrialising machine learning"	Using machine learning to solve problems and make decisions. Improving the efficiency of machine learning processes.	Investment in this will continue to grow and we can expect to see major advances in the technical capacity.
"Advanced Connectivity"	Advances in the speed and quality of connections.	This will certainly develop further but we have concerns about increasing the divide between different sectors of the population with different access.
"bioengineering"	Further convergence between biological and information technologies.	This will continue to grow along the lines of the development we outlined in Box 5.2.
"clean energy"	The search and drive for cleaner energy sources to respond to climate change.	These are all trends which we as individuals (and all organisations) need to worry about and try to act upon. For example, can we make choices in favour of more sustainable consumption both at home and work?
"mobility"	Improvements in efficiency and sustainability of transportation.	
"sustainable consumption"	Transforming consumption to address climate issues.	
"Web3" and "Immersive-reality technologies"	The next generation of internet development. Using "sensing" technologies to offer different views of the environment through VR and AR.	We discuss these in more detail later in this chapter. These technologies are strongly linked in notions of the metaverse.
"cloud and edge computing"	Distributing computing workloads across data centres	The increasing distribution of data will place more emphasis on issues of cybersecurity.
"trust architectures and digital identity"	These are the technologies which will persuade us to trust the organisations which have our data.	
"space technologies"	Developments in satellites and other space-related technology	The developments in these areas should enable organisations to use more reliable software on more powerful computers.
"quantum technologies"	These are promised to deliver "exponential increase in computational performance"	
"next-generation software development"	Tools such as "AI-enabled development" are promised to help in the development of better software.	

BOX 5.3

The computer is in charge: nothing can go wrong, go wrong, go wrong...

While the technology has developed at an astonishing rate, the human capacity to manage it has not advanced at the same rate. Back in 1996, Stephen Flowers analysed "failed" computer systems and highlighted several common factors, many of which relate to communication. These factors are still relevant and include:

- "hostile culture", where staff feel unable to comment openly on errors and possible problems. Staff may still try to continue a project which is failing rather than admit the problems. And this will usually make things worse in the long run.
- "poor reporting structure", a situation where senior management do not have a clear idea of the progress of the computer project.
- "technology-focused developments", where system design has focused on technological possibilities and has ignored important human factors.
- "poor consultation" with users and other stakeholders.

The case of the UK Post Office (see Chapter 4) illustrates the fact that these problems are still with us.

Another example of a system that does not yet seem to have fulfilled its promised outcomes is the "Common Platform" which was introduced to support the Law Courts in England and Wales in the UK. The idea of having one system where legal staff can access all the details of all past and present course cases is obviously useful – but what happens if it does not work effectively all the time? Missing data can have horrendous implications for individuals who may be wrongly imprisoned or released, and this sort of problem was publicised in professional publications and in the mass media in 2021 and 2022 (Fouzder, 2021; Harte and Robinson, 2022).

Exponential growth as the future for computing?

We have become used to advances in computer technology which follow "Moore's Law" which suggested that the number of transistors we could place on a silicon chip would double every two years, with a corresponding increase in computing power. While this has been a reasonably accurate prediction, and although some manufacturers have exceeded this rate of growth, there are concerns that we are approaching the limits of our manufacturing ability (Hughes, 2022).

Azeem Ashar suggests we are now in a different era – what he calls the "Exponential Age". This is characterised by *exponential* growth in the power and capacity of computer technology. Unfortunately, this is happening alongside much slower change in our responses to this technology growth. As a result, he discusses the "widening gulf between technology and our social institutions" (Ashar, op cit, page 10).

Computer technology as a neutral tool?

This is another issue that Azeem Ashar raises, highlighting quotes from industrial leaders such as Google's Executive Chair in 2013, Eric Schmidt. Schmidt argued that "The central truth of the technology industry…(is)…that technology is neutral but people are not". (Ashar, op cit, page 5). In contrast, we agree with Ashar's perspective:

> *Technologies are not just neutral tools to be applied (or misapplied) by their users. They are artefacts built by people. And these people direct and design their inventions according to their own preferences.*
>
> (Ashar, op cit, page 6)

Unfortunately, a growing number of examples demonstrate that many technologies, including computer systems and software tools, are designed with "built-in" biases and limitations which are not recognised by the designers, including:

- the algorithms in recruitment software which discriminate against women (O'Neil, 2016).
- the car safety systems based on the male body which can cause serious harm to female passengers and drivers (Criado Perez, 2019).

Learning from the pandemic?

Many organisations learned that they did not need a central office or location to operate effectively and have abandoned their previous premises in favour of virtual and homeworking. They have adopted various strategies to provide sufficient social interaction to keep staff committed and involved.

We all learned to use meeting software like Zoom or Teams but not necessarily very well. We discovered some of the disadvantages of this software (e.g. "Zoom fatigue") which we also discuss later in this book.

A Microsoft survey in 2022 revealed strong disagreement between staff and senior management over the value and future of hybrid/virtual working. Based on a survey from over 20,000 people in 11 countries and other data sources, they found very different perspectives which you can see in the following quotes:

> *85% of leaders say the shift to hybrid work has made it challenging to have confidence that employees are being productive.*

The majority of employees (87%) report that they are productive at work.

73% of employees say they need a better reason to go into the office than just company expectations.

(all three quotes from Work Trend Index, 2022, where you can also find a link to the full report)

The robots are coming (or are they?)

Automation through computer technology will continue to expand. But how will this eliminate or modify human jobs? Daniel Susskind argues that:

> *In the next 100 years, technological progress will make us more prosperous than ever before. Yet that progress will also carry us towards a world with less work for human beings.*
>
> (Susskind, 2021, pages 237/238)

This will create three major problems which society will need to resolve: inequality; political power; and "meaning" (how do people find meaning in their lives without work as a central core?) (page 238). His book was written before Russia invaded Ukraine and so does not take account of either the terrible damage caused by this conflict or the restructuring of international relationships which is ongoing as we write. He does offer some convincing data to support his central argument but the upheavals caused by the conflict in Europe and its economic impact do have implications for technological progress which are difficult to assess at the moment. We think the trends that Susskind identifies will continue but probably at a different and much slower pace.

A different perspective is offered by Paul Daugherty and H. James Wilson (2018). They argue that the most successful companies now and in future will be those that adopt a new "organisational mindset". This is:

> *a radically different approach toward business by re-imagining work around the missing middle, wherein people improve AI and, in turn, smart machines give humans superpowers.*
>
> (2018, page 13)

They offer numerous examples of organisations that are already taking advantage of the creative power of human operators allied to the processing power and precision of machines controlled by AI. For example, Daugherty and Wilson describe the experience of Mercedes who replaced some of their robots on the production line with a human plus robot combination (what they called "cobots") in order to produce more individually customised cars. This combination of the human making the choices and the robot doing any repetitive or high precision tasks (and also the heavy lifting) proved more efficient than either robot or human on their own.

Whatever the future, this trend must be taken very seriously by organisations looking to their future survival.

The need for a digital mindset?

Daugherty and Wilson suggest five steps to "reimagining business processes" (op cit, page 153), recommending that organisational leaders need to "imagine a blended culture of people and machines" (op cit, page 166). Leonardi and Neeley also present a convincing case for developing a "digital mindset" which for them means "redefining fundamental views of approaching three key processes:

- collaboration.
- computation.
- change.

(Leonardi and Neeley, 2022, page 10)

Under the heading of collaboration, they point out that we need to develop a better understanding of the ways that machines such as chatbots work so that we do not make mistakes by treating them as humans. We also need to make more effort to work with real humans when a major proportion of our work is virtual or online – they talk about "cultivating your digital presence".

Under the heading of computation, they highlight the increasing use of data analytics but emphasise that this must be done carefully (and that we need to develop a more sophisticated understanding of statistical methods and analysis). They warn against applications which have not identified possible limitations or even unintended bias in the results and outcomes, such as the gender bias found in facial recognition software. As with many examples we mention in this book, we always need to identify and interrogate the assumptions that are built into the design of the systems we use.

Under the heading of change, they recommend a stronger emphasis on cyber-security and privacy and encouraging digital experimentation. They talk about "creating a learning agenda" across the organisation which "helps you experiment intentionally rather than willy-nilly" (op cit, page 149).

Welcome to the metaverse?

In 2021, Facebook announced its new brand identity – Meta – claiming that:

> *The metaverse is the next evolution in social connexion and the successor to the mobile Internet.*
>
> (https://about.facebook.com/what-is-the-metaverse/)

Since then other influential tech companies have agreed that the future of the internet and our online communication will involve this new concept and approach, and there are now some very enthusiastic advocates. In a book subtitled "A guide to limitless possibilities in a Web 3.0 world", Cathy Hack and her two co-authors suggest their individual perspectives on this development before offering a more formal definition as follows. The metaverse is:

- "a convergence of our physical and digital selves", or
- "like a parallel, immersive world that blurs with the real one where people assume one of multiple identities", or
- "the next generation of consumer engagement: an immersive experience with a self-sustaining, community-driven economy at its centre".

They then offer a "consolidated" definition:

> *The metaverse represent the top-level hierarchy of persistent virtual spaces that may also interpolate in real life, so that social, commercial, and personal experiences emerge through web 3.0 technologies.*
>
> (Hack et al., 2022, page 9)

This definition may not help you if you have not already come across some examples of new applications. And this is part of the reason why other technology commentators are more sceptical of this development. For a recent description of its potential which raises important questions for the future, see Wakefield (2023) and our update on the website.

What we can say is that we can expect significant development in the technologies which underpin the metaverse such as virtual reality (VR) and augmented reality (AR) alongside ways of merging these technologies into our routine communications (see Box 5.4 for a few recent examples).

We can also suggest that trends in the application of these technologies need to be monitored by everyone who is interested in the future of our online communications.

BOX 5.4 FUTURE TECH IN THE METAVERSE?

While, at the moment, we are a little sceptical about some of the hype attached to the metaverse, we can find an impressive range of applications at the website of the virtual reality society (https://www.vrs.org.uk). And we are convinced that the next decade will bring dramatic developments in computing, due to the exponential increase in computing power we mentioned earlier and clever integration of different functions and services. We can also see computers advancing in areas which make distinctions between human and machine abilities more difficult to define. A few examples to illustrate these trends:

Computers as storytellers

Consider the following start to a short article:

> Since the earliest days of writing, authors have had to spend a lot of time thinking about how to get people to read their books. AI storytellers will make this task much easier by generating material that is automatically appealing.

This extract from the book by Sharples and Pérez y Pérez (2022) may not seem especially remarkable until the authors reveal it was entirely composed by computer software after being supplied with the prompt "describe a future with AI story generators". Their book discusses the history of this technology and speculates on its future. We have already seen examples of the same software generating student assignments good enough to achieve pass grades at university. So will this technology replace human storywriters? They anticipate that this technology will move from a research exercise to practical applications *in support of* human activity. It will enable tasks such as summarising large quantities of digital text, or perhaps acting as a set of tools to support writers.

This debate over the future of this type of software 'exploded' over the internet and social media at the end of 2022 when OpenAI.com released ChatGPT and made it freely available. Instead of producing the list of websites you expect from a 'traditional' websearch, ChatGPT produces a coherent text which answers the question or prompt you have given it.

Following significant investment in the OpenAI company, Microsoft announced new initiatives in March 2023 – 'Copilot' and 'Business Chat' – which embed AI in their office software. In the same week, Google announced their "new era for AI and Google Workspace."

This will affect *all of us* in some way: from students looking for help with assignments, to software engineers producing code, to managers drafting a quick press release or planning a presentation or reviewing email threads or meeting minutes, and so on. Many educators are concerned about implications for plagiarism and academic integrity while some have already built it into their assignment tasks. As this development is moving so fast, see the website for updates.

Seeing a conversation?

Xrai Glass in the UK have integrated speech recognition software into spectacles so that anyone wearing them can "see" the conversation presented through AR in front of them (https://xrai.glass/about). An early user with hearing disability described them as "life-changing" on a recent radio programme. These sorts of devices will become more effective and more affordable in the next few years.

How fast are organisations really changing?

Although advocates of new organisational forms may offer persuasive examples, we cannot assume that all organisations are so progressive. Nor can we ignore the political implications of new forms of working. In our previous edition, we noted a more pessimistic picture which was painted in papers from the annual International Labour Process Conference (Thompson and Warhurst, 1998). Although mentioning some areas and examples of positive change, these papers suggested that claims of "revolutionary" and "wholesale change" were exaggerated.

These concerns are now 25 years on, but we can still see them alive and kicking in many current organisations. We list them in the table below with a comment against each about current and future relevance:

Table 5.3 Have companies progressed?

The concerns	Our comments
Much "knowledge work" is in fact extremely routine and repetitive.	This is still true. Some organisations have automated many of these routine tasks (not always successfully as anyone who has negotiated automatic answering services will testify).
Organisations may wish to ensure consistency and "quality" by using strong control principles akin to the ideas of "McDonaldization" (see Box 4.3).	We see many organisations still adopting strategies like McDonaldization.
Some modern human relations practices which claim to "empower" workers are devices "to achieve nothing less than the total colonisation of the…workforce" (page 7).	This is echoed in modern criticisms of some organisations' attempts to improve "staff wellbeing" through courses and training while ignoring the everyday staff issues re workload etc.
"most companies…remain traditionally managed, wedded to a low-trust, low-skill, authoritarian route to competitiveness" (page 9).	Again we still see examples of this.
Relatively few workers are currently able to take advantage of the flexibilities which are offered by information and communications technologies.	This has changed. But are most organisations taking full advantage of these flexibilities?

Will there be unforeseen effects or outcomes?

If organisation cultures, structures, and technologies do change (if only partly) in the ways advocated in our previous sections, then organisational communication must also change. For example, if we assume a broadly networked organisation with lots of external links and sub-contracting, then the managers in the "core" of the organisation will have to adopt a much more trusting, co-operative, and less directive style. There will also be increased needs for horizontal co-operation and the need to manage the growing importance of teamwork.

But there are inherent contradictions which are difficult to reconcile. Fisman and Sullivan (2014) argue that, by providing more information to everyone in the organisation, computer technology enabled the flattening of many corporate hierarchies. At the same time:

> *improved communication systems...actually push decisions back up the hierarchy.*
> (op cit, page 259)

When the boss is available 24/7 on her mobile then why do I need to take responsibility to make that decision? The answer to this question depends on the broader organisational culture.

How much disruption can we anticipate?

The word "disruption" is often associated with the emergence of technologies that create major and sudden changes in how we work, learn, and live. Digital photography and video is such an example. Technologies now commonplace on smartphones and tablets disrupted many businesses, such as Kodak, which did not adapt its business quickly enough (Mui, 2012).

Crowdfunding is an example of one of the more truly disruptive examples of the use of social media. This includes peer-to-peer funding, based on collaboration/community membership, shared knowledge, and transparency, to support the development of innovations and ventures, including those focused on socially good projects such as micro-loans in developing countries, and charity-donation communities. More recently, online companies have started up to support new ventures in different markets such as the creative industries (e.g. music, film, and publishing) and health sector, which could begin to shape investments in these sectors – and bring with it a "power of the people", e.g. ethical perspectives.

Divergence, convergence, and divergence?

The number of options for online communications is growing e.g. email, discussion groups, social networks, blogs, and wikis – combined with the growing availability of low-cost media devices and the ability to manipulate and store multimedia information online. The rapidity of change is also remarkable. For example:

- writing before Musk's takeover, Quinn (2022) noted that Twitter (created in 2006) had 396.5 million users, with 66% of larger organisations (more than 100 employees) using it for marketing. It will be interesting to see how (and how fast) these figures change.
- in 2014, Facebook took over the WhatsApp messaging app, founded in 2009.
- Facebook now has 2,920 million monthly users; WhatsApp has 2,000 million; and TikTok has 1,000 million (Statista, January 2022).

This trend will continue, presenting users with rich but complex environments in which to communicate where for some, there are just too many choices to cope with. Such trends illustrate "divergence", where innovative technologies introduce new ways of doing things. Alongside this, we also see technology convergence – technologies merging into new forms that bring together different types of media and applications. Convergence can be seen in computers, mobile phones, tablets, and TVs. For example, TVs include network connections for internet access. Another example would be the 2022 e-reader from Amazon – the Kindle Scribe – which is no longer just an e-reader. It "was designed for note-taking and journaling, with the stylus designed to feel like a real pen in use" (Bedford, 2022). So, we have a convergence of facilities previously associated more with tablets than e-readers into one device. If you are a consumer then you now have to decide whether you want a multi-purpose device or one that offers a more specialist experience for notetaking and annotating such as the reMarkable 2 which claims to be "the only tablet that feels like paper".

Converging technologies bring both positives and negatives. For some, devices such as smartphones enable just one device to be carried allowing users to e-mail, text, use social networks, listen to music, use e-books, watch videos, and make phone calls. Others find that a single device can rarely be fully effective for all these different uses. For example, the small screens on smartphones can be a limitation which manufacturers are attempting to resolve by increasing size, hinged screens etc.

There is another downside to convergence: it can begin to stifle innovation and lead to a lack of variety and in some instances can encourage monopolistic practices. The future trend is therefore likely to be one of periods of divergence, convergence, and then more divergence alternating cyclically.

Anytime, anywhere communications

The year 2014 was a turning point:

> *Americans used smartphone and tablet apps more than PCs to access the Internet last month – the first time that has ever happened.*
>
> (O'Toole, 2014)

This trend will continue, thanks to several technological developments, including:

- the growth in both mobile phone data networks and wireless networks.
- having said that, there are several problems associated with mobile phone data networks from reliability in access (using data networks on trains remains a less than satisfactory experience) to issues associated with international roaming and billing (we still hear of mobile phone customers unwittingly running up bills in the thousands of pounds when on an overseas trip).
- availability of low-cost connected consumer devices (e.g. smartphones, tablets, laptop computers).
- cloud computing, where data and software applications are stored and used in the cloud.

This will not always provide a single approach to computing – there will be times where people do not have access to a broadband connection and will need to use their offline computer to work. To this end the concept of synching is often adopted, where resources stored in the cloud can be synched to local computers. The need for such synching capability is likely to persist for some while until telecommunications companies can provide comprehensive coverage with the same reliability as a data connection through landline and at sensible costs for international travelers.

Computing as ubiquitous utility?

The concept of computing as a ubiquitous and reliable utility will drive demand for connectivity, especially for those in remote rural areas and those on the move (both nationally and internationally). It will also (hopefully) reduce the "digital divide" in respect of access.

The utility concept also implies further integration of computer processors into a whole range of devices, many of which will be small and inexpensive and focused on common-place functions and linked to the internet. Home automation systems are an example, which provide facilities to remotely control different devices in the home, such as the heating, lighting, home alarms, security devices, and curtain-closing. Some of these developments will be supported by legislation, e.g. recent Scottish laws requiring domestic fire alarms to be electronically linked.

The intelligent web and smarter devices?

Increasingly, devices connected to the internet will be designed to be smarter and to support humans in decision-making and some will include sensors to help input local data. Our everyday devices will get "smarter".

"Intelligent agents" is another fast-developing concept and application, designed to make computing easier. For instance, they can monitor how you use the web and what you search for and then make suggestions for future searches that are more personalised to your online history. There are of course issues associated with such technologies, for instance, users do not know what "decisions" the intelligent agent is making on their behalf. However, there are some very useful examples of "smart" devices e.g. low-cost car satellite navigation systems, which can be used not just to help drivers navigate, but will also take data from a range of sources, such as traffic density and flow and recommend optimum routes that will meet driver preferences, e.g. fastest and least hassle route. Overall, this leads to a future where people are more connected to devices which are aware of their contexts and location. But even these may have unforeseen complications – for example, the suggestion based on some evidence that drivers of "very safe automatic cars" can adopt a riskier driving style.

The future for big data?

According to SG Analytics in 2020,

> *more than 2.5 quintillion bytes of data are generated every single day.*

You should be able to find a more recent estimate – this figure will certainly have grown!

This is definitely big data - which IBM define as:

> *datasets whose size or type is beyond the ability of traditional relational databases to capture, manage and process the data with low latency.*
>
> (IBM. See at: https://www.ibm.com/analytics/big-data-analytics,

As a result, we need new data analytic techniques to make sense of this data.

Such data comes from a wide range of sources – not just from computers, but also from devices, sensors, audio, video, and so on – and a vast array of sources. Out of all this comes both opportunities and threats in respect of analysing this data and making use of it. Companies use data analysis tools to build up pictures and trends e.g. how their customers use products. This can all be fed back into product development. Credit card companies build very detailed profiles of customer buying habits and telecommunications companies keep track of how individuals use the internet. From an individual perspective, all this can be both good and bad. Systems can be designed to help individuals make choices from huge ranges of possibilities, drawing on patterns of behaviour of both the individual and others. However, not everyone will be happy with this and the collection of such data can be used for purposes that individuals may not welcome, such as junk mail.

However, the more worrying area of concern is when different systems are joined together enabling the joining up of "big data", e.g. linking surveillance camera networks with facial recognition systems, tracking of devices (such as mobile phones) and purchasing/travel data – allowing those with access to these different systems to comprehensively intrude into an individual's working and social life. There are positives, of course, e.g. the ability for Government health departments to spot and predict health trends and generally for Government departments to target services more towards community needs. However, there have been numerous examples where both companies' and Government departments' rhetoric about data privacy and security are not matched by practice or adequate procedures and this rekindles the concept of Big Brother watching over us.

A useful introduction to this area is by Victor Mayer-Schonberger and Kenneth Cukier (2013). They suggest that big data "represents three shifts in the way we analyse information that transform how we understand and organise society" (page 12):

- we can now analyse and integrate more data than ever before.
- the availability of these enormous datasets means that we do not have to be as precise or as exact with specific details as we did when we were only using small datasets.
- the final shift is what they call "a move away from the age-old search for causality" (Page 14).

Using big data allows us to reveal previously hidden patterns and correlations which we can then investigate to discover what they mean. Of course, we need to be very careful in interpreting the meaning of any correlation. We need to beware of spurious correlation where a direct link or strong association does not mean that we can easily work out what causes what. How would you explain the very strong relationship between the per capita consumption of cheese in the USA and the number of people who died by becoming tangled in their bedsheets? See the "spurious correlations" website for this and other examples – http://www.tylervigen.com

The future is open?

Openness is a growing movement in the area of technology and education which has certain characteristics associated with it, such as those described by Educause:

- the use of open standards and interoperability of systems.
- open and community source software development.
- open access to research data.
- open scholarly communications.
- open access to, and open derivative use of, content (often referred to as "open educational resources" (OERs).

For a practical example, we mentioned MOOCs (massive open online courses) in Chapter 2 and these are based on open approaches. There is insufficient space in this book to fully explore the pros and cons of open approaches particularly in relation to how such approaches will evolve over time. However, at the very least, it is an important aspect of being a good communicator that developments in open approaches are monitored to identify how effectively such approaches can be exploited in communications and education.

How green is your computing?

The commitment to carbon neutrality by various governments and by many organisations has significant implications for the devices we buy and the ways we use them.

For example the McKinsey management consultancy has its own policy statement – https://www.mckinsey.com/about-us/environmental-sustainability – and has researched other organisation strategies such as the use of quantum computing. They suggest that:

> *Quantum computing, an emerging technology that uses the laws of quantum mechanics to produce exponentially higher performance for certain types of calculations, offers the possibility of major breakthroughs across sectors*
>
> (https://www.mckinsey.com/featured-insights/themes/how-quantum-computing-could-change-the-world)

We still have a long way to go. The Electronics TakeBack Coalition in the USA offers some sobering statistics. For example:

> *in the US, we throw away over 3 million tonnes of e-waste every year. Only 15% is recycled.*

We are concerned that many manufacturers (and consumers) still don't generally seem to have an appetite for such green approaches. Some of the most popular electronic devices (e.g. tablets and smartphones) seem to be manufactured with obsolescence in mind (e.g. through the use of sealed cases and batteries and components that cannot be replaced). This has been a regular criticism of Apple – many of their devices are difficult if not impossible for anyone other than Apple to adapt or repair. Their initiative to provide more access to repair resources may change this – we will wait and see.

The dark side of technology?

Whilst all the trends in technology are driving greater social interaction across the world – and this can be very positive for communications – it is not set in stone how such interactions will continue. We have already mentioned the dramatic changes at Twitter following its sale to Elon Musk (Chapter 4) and speculation about its future. We wait to see the long-term impact of these changes on both its users and its commercial future.

There is no shortage of evidence of problems in digital social interactions – cyber-bullying, criminal activity, non-stop spam, cyber-terrorism etc. Advances in AI have enabled the production of "deepfake porn" at a fraction of the costs of this technology only a few years ago. Victims of tragedies such as mass shootings have been pursued and abused online by so-called "disaster trolls" which adds an extra unwanted dimension to their grief and suffering. So all the positive moves towards sharing and interaction could be disrupted by unforeseen events: for instance, increases in crime against children on the web could start to affect the culture of sharing and openness. Social resistance could develop as quickly as social interaction has developed!

And finally

As well as these broad changes in technology, we suggest you review your personal use of technology to decide whether it fully supports your future plans. An exercise we do with student groups is to ask them to prepare a "technology map" to see if they are equipped for the task they have taken on – and you can use this exercise as an individual (Hartley et al., 2022).

SUMMARY OF KEY POINTS

- following the pandemic we may well be entering a new phase in our use of computing technology in the workplace, taking advantage of developments in computing power, portability, and communication across networks.
- these developments support new applications which take advantage of the fundamental characteristics of computing technology, e.g. automating, informating, and integrating.
- in the next few years, we foresee further rapid development, especially in integration and embedding.
- there is a fair degree of consensus on the most important and likely trends in specific areas such as AI, VR, and AR.
- there are important concerns which we all need to take into account such as digital security and privacy.
- there are also worries that many organisations are not taking full advantage of the opportunities offered by technological development.
- we also need to worry about the implications for climate change in the ways that we (and our organisations) both adopt and use computer technology.

References

Azhar, A. (2021) *Exponentia: Order and Chaos in an Age of Accelerating Technology*. London: Penguin.

Bedford, T. (2022) New Amazon Kindle scribe arrives with three surprising upgrades. *Tech Radar*. https://www.techradar.com/news/new-amazon-kindle-arrives-with-two-massive-upgrades.

Clute, E. (2022) Three mile island true story: Biggest things the documentary leaves out. *Screenrant*. https://screenrant.com/three-mile-island-true-story-meltdown-missing-details-documentary/.

Criado Perez, C.. (2019) *Invisible Women: Exposing data bias in a world designed for men*. London: Chatto and Windus.

Daugherty, P.R. and Wilson, H.J. (2018) *Human + Machine: Re Imagining Work in the Age of AI*. Boston, MA: Harvard Business Review Press.

Fisman, R. and Sullivan, T. (2014) *The Org: How the Office Really Works*. London: John Murray.

Fouzder, M. (2021) Early users warned HMCTS about Common Platform problem. *The Law Society Gazette*.

Gall, R. (2020) Explained: Surveillance capitalism (and what Shoshana Zuboff's definition gets wrong). https://thecookiemag.com/explained-surveillance-capitalism-and-what-shoshana-zuboffs-definition-gets-wrong/.

Hackl, C., Lueth, D. and Di Bartolo, T. (2022) *Navigating the Metaverse: A Guide to Limitless Possibilities in a Web 3.0 World*. New Jersey: John Wiley.

Harte, A. and Robinson, B. (2022) Court IT system 'putting justice at risk', staff claim. https://www.bbc.co.uk/news/uk-62722855.

Hartley, P., Dawson, M. and Beckingham, S. (2022) *Success in Groupwork*, 2nd edition. London: Bloomsbury Academic.

Hobshawm, J. (2022) *The Nowhere Office: Reinventing Work and the Workplace of the Future*. London: Basic Books.

Hughes, A. (2022) What is Moores law and is it still relevant today? *BBC Science Focus*. https://www.sciencefocus.com/future-technology/moores-law/.

Leonardi, P. and Neeley, T. (2022) *The Digital Mindset: What it Really Takes to Thrive in the Age of Data, Algorithms, and AI*. Boston, MA: Harvard Business Review Press.

Liu, X. (2020) *Tracking How Our Bodies Work Could Change Our Lives*. World Economic Forum. https://www.weforum.org/agenda/2020/06/internet-of-bodies-covid19-recovery-governance-health-data/.

Mayer-Schonberger, V. and Cukier, K. (2013) *Big Data: A Revolution That Will Transform How We Live, Work and Think*. London: John Murray.

Meredith, N. (2019) *£20m Research and Technology Centre to enable people with dementia to live in own homes for longer*. Press Release from University of Surrey at https://www.surrey.ac.uk/news/ps20m-research-and-technology-centre-enable-people-dementia-live-own-homes-longer.

Mui, C. (2012) How Kodak failed. *Forbes*. https://www.forbes.com/sites/chunkamui/2012/01/18/how-kodak-failed/.

O'Neil., C. (2016) *Weapons of Math Destruction: How big data increases inequality and threatens democracy*. UK: Penguin Random House

O'Toole, J. (2014) Mobile apps overtake PC Internet usage in U.S. *CNN Business*. https://money.cnn.com/2014/02/28/technology/mobile/mobile-apps-internet/index.html.

Quinn. (2022) How many people use Twitter in 2022? (Twitter Statistics). *Quantum Marketer*. https://quantummarketer.com/twitter-statistics/.

Susskind, D. (2021) *A World Without Work: Technology, Automation and How We Should Respond*. London: Penguin.

Thompson, P. and Warhurst, C. (editors) (1998) *Workplaces of the Future*. London: Macmillan.
Wakefield, J. (2023) *Will the metaverse be your new workplace?* At: https://www.bbc.co.uk/news/business-64173594
Zuboff, S. (1988) *In the Age of the Smart Machine*. New York: Basic Books.
Zuboff, S. (2019) *The Age of Surveillance Capitalism*.

PART 2

Presenting information: effective methods and media

CHAPTER 6

How should we plan and organise professional written communication?

Introduction

This chapter invites you to consider your approach to professional written communication and start thinking about the choices you must make when you choose different forms, styles, and channels for your written documents, both printed and online.

We start by examining different approaches to writing – we summarise the various stages or steps that have been identified as important and discuss whether these should be followed in a specific order.

We highlight the way that structure affects our perception and how the organisation of a document influences how readers respond to it. This reinforces the need for clear objectives, and we suggest ways in which these might be prepared and phrased. Finally, we discuss different methods and techniques for planning the structure of documents and show how particular structures can support specific objectives.

OBJECTIVES

This chapter will:

- review different approaches to writing and suggest that you decide which approach suits you best.
- explain why organising and structuring information is so important.
- discuss how to establish clear objectives.
- explain different methods and principles for structuring information and show how these can be used to plan documents.
- show how we can also use these principles to organise information at different levels.
- show how the structure of a document can and should support its objectives.

DOI: 10.4324/9781003297550-9

How effective is written communication in your workplace?

All documents would have clear and appropriate purposes. These purposes would normally include most, if not all, of the following, and would be to:

- inform (providing the necessary information for effective decisions).
- educate or guide (proving the opportunity for staff development).
- motivate (providing the incentive for action).
- influence (persuading readers to act in certain ways in the future).

The documents should achieve this by:

- explaining clear and appropriate aims and objectives.
- demonstrating awareness and understanding as to who receives the communication.
- providing the right level of facts, information, and data.
- presenting appropriate findings and analyses, conclusions, and recommendations to guide the reader.

Such documents would deliver their messages, without unnecessary length, and without any confusing information that is difficult to read and/or understand.

Unfortunately, we have yet to find an organisation where this is always the case.

When we talk to colleagues in various organisations, the more common picture includes:

- documents which do not appear to have any clear purpose.
- documents which confuse (and often) annoy their readers.
- writers who are not really sure (or confident) about their audience(s) or their own purposes.

Box 6.1 includes a few real examples which illustrate what and how things can go wrong.

BOX 6.1

Nothing can go wrong?

The following quotes are from staff and individuals experiencing communication issues – illustrating ideas discussed later in this chapter. They are all real events but we have left them anonymous:

we received the 'consultation paper' from senior management which set out only one option for a new structure. This led us to question what they meant by 'consultation' and created very bad feeling towards senior management.

our working group had to review and to report on the committee structure. We struggled to present this until someone suggested a diagram showing links between committees (we happened to use Cmap). This revealed one longstanding committee, chaired by a senior manager, which did not appear to have any useful links with any other parts of the organisation! It was disbanded shortly afterwards.

I was discharged from hospital but did not receive any information as to how to manage my condition. I had to try to find it out for myself when t got home. I found conflicting advice on the internet. In contrast, my friend, a cardiac patient, received a 'discharge summary.' Luckily, the nurse explained this to her as it is written for doctors with lots of technical jargon, and pointed out really helpful online information from British Heart Foundation.

Where do you start?

Many books on professional writing start by offering advice on the most appropriate writing style which we talk about in the next chapter. We suggest a different starting point – taking a step back to *reflect* on your approach to writing and the way you organise information. This raises questions about what sort of document is needed (including all the possibilities now offered by online media) and we focus on that in Chapter 9.

Our starting point is represented in the following quotes from well-known British researchers and consultants in communication:

> *the real effort in writing is in the thinking required for planning and preparing.*
>
> (Turk and Kirkman, 1989, page 126)

> *Planning comes first...Many authors reckon the best way to start is not to write but to plan.*
>
> (Cutts, 2020, pages 1,2)

This idea is not new but is often ignored.

Kirkman and Turk go on to propose *three* critical steps which we reflect in this book:

- planning.
- organising the material.
- choosing the best way to express yourself.

This puts the initial emphasis on planning and preparing.

How do you plan and prepare?

Is there a best way of going about this process? For example, we have already emphasised the importance of clear objectives. A document, whether paper or online, can be beautifully written but if it does not have clear objectives and does not satisfy the needs or expectations of its readers then it is *not* going to be effective.

Martin Cutts recommends two useful starting points:

- the "core statement".
- This is a "rigidly constructed sentence in seven segments" which includes the intended audience, the main topics, and the purpose (this is the verb in the sentence such as "analyses", "evaluates" etc.). (Cutts, op cit, page 4)
- the "horizontal document plan".
- This translates the core statement into a series of boxes where you make a note of possible topics (Cutts, op cit, page 5ff).

What are the best steps or stages for effective professional writing?

Another common recommendation is that writing is best achieved through a definite sequence of steps. Different writers use different labels for the steps, but their ideas are often very similar, as Table 6.1 shows. These recommendations can be applied to both word-processed/printed and online documents. Stages of testing and maintenance are also often added to the timeline for online documents.

Figure 6.1 offers our interpretation of these stages in terms of the main tasks. You can use this as a checklist for any/every document you have to write – have you answered all these points in every document you write?

Should we always follow these suggested steps in the same order?

Is this advice supported by research evidence?

Can we assure success by following these steps?

As with most aspects of human communication, reality is more complex than some of the advice. In one of the most accessible and interesting reviews of what we know about the writing process, Mike Sharples concluded there are three "core activities" in writing – planning, composing, and revising – but the "flow of activity. . .is not just in one direction" (Sharples, 1999, page 72).

His model is reproduced in Figure 6.2. It shows a flow of material in a clockwise direction – from notes and plans to draft to final copy – *and* a flow of ideas in

Table 6.1 Stages of the writing process

	Authors		
	Chartered Management Institute, 2015	*Bovee and Thill, 2014*	*Timm and Bienvenu, 2011*
Steps involved in creating business documents	Define the purpose and objective	Decide what you want to say	Define the context (including your objectives)
	Gather and organise the information		Consider your media, source, and timing options
	Structure	Research information	Select and organise your information
	Write	Write your draft	
	Include graphics	Write your draft	
	Review what has been written	Edit and revise	Deliver your message
	Check		Evaluate feedback for continued success

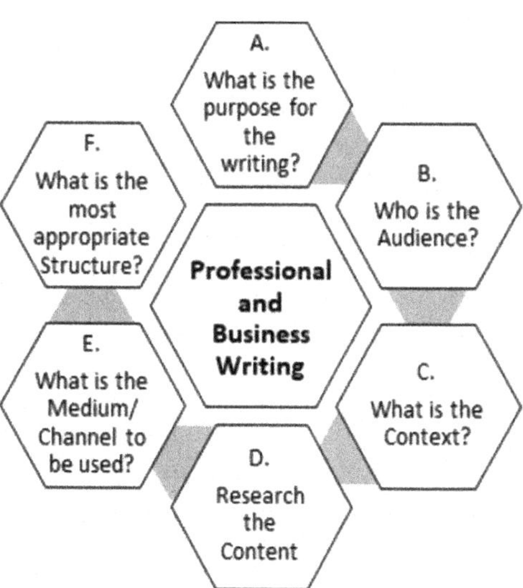

Figure 6.1 Key tasks in professional writing

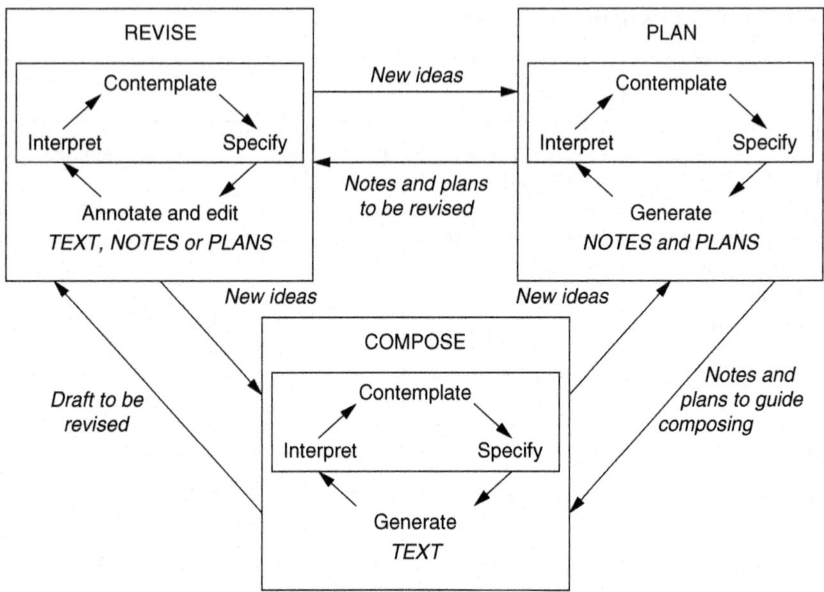

Figure 6.2 Sharples' model of writing as creative design (Sharples, 1999, page 72)

the opposite direction. For example, reading a draft may generate an idea which alters the plan.

Sharples also reviewed specific studies on the impact of the initial planning phase, as well as looking at some of the methods we cover in this chapter. He concluded that "time spent on planning is time well spent" (page 88) but that there are different ways to plan. You need to find the combination of methods that best fit your situation rather than relying on a single "model approach", as per Table 6.1 above.

We can extract practical conclusions from this brief review:

- it is important to develop plans and objectives.
- this does *not* mean that you have to write in a rigid sequence of steps.
- you should continually review your initial plans and objectives as your writing develops.
- you need to find an approach to planning and organising your writing which suits you.

An important research finding is that writers have very different ways of approaching all **three** main components of the writing process, and we summarise some important differences below.

We can apply these conclusions equally to writing online content, although you also need to consider specific characteristics of online media. There are now many online sources offering useful advice here and we have listed some on the website, including suggestions about ChatGPT and similar software.

Are you a bricklayer or an oil painter?

Several research studies have tried to investigate the main strategies used by writers. Sharples identified major studies which came up with very similar results (Sharples, 1999, pages 114ff). Table 6.2 below highlights major differences between strategies:

Some writers seem to use one strategy almost exclusively; some writers adopt different strategies for different tasks. We can find examples of successful professional authors who use each of these strategies. The key to successful writing is being aware of what you need to produce rather than following a specific process. As Sharples concludes:

> *Being a writer is, above all, having control over how you write and trust in your ability to make progress.*
>
> (Sharples, 1999, page 128)

We have included some comments on our own collaborative writing process later (see Chapter 16) to illustrate the point that you can use technology in very different ways to achieve the same outcomes. This account of our process is already out-of-date as we expect to be able to work very differently when the AI developments from Microsoft and Google become part of our everyday experience (see website for update).

Table 6.2 Writing strategies (taken from Sharples, op cit)

Writing strategies				
"Watercolourist"	*"Architect"*	*"Bricklayer"*	*"Sketcher"*	*"Oil painter"*
Tend to write "in one pass" from mental plan	Make detailed plan	Build the text up, sentence by sentence	Produce rough plan	Start by drafting rather than planning, working from broad headings
Tend to review and revise on screen rather than print out drafts	Do a draft, then print out. Revise paper version and then return to computer	Revise on screen as they go	Make frequent revisions and review/revise both on screen and from paper draft	Review drafts on paper

Planning is more than the text

Another important point which is not always emphasised is that planning should not just be about the words or the text – it should consider the whole of what we call "document design". You need to consider ***four*** interlinked aspects which will create the finished document:

- style of writing, i.e. choice of words, jargon, the way you address the reader, and so on. We cover this in Chapter 7.
- layout and design, i.e. the design of the page, whether printed, online or both, and the use of any visual aids such as illustrations or diagrams, and so on. We cover this in Chapter 8.
- the way the information is structured, which is the focus of the rest of this chapter.
- choice of media. For example, it is not enough to simply think of the distinction between print and online. There are different possibilities depending on which type of print or online document you may choose and we say more on this in Chapter 9.

One advantage of a clear plan is that the completed document should be easier to understand from the reader's point of view.

Why is structuring information so important in professional communication?

We know from decades of research into human perception, cognition, and memory that our brain continuously anticipates, organises, and reorganises the information it receives (we introduced the idea of the brain as an "anticipation machine" in Chapter 1). A lot of the time we are not conscious of the amount or extent of this processing. As a result, we can be misled by the way information is presented. A few examples will illustrate this:

in his summary of research on human decision-making and problem-solving, Scott Plous (1993) described research where students had to comment on film clips of road accidents. When he asked how fast the cars were going when they "smashed", students estimated an average speed which was 30% higher than students who were asked about the speed when the cars "hit". Students who were asked about "smashed" cars were also likely to "remember" a week later that the accident involved broken glass – something which was *not* on the film clips. In other words, these students had not just remembered – they had *reconstructed* an image of the accident based on the notion of a "smash" and subconsciously exaggerated elements of what they had actually seen.

Other research demonstrated the power of suggestions in particular formats of questions – for example, it makes a difference to people's estimates if you ask "how *long* was the movie?" rather than "how *short* was the movie?" (Plous, 1993, pages 32ff and 66ff).

More recent studies have emphasised the way we actively construct our interpretation of events. For example, we can be influenced in our thinking and judgements by perceptual biases such as priming, anchoring, and framing.

Priming

Imagine you have volunteered to participate in a psychology experiment. Your first task is to assemble four-word sentences from a set of five words. You are then asked to walk to another room to do another task. Suppose the words that you were using in the first task contained a lot of words relating to old age and getting old. Would that influence your later behaviour?

The short answer is "yes". Researchers compared the behaviour of participants who worked with a lot of "elderly" words and those who did not. They measured the time it took them to walk to the next room and discovered that those participants who had been "primed" to think about associations with old age walked more slowly down the corridor. This classic experiment and other similar studies are discussed in detail by Daniel Kahneman (see Kahneman, 2011, Chapter 4).

Anchoring

Anchoring is a similar process. You subconsciously use an estimate that you already have in your mind to make a decision or solve a problem. Again, the best way to understand this is through an example. Consider your response to the following two questions:

- is the height of the tallest redwood tree more or less than 1,200 feet?
- what is your best guess about the height of the tallest redwood tree?
- is the height of the tallest redwood tree more or less than 180 feet?
- what is your best guess about the height of the tallest redwood tree?

These are variations of the same problem – how tall is the tallest redwood tree?

But the first variation gives you a much bigger anchor – 1,200 feet – and this has a significant impact on the way that most people answer the question. When these questions were presented to different visitors at San Francisco Exploratorium, the answers were 844 and 282 feet respectively – in other words, the average answer added over 50% of the anchor figure (Kahneman, 2011, p.123ff).

Framing

The way that we introduce a topic or an argument – the way that we "frame" it – can have a powerful impact.

> *The way in which we frame an issue largely determines how that issue will be understood and acted upon.*
>
> (Scott, 2013)

This quote starts the article by Scott which provides a very detailed analysis of the framing techniques used by Barack Obama in his Nobel Prize acceptance speech.

Another research area which demonstrates the "power" of framing is the work on "attentional blindness". If you are focusing on one particular task or object then you may well not notice other changes in your environment, no matter how unusual or unexpected these changes may be. You can be attentionally blind not just to what you see but also to what you hear and also to physical touch. And you can test yourself to demonstrate this process using examples we discuss on the website.

Practical implications?

The important practical implication of these studies is that we have to be very aware of possible interpretations which our readers may make and which could be avoided by different structuring.

Our retention and understanding of messages depend on how they are presented. We cannot easily absorb or remember information which is not clearly structured.

Defining objectives

Many discussions of objectives imply that you must have them "perfectly" worked out before you do anything else. We see objectives as more flexible in line with the more fluid description of the writing process we gave earlier. There are two aspects of objectives we want to highlight in this chapter:

- phrasing your objectives in a particular way can help you decide what information to provide.
- clear objectives help you to improve the document by revising or redesigning it.

After we have discussed these will look at one common business objective – to persuade – and show some of the complexities of translating this into writing.

Clear objectives can lead to new (and better) documents

David Sless analysed how a large company used several rounds of customer testing to refine the format of what had been a complex multi-page document – a traditional letter plus several forms (Sless, 1999). The single page which resulted satisfied all the necessary objectives:

- telling the customer that their insurance policy would be cancelled if payment was not received by a certain date.
- reminding the customer of the details of the policy in question.
- providing a payment slip which customers could use by mail or at a post office.

The previous design put these objectives on separate pages. This created practical problems – all the customer needed to do was separate the letter and the forms and they had no idea which policy was being chased up. Using a single sheet eliminated this problem. The layout of the new form also clearly highlighted the three sections by the use of shading behind the text:

For current examples of similar restructuring and simplification, see the work of the Simplification Centre in the UK (and especially their "Simple Actions" reworkings) – http://www.simplificationcentre.org.uk

When the objective is to persuade

The study of persuasion goes back about 2,500 years to the time when the Greek Sophists taught people to argue their cases in courts and in public forums. Many modern theories of persuasion are still based on the three basic elements identified by Aristotle:

- ethos – establishment of sender credibility, or believability.
- logos – appeal to reason.
- pathos – appeal to emotions.

Sender Credibility

Aristotle correctly reasoned that if people could impress an audience with their credibility, then what they said was likely to be accepted.

Rational argument

We cannot just rely on the strict rules of logic which the ancient Greeks used. In most situations, you do not progress from irrefutable facts to logical conclusions; rather, you have a mass of evidence, often contradictory, which has to be weighed before a decision is taken. You have to show that the weight of the evidence favours certain conclusions, and that these conclusions suggest certain actions.

So, persuasive argument in professional writing usually consists of:

- a clear presentation of facts and inferences.
- an objective analysis of this information.
- reasoned conclusions from the analysis.
- a proposed course of action based on these conclusions.

There are some further issues to worry about:

Emotional appeal

Your audience will often react emotionally to a message. It is important to know those areas where an audience is influenced by strong emotion, particularly where political, religious, and moral beliefs and values are concerned.

Audience analysis

Persuasion aims to change the audience's world view in some way, so it is important to have some idea of the audience's *present world view* and the factors that are likely to *motivate* the audience to adopt the desired view.

Format of correspondence

All writing should encourage the audience to read it as there is usually no compulsion to do so. The minimum requirement for a persuasive letter is that it is clear and well set out.

Deciding on the content of persuasive writing

You can use all three of Aristotle's principles. For example, when applying by correspondence for financial support, sender credibility (*ethos*) can be established by a number of methods, such as:

- the high status of the writer or the organisation.
- the obvious legality of the document, e.g. proper organisational stationery, fund-raising number, etc.
- stating (briefly) some achievements of the organisation.

We must also use logical argument and provide some evidence that the appeal is necessary. Such evidence can come from:

- facts and figures.
- expert opinion.

The emotive appeal must be carefully handled. It has been shown that overly emotional appeals do not necessarily result in the desired action, although they may often elicit an emotional response. For example, people usually want to forget unpleasant emotions as soon as possible. Charities have found that focusing on a bad situation during appeals is less successful than placing some emphasis on the potentially happy outcome of a successful appeal.

Modern techniques and approaches to persuasion tend to build on these ideas and emphasise the importance of building conducive relationships. For example, Robert Cialdini (2021) suggests six principles, summarised in Table 6.3.

Kevin Dutton reviews a wide range of studies and his own analysis of persuasive techniques in action to propose "five major axes of persuasion": simplicity, perceived self-interest, incongruity, confidence, and empathy. (Dutton, 2011) We have summarised these in Table 6.4 below and you can use this as a checklist for your own persuasive messages, both written and oral.

Table 6.3 Principles of influence (adapted from Cialdini, 2021)

Principle	Meaning?	Practical implications?
Reciprocation	Give a little something to get a little something in return	Would this make a regular site user be more inclined to pay towards a training course of tips and expertise?
Commitment and consistency	People want their beliefs to be consistent with their values	By identifying regular site users as customers and aligning their self-belief and perception with yours, can they be more easily persuaded?
Social proof	There is nothing like feeling validated based on what others are doing	Does the "wisdom-of-the-crowds" philosophy work if safety in numbers is evident?
Liking	The more you like someone, the more you will be persuaded by them	Does the Richard Branson liking principle work? Does his persona and ideals persuade customers to buy Virgin?
Authority	Will you obey me?	Do influencers truly influence? What authority do they hold to persuade others to accept what they say, or do what they do?
Scarcity	When you believe something is in short supply...you want more of it!	Remembering the scarcity of toilet rolls and pasta at the beginning of the pandemic, the use of fear is a persuasive tool to encourage consumers to act fast.

Table 6.4 Characteristics of persuasive messages (adapted from Dutton, 2011)

Characteristics of persuasive messages	Meaning	Checklist question
Simplicity	Simple messages are more memorable.	Can you summarise your main message in a simple phrase or sentence? Does your use of language make the main message easy to remember?
Perceived self-interest	Your main message should appeal to what the audience sees as its own advantage.	What does your audience want? Does your main message offer them an advantage?
Incongruity	Persuasive messages often contain an element of surprise which captures attention.	Does your presentation contain novel elements which will catch your audience's attention?
Confidence	Persuasive messages are expressed confidently.	How does your presentation inspire confidence?
Empathy	Persuasive messages demonstrate that you appreciate the feelings and circumstances of your audience.	How does your presentation demonstrate that you have recognised the main issues or interests of your audience?

Methods and principles for structuring information

There are several different ways of looking at structure.

Chunking, ordering, and signposting

Much of the communication skills training that we have been involved in over the last few decades has used these three basic principles (Hartley, 1984):

- chunking – dividing information into sections or "chunks" which make the information easier to digest.
- ordering – putting those chunks into an order which will make them more or less useful or meaningful.
- signposting – providing clues or signals to explain or demonstrate the way the information is structured.

We can illustrate these principles with an everyday example. The news bulletin on US or UK television is usually organised along the following lines:

- the bulletin is presented in a series of specific events with some use of overall categories – for example, the sports stories are clustered together towards the end (chunking).
- the introduction at the beginning lists the main stories (signposting). This is repeated at the end and sometimes also about halfway through.
- the most "important" stories come first (ordering). There is often a short funny story or unusual event at the end to provide light relief.

All the methods we go on to describe use some combination of these three basic principles. They often use a visual analogy as a basic idea and so we start with the "magic" of pyramids.

The pyramid principle

This comes from the book of the same name by Barbara Minto, first published in the USA in 1987 and since published in several different editions (Minto, 2002). It is based on the idea that the human mind will look for patterns in the information presented:

> *the clearest written documents will be those that consistently present their information from the top down, in a pyramidal structure.*
>
> (Minto, 2002, page 11)

She explains how to construct pyramids which can then be translated into documents, emphasising that

- any level in the pyramid must summarise the ideas grouped below it.
- you must logically order and cluster ideas into sensible groups (what we would call "chunking").

She recommends a top-down approach although she also shows how you can build a pyramid from bottom-up, where you have a collection of information but do not have a clear idea of how to put it together.

With a clear objective, you can use the top-down approach. You start by defining the top-level of the pyramid. To do this you need to decide what question you are dealing with and what is your recommended answer. This answer then fills the box at the top of the pyramid. For example, suppose that you have been asked to produce a written report which evaluates a proposal to replace an existing information system with a new one. If you decide that the new information system is a good idea, then this proposition becomes the top box in the pyramid.

You then have to ask yourself how to convince your reader to go along with the proposition. For example, you may want to argue that a new system will actually provide more comprehensive information than the present one. It may

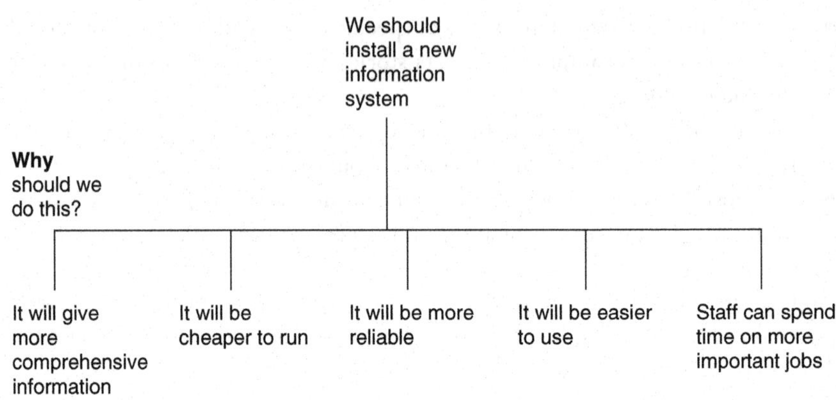

Figure 6.3 Pyramid example

be cheaper to run. It may be easier to use and allow staff to spend more time on other more important jobs. You can see from Figure 6.3 below that you can use these ideas to build the second layer of the pyramid.

By generating a logical question which follows from these three propositions, you can produce of the third layer of the pyramid. The key question here is "how?" How will the new system deliver more comprehensive information? How will it be cheaper to run? How will it allow staff to spend more time doing more important jobs? To construct the complete pyramid, you simply repeat this question and answer sequence to generate as many levels as appropriate.

Minto also provides a very interesting model to form the introduction to any document. This is based on her suggestion that we need to spell out the history of events which have led up to the document. This can be represented by what she calls a "classic pattern of story-telling" – situation, complication, question, answer. This sequence is explained in a bit more detail below.

Spider diagrams and mind maps

The Pyramid Principle advocates that we should visualise the structure of our argument as a pyramid. But what other visual analogies can we use?

The spider diagram

Another way of developing a structure of ideas is to create a spider diagram. You write your central idea or topic in the middle of the page and then build a "spider's web" of associated ideas which link from it. This then gives you a structure which you can amend and revise until it covers what you want. We have used this very simple method of summarising ideas in various ways – to take notes of lectures, to plan lectures, to give as handouts, to plan reports and papers, and so on. The spider diagram has a number of potential advantages over linear notes or a full transcription:

- it is quick and easy to do.
- it gives a visual map of the topic which can make it easy to remember.
- it can summarise complicated ideas.

Mind maps

A more sophisticated development of this idea was originated by the late Tony Buzan, one of the leading advocates of the Mind Map®, which he described as:

> *a revolutionary thinking tool that, when mastered, will transform your life. It will help you process information, come up with new ideas, strengthen your memory, get the most out of your leisure time and improve the way you work.*
>
> (Buzan, 2018, page 13)

He argued that these maps work best when you incorporate a variety of techniques, such as:

- emphasis, by including images, colours, and spacing on the page, and by variations in the size of lines, text, and images.

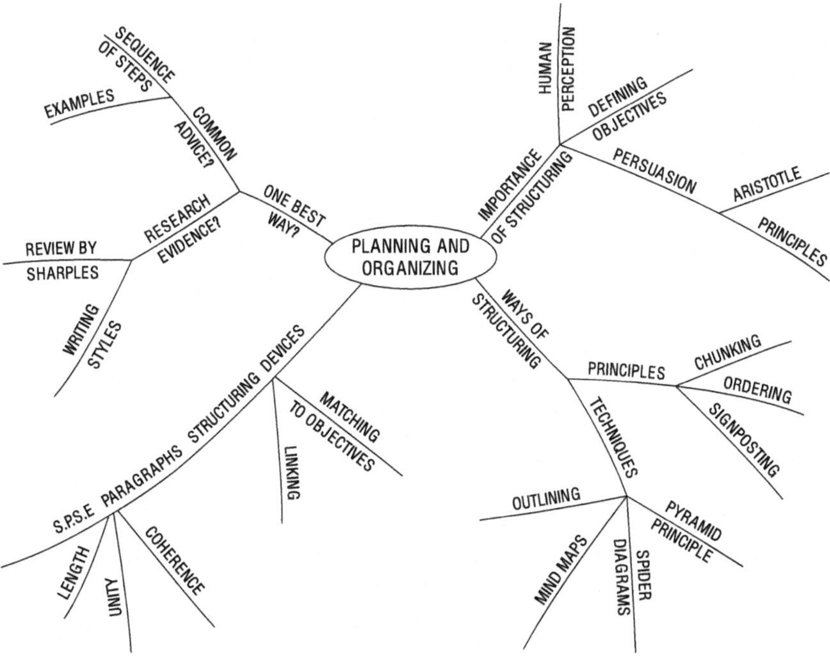

Figure 6.4 Spider diagram

- association, by making links across the diagram and by developing your own codes to represent ideas.

According to Buzan, there are three essential characteristics of a good mind map:

- "a central image that captures the main subject under consideration".
- "thick branches radiating out from the central image". These represent the key themes and should be "represented by a different colour".
- "a single key image or word placed on each branch".

As a result of his emphasis on colour and images, many of the examples in his books and on the website which is carrying on in his name (https://tonybuzan.com) are much more visually complex and colourful than the diagrams we have tended to use in this book.

Buzan offered strong arguments in favour of mind maps, as in:

> *recent scientific research support growing evidence that the Mind Map is the natural manifestation of the human brain's thinking processes, and that we actually all think in internal Mind Maps.*
>
> (Buzan, op cit)

We think this claim is overstated but we are persuaded that many if not most of us can benefit from using some form of visual thinking to help us in our professional writing. As with your approach to writing in general, you should investigate alternatives and find the tools that best suit your approach and personality.

Concept Maps

Several of the diagrams in this book were prepared using concept mapping software (Cmap) which offers an alternative approach to mind maps which may be more useful in many situations. One leading exponent of concept mapping in the UK describes mind mapping as a 'helpful study tool' but suggests that concept mapping is a tool that promotes a greater level of reflection. (Kinchin, 2014)

As with mind maps, different software packages are available. We use Cmap which has several advantages:

- as "Freeware", it can be downloaded (from https://cmap.ihmc.us) and used freely (we do recommend a donation to its parent institution).
- it is very easy and quick to learn.
- maps start from a clear/relevant "focus question".
- coherent links between concepts can encourage thinking and test your understanding.

- it works cross-platform (PC/Mac/iPad) and there are also web and server versions.
- because they are based on propositions, they can be easier to "read" and understand than many mind maps.
- you can include docs/links in the map (e.g. weblinks).
- a presentation can be stored in the map.

There is an international community of "Cmappers" and you can find multiple examples of its application as well as research and analysis of its impact and benefits.

Visual thinking: Sketchnoting and Infographics

If you have attended an annual conference or an organisation's strategy meeting or a public consultation meeting in the last few years, the discussion in the room or online may well have been summarised in graphic form by a facilitator using visual thinking and sketch-noting techniques. These often use colour as well, so we have included some examples on the website.

While these facilitators are usually skilled graphic illustrators, basic techniques can be used by everyone. For example, Brandy Agerback (2016) offers a practical manual explaining and illustrating techniques which she has used with a wide range of organisations, and which includes the five steps described in Table 6.5 and 24 "Idea Shapers" (specific tools which you can use and adapt in your own plans).

Where sketchnoting is typically based on hand-drawn sketches, infographics primarily use software. As they are mainly used for presentations rather than planning or structuring ideas, we will discuss them in more detail in Chapter 8.

Table 6.5 Sketchnoting principles

Step	Title	Where you/you are...
1	Chunk	"identify and isolate discrete, relevant ideas from a big messy pile" (page 49)
2	Sort + Group	"arranging related chunks of information into useful groupings" (page 105)
3	Connect + Contain	"using lines and shapes to express relationships" (page 183)
4	Scale	"adjusting size to shift thinking and create organization" (page 277)
5	Grasp	"strengthening your drawing and making meaning from it" (page 327)

A fairly typical definition of infographics comes from Nediger (2022):

An infographic is a collection of imagery, data visualisations like pie charts and bar graphs, and minimal text that gives an easy-to-understand overview of a topic.

Walsh (2020) provides a set of influential infographics which illustrates the variety of formats and objectives, and we discuss this further in Chapter 8.

Outlining

Even the simplest written communication needs some form of planned structure. This can vary from a three-or-four point outline for a response to an enquiry letter, to an outline with headings and sub-headings for an investigative report. Your word processor includes an outliner so you can either type in your text in normal page fashion or directly into the outliner. Provided you have used the hierarchy of headings which your word processor allows then you can also review your text in outline at any time. You can also move the text around in outline view which can be easier than using "cut and paste" in normal view.

So you can produce an outline straight into the word processor to see if your plan looks sensible and then expand it. For example, after several staff in a training department had expressed interest in using infographics, one was asked to produce a short report on possible ways forward. They started with the following outline:

- what are infographics? (definition plus examples.)
- how are they used by organisations? (what benefits do they offer?)
- how could we use them? (are there any disadvantages?)
- what software is available (and what would it cost?)
- how could we become expert in them? (what training would we need? Or could we do it ourselves?)
- what would the plan of action be if we decided to adopt them?

For longer documents, such as reports on investigations, you can use the outliner function to produce a plan of action as a guide before you start your investigation. Once the investigation is complete this can be expanded in the outline for the report. For example, if you were asked to investigate the copier needs of your department/organisation for the next five years, your plan could look something like this:

- present copying facilities.
- estimate of future requirements.
- technology – current and developing.

- operating costs.
- back-up service and spares.

Once the information has been collected and examined you could develop this plan into a more comprehensive outline. For example, under operating costs you would want to investigate the comparative costs of purchase or lease and the different forms of lease available.

But would this approach meet the needs of your audience?

This example also illustrates one possible issue with any request for a document – what is the actual objective? Are there hidden agendas behind this request?

If you are asked to "investigate copier needs", what could this mean?

- is this an invitation to consider whether the organisation needs to use photocopiers at all? (are you or should you be heading for the "paperless office"?)
- is there a "hidden agenda" as the boss suspects some staff of doing too much copying?
- does "the boss" expect a simple recommendation on how we can "replace that old cranky machine in the corner" as cheaply as possible?

These are very different requests which need very different approaches, or at least further discussion about what is really required.

In the next few years, we are likely to see further advances in the way computer software supports our writing through functions like outliners. And you should check whether your default word-processor software is offering you the facilities you really need as in Box 6.2.

BOX 6.2

Are you using the "right" word processor?

If you have been through a school/college/university career in the UK, you have probably been provided with a copy of Microsoft Office. You may never have considered using an alternative word processor to Microsoft Word.

But there are a number of alternatives which offer different facilities. For example:

- Google Docs allows collaboration online but does not have such a wide range of formatting.
- one of us (PH) prefers Apple's Pages to Word for specific tasks because of the more flexible ways it manages page layout.
- some word processors are designed for particular tasks. For example, Scrivener advertises itself as "tailor-made for long writing projects"

(https://www.literatureandlatte.com/scrivener/overview). It is worth taking some time to review alternative software as you may well find one which saves you both time and effort.

See the website for an update and further discussion.

Structuring devices in written documents

We can use several techniques in documents to make the structure clear to readers. To illustrate this, we shall identify features of paragraphs: structure, length, unity, coherence, and linking devices. In later chapters, we show how features like typefaces and page design can supply similar cues, including the use of headings and sub-headings linked to page layout.

Structure of paragraphs

One common paragraph structure presents the following logical progression:

Situation

Problem

Solution

Evaluation

You can also use this structure as a model for structuring documents.

Often you only need to use two or three of the components but they follow the same sequence:

- situation – problem – evaluation.
- situation – evaluation.

For example, the following paragraph follows the "situation – evaluation" pattern:

Any substantial written professional text contains a number of different pieces of information that are part of a presentation to achieve some communication objective. These pieces are usually related in a structured way.

Another common structure is to follow the time sequence:

We were travelling by car to Springfield. Near Halfway House the left-front tyre burst and the car skidded off the road into a barrier. We were extremely lucky to escape without injury.

This paragraph also follows the "situation – problem – evaluation" sequence.

Length of paragraphs

As you have just seen, a paragraph can consist of a single sentence.

Short one-sentence paragraphs are often used to emphasise a point, like this one.

There is no upper limit to the number of words in a paragraph. Good business writing tends to have short paragraphs compared with literary writing. For long documents like reports, a maximum of 100 words per paragraph is a rough guideline. For shorter documents, about 60 words is suitable, but you should not destroy the unity of a paragraph in an effort to reduce its length.

To maintain the reader's interest, you should use paragraphs of varying lengths.

Unity

Unity here means that the paragraph deals with a single topic. Any sentence that does not refer to the topic should be excluded and moved to a new paragraph. This enables the reader to follow your train of thought one step at a time.

Coherence

It is not sufficient that all sentences in a paragraph refer to the topic; they should also develop the theme in a logical way. Each sentence should follow on naturally from the previous one.

A typical practical translation of these sorts of ideas comes from Suzanne Sparks who advises that you should "structure your writing to reach your reader" (Sparks, 1999, page 48). She offers five possible structures for short documents which are similar to the paragraph structures we talked of above. For example, she suggests that a persuasive communication should be based on the following five paragraphs:

1. you try to establish some common ground.
2. you explain the problem which will be resolved if the reader agrees to your request.
3. you explain the solution and show how it has significant advantages for the reader which outweigh any disadvantages.
4. you list all the benefits for the reader.
5. you clearly specify what you want the reader to do.

Matching structure to objectives

To conclude this chapter, we would emphasise our main message: the structure of your written communication should support your objectives (this also applies to face-to-face communication as we shall discuss later in this book).

We can illustrate this by looking at possible structures for a persuasive flier/ letter. The following are some of the elements that may be included. Not all of these elements will suit every case and they do not necessarily follow this exact sequence given.

- attention-getting introduction.
- statement of problem or situation.
- statement of needs of or advantages to receiver.
- statement of needs of sender.
- visualisation of outcome.
- reconciliation of sender's and receiver's needs.
- call for action.

But will this letter work?

Will it achieve its objectives?

Consider your answer to these questions and then have a look at an example and our further analysis on the website.

SUMMARY OF KEY POINTS

- many texts divide the writing process into a series of steps and suggest you follow them in that order, moving from preparation and research, to organising the material, and on to writing and revising.
- research suggests that life is more complex. Writers need to find the combination of methods that suit their situation – it is important to develop plans and objectives but this does not mean that you have to write in a rigid sequence of steps.
- research shows that if we can present information which is clearly organised *and* organised in a way which makes sense to the audience, then that audience will find the information easier to understand and remember.
- clear objectives are an important part of planning. Phrasing your objectives in a particular way can help you decide what information you then need to provide.
- persuasion is an important function of many documents. We need to consider whether our writing can use appropriate tactics and techniques.
- there are various ways of structuring information which you can use as the basis for a written document. They are all based on three basic principles: chunking, ordering, and signposting.
- there are many useful techniques for structuring material which often use some visual analogy as a basic idea. It is worth considering the Pyramid Principle, the use of Concept and Mind Maps, sketchnoting, and the use of outliners.

- there are also devices we can use in documents to make the structure clear to readers. To illustrate this, we concentrated on features of the paragraph: argument structure, length, unity, coherence, and linking devices.
- the structure of your written communication should support your objectives, and we illustrated this by looking at possible structures for a persuasive letter. But this then raises the question of the appropriate media for particular messages.

References

Agerback, B. (2016) *The Idea Shapers: The Power of Putting Your Thinking into Your Own Hands.* Loosetooth.com.

Bovee, C. and Thill, J. (2014) *Business Communication Today.* London: Pearson.

Buzan, T. (2018) *Mind Map Mastery.* London: Watkins.

Cialdinii, R.B. (2021) *Influence: The Psychology of Persuasion.* New York: HarperCollins.

Cutts, M. (2020) *Oxford Guide to Plain English*, 5th edition. Oxford: Oxford University Press.

Hartley, P. (1984) *Principles For Effective Documents. Paper to Scottish Communication Association Annual Conference.* Edinburgh: Napier university.

Dutton, K. (2011) *Flipnosis: The Art of Split-second Persuasion.* Croydon: Arrow.

Kahneman, D. (2011) *Thinking, Fast and Slow.* London: Penguin.

Kinchin, I. (2014) Concept Mapping as a Learning Tool in Higher Education: A Critical Analysis of Recent Reviews. *The Journal of Continuing Higher Education,* 62(1): 39–49. At: https://www.researchgate.net/publication/journal/The-Journal-of-Continuing-Higher-Education-0737-7363

Minto, B. (2002) *The Pyramid Principle: Logic in Writing and Thinking*, 3rd edition. London: Pearson.

Nediger. (2022) https://venngage.com/blog/what-is-an-infographic/.

Plous, S. (1993) *The Psychology of Judgment and Decision Making.* New York: McGraw-Hill.

Scott, B. (2013) *Framing an argument.* At https://www.diplomacy.edu/people/biljanascott/

Sharples, M. (1999) *How We Write: Writing as Creative Design.* London: Routledge.

Sless, D. (1999) The mass production of unique letters. In Bargiela-Chiappini, F. and Nickerson, C. (eds) *Writing Business: Genres, Media and Discourses.* Harlow: Longman.

Sparks, S.D. (1999) *The Manager's Guide to Business Writing.* New York: McGraw-Hill.

Timm, T. and Bienvenu, P.R. (2011) *Straight Talk.* London: Routledge.

Turk, C. and Kirkman, J. (1989) *Effective Writing: Improving Scientific, Technical and Business Communication*, 2nd edition. London: E and FN Spon. Close.

Walsh, S. (2020) *14 Influential Infographic Examples To Inspire You.* https://www.semrush.com/blog/infographic-examples/?kw=core_bu_82&cmp=Core12_SRCH_DSA_Blog_Core_BU_BING&label=dsa_pagefeed&Network=s&Device=c&utm_content=&kwid=dat-2333507271648916:loc-188&cmpid=412591844&agpid=1307319654896571&BU=Core&extid=&adpos=&msclkid=fb4893cdc07d11f75710f132ba0a9d3d&utm_source=bing&utm_medium=cpc&utm_campaign=Core12_SRCH_DSA_Blog_Core_BU_BING&utm_term=core_bu_82.

CHAPTER 7

What is an effective writing style?

Introduction

As we said in the last chapter, professional writing should achieve clear objectives – it should help to get some necessary job done. For example, you might be writing to give someone accurate information (as in a product information sheet) or to persuade someone to set up a project (as in a project proposal).

How effectively you achieve your objective will depend in part on your writing style. We need strategies which will increase the likely effectiveness of professional language. These strategies are what this chapter is all about – how to write in an effective style for various forms of professional communication.

We start by identifying some common criticisms of official and business language, using examples from communication specialists such as the Plain English Campaign and the Plain Language Commission. We then work through the main criteria we use to identify the main features of effective style – appropriate content and appropriate tone. Many business communicators advocate Plain English or Plain Language as the appropriate style to meet these criteria and we review the main supporting claims and possible limitations of this approach.

Finally, we look at some detailed strategies for improving writing and assess the value of methods such as measuring the "readability" of a document. But we must treat tools like this with caution – we cannot offer a "magic solution" to language problems which can deal with every situation. Throughout this chapter, we shall point out the difficulties and pitfalls of relying on simple or absolute rules of "effective" language. As we must keep saying, communication is both complex and dependent on context.

OBJECTIVES

This chapter will:

- identify common criticisms of professional writing.

DOI: 10.4324/9781003297550-10

- explain the main criteria we can use to identify an effective professional writing style.
- outline the main characteristics, potential advantages, and possible limitations of the Plain English/Plain Language approach.
- summarise important strategies of "plain language" and suggest how to improve your style by using appropriate words and effective sentences.
- evaluate methods to measure the readability of a document.

What do we need to "fix" in business writing?

There are two main forms of communication in organisations – how the organisation communicates to its customers/clients and the general public, and how it communicates within its own walls. Both aspects of professional writing have come in for their fair share of criticism. For current examples of baffling prose, we only need to consult the "Golden Bull" awards from the UK Plain English Campaign (PEC). As well as awards for examples of excellent communication, the Campaign publicises organisations and individuals who have managed to confuse and/or mislead their audiences. These brief descriptions of some of their awards are taken from the PEC website (https://plainenglish.co.uk):

- The Golden Bulls ("for the worse examples of written tripe").
- Heroes and Villains ("for those who have performed plain English heroics and for those that have done the opposite").
- The Foot in Mouth Award ("for baffling quotes by public figures").
- Web award ("for clear and usable websites").

The following examples demonstrate some of the language misdemeanours which the Campaign aims to eliminate. For each one, you might like to contemplate how you would feel if the message had been aimed at you:

Example A – from the Golden Bull Awards 2021:

This extract from the NHS England Primary Care Bulletin baffled many readers.

> The ICS Design Framework set an expectation that provider collaboratives will be a key component in enabling ICSs to deliver their core purpose. This guidance outlines minimum expectations for how providers should work together in provider collaboratives, offering principles to support local decision-making and suggesting the function and form that systems and providers may wish to consider.

This Bulletin "provides resources on health policy and practice" aimed at "teams across general practice, dentistry, community pharmacy and optometry" (NHS England, 2022).

Example B – Golden Bull Awards 2021:

Customers were not impressed by this email from SP Energy Networks which assumes a significant level of technical expertise and understanding of acronyms:

> As your local Distribution Network Operator (DNO) – the company responsible for the connection of your power generation assets to the local electricity network – we have previously notified you of an important change to the Distribution Code.
>
> To further update you all, EREC G59 requirements must be implemented by generation owners by 1 September 2022. Where Loss of Mains (LoM) is provided by Vector Shift, it must be removed and/or replaced with Rate of Change of Frequency protection (RoCoF)

The email continues in a similar vein, and you can find further paragraphs on the PEC website.

Example C – Foot in Mouth Award, 2021

British politician, Dominic Raab, managed to demonstrate his complete misunderstanding of misogyny:

> *Misogyny is absolutely wrong – whether it's a man against a woman or a woman against a man.*

Example D – Plain English Villains Award, 2021

Former British politician, Nick Clegg, now working for Meta, was recognised for his attempts to divert attention from criticisms of Facebook. Responding to accusations of "allowing dangerous misinformation to run unchecked on its pages", PEC highlighted this quote from Clegg:

> *The vast majority of content on Facebook is babies, barbecues and bar mitzvahs.*

Example E (showing that official pomp and long-windedness has a long and undistinguished history) – Golden Bull from 2012

> The Committee concluded, having regard to the totality of the factors considered above that choice could not be given significant weight and that there was not currently a gap on the spectrum of adequacy sufficient to conclude that

> the provision of pharmaceutical services is not currently secured to the standard of adequacy. Accordingly, the Committed concluded: The application was neither necessary nor expedient to secure the adequate provision of services in the neighbourhood, and therefore dismissed the appeal in this respect.

NHS Litigation Authority explained their rejection of an application to open a pharmacy – their Appeals Manager is quoted as admitting the error and promising to do better in future.

These awards do generate considerable adverse publicity and can have an immediate impact. All "award-winners" are also preserved for posterity on the PEC website.

All these examples would have been seen both inside and outside the organisations concerned. Criticisms of the written materials which circulate only *within* organisations can be equally scathing. Again, this is nothing new.

Exasperation with poor professional writing has a long history. For example, we can go back to World War 2. At the height of the Battle of Britain, the British Prime Minister, Winston Churchill, still found time to write a memo to his staff recommending "reports which set out the main points in a series of short, crisp paragraphs". He complained that most official papers were "far too long"; wasted time and energy by not highlighting the main points; and contained too many "woolly phrases".

If professional and business writing is still often ambiguous, overcomplex, and unattractive, what can we do about it?

Suggestions to resolve these problems also have a long history. Back in the 1990s, William Horton suggested we need a new type of business document – "one that answers questions in a hurry" (Horton, 1997, page 3). Through advances in electronic communications (perhaps most notably email and/or text messaging) have we now answered Horton's suggestion?

One common response is to adopt Plain English. Before we investigate this in detail, we need to examine *general criteria* for good style which are often applied to professional writing.

What is "good style" in professional writing?

To demonstrate good style, professional writing must be concise, clear, and convey information and ideas quickly. This style of writing is to inform or persuade and/or to clearly convey information and ideas.

> *Style in writing is concerned with choice.*
>
> (Kirkman, 1992, page 6)

Even if you work in an organisation with very strict rules about how emails, letters, and reports are presented, you still have to make choices about which words and phrases to use, how to organise your content or paragraphs, and so on. You have to make stylistic choices to create a document with the appropriate content and tone – and we shall investigate these two aspects in search of the "best" business style. A more recent consideration is the use of gender or un-gendered terms in professional writing.

There are numerous guides to good style written by experienced consultants and language experts. Table 7.1 compares recommendations from a

Table 7.1 Agreement on Plain Language

Language characteristic	Cutts (2020) *	Timm and Bienvenu (2011)	Bovee and Thill (2013)
Use short sentences	Average 15–20 words	"Sentences should average about 16 to 18 words in length". (Page 16)	"Look for ways to combine a mixture of sentences that are short (up to 15 words or so), medium (15–25 words), and long (more than 25 words)". (Page 108)
Use familiar words	"Use words your readers are likely to understand"	"Use simple, everyday wording". (Page 21)	"Choose familiar words". (Page 89)
No unnecessary words	"Use only as many words as you need".	"A sentence should contain no unnecessary words". (page 1)	"Readers want messages that convey important content clearly and quickly". (Page 105)
Prefer active to passive voice	"Prefer active-voice verbs unless there's a good reason for using the passive".	"Minimise the use of passive voice in workplace writing". (Page 218)	"In most cases, the active voice is the better choice". (Page 86)
Direct style	"Put your points positively when you can".	"Write the way you would talk in a planned, purposeful conversation". (Page 19)	"Achieve a tone that is conversational but still business-like". (Page 85)
'Good' grammar and punctuation	"Put accurate punctuation at the heart of your writing".	"We conspicuously display our professionalism in our writing". And this includes "Avoiding common grammar, punctuation and usage mistakes". (Page 194)	"If you make errors of grammar or usage, you lose credibility with your audience". (Page 87)

*All quotes taken from his summary of guidelines (Cutts, 2020, pages xxvi to xxxvii)

number of leading experts (one from the UK and two from the USA) demonstrating substantial agreement.

BOX 7.1

Good style can be dangerous?

Frank Luntz has an impressive track record of working with corporations and political leaders on their use of language. His 2007 book is based on the "basic advice" listed in Table 7.1 which we would echo:

> *It's not what you say, it's what people hear.*

And so:

> *The key to successful communication is to take the imaginative step of stuffing yourself right into your listener's shoes to know what they are thinking and feeling (page xi)*

He offers ten "rules of effective language":

- credibility.
- brevity.
- simplicity.
- consistency.
- novelty.
- sound.
- aspiration.
- visualisation.
- questioning.
- context.

He introduces some ideas which are not in our recipe below and which are worth considering in your own context, such as the value of explaining things in a way which your audience can visualise.

These techniques can be used to mislead readers. Steven Poole (2007) highlights a leaked memo from Luntz back in 2003 which advised US Republican politicians to "refine" the terminology they should use in an environmental debate – "It's time for us to start talking about 'climate change' instead of global warming" as "'Climate change' is less frightening ..." Poole discusses the effectiveness of this strategy of "redefining labels" to serve political and economic ends (page 42ff).

More recently Lundt has changed his political stance on issues such as climate change, but his advice was influential at the time. The important lesson from this example is that language can be (and is often) used to mislead. For this reason, we suggest "accuracy" as our first content criterion below.

An example where accuracy is essential relates to the specific requirements for prepacked for direct sale (PPDS) food labelling. Relevant law was changed in England, Wales, and Northern Ireland on 1 October 2021. New legislation known as Natasha's Law (Introduction to allergen labelling changes (PPDS) | Food Standards Agency) helps to protect consumers – all labelling provides life-saving allergen information on the packaging. The need for such accuracy on packaging followed the tragic death of teenager Natasha Ednan-Laperouse from an allergic reaction – caused by a baguette without allergen labelling.

Content criteria

What criteria can we use to evaluate the content of a business or official text?

We suggest you start from these criteria:

- accuracy.
- brevity.
- clarity.
- emphasis.

Accuracy

Accuracy is the most important criterion. Inaccurate and incorrect information can often be more harmful than no information at all. Would you wish to travel on an aircraft that had been serviced according to an inaccurate manual?

But this raises a problem: *how* accurate must your writing be? A high degree of accuracy often requires considerable detail and qualification of the information. The result could be long and turgid texts which nobody can bring themselves to read. So, you need to strike the right balance in terms of the level of detail.

Brevity

Overlong documents are usually caused by unnecessary material and/or long-winded writing. In any communication situation, the writer usually has more information than is necessary and must therefore determine:

- what the audience already knows.
- what the audience needs to know.
- what the audience wants to know.

Once you have a clear idea of this, you can trim the message without leaving out important information. However, this is not as easy as it sounds – your audience may contain distinct subgroups with different needs.

Clarity

Lack of clarity is often due to poor style, rather than difficult subject matter, and may be caused by:

- stilted phrases and cliches.
- too much detail and repetition.
- lack of logical structure.
- excessive use of abstract and generic terms.

Emphasis

Important information should be emphasised. But how do we decide what is important? It is:

- information that is important to the audience.
- information that will support your arguments as a writer.

Less important information should be left out or placed later in the text.

Apart from ranking items in order of importance, emphasis can be achieved by other methods, such as:

- format and typography.
  The layout and typography of a document can be used to highlight important points. We say more on this in Chapter 8. Techniques include the use of white space, use of lists and bullet points, use of headings etc.
- grammatical structure.
  We can emphasise a word by making it the subject of a sentence. For example, rather than "The temperature was measured by an optical pyrometer", you can say "An optical pyrometer measured the temperature". This puts the emphasis on the means of measurement.

Of course, emphasis should not be carried to the point where information is distorted or where important facts are concealed.

Balancing the content criteria

A good text depends on achieving a successful *balance* of the four criteria to meet the reader's needs. In the simple examples we have used above, the criteria are relatively easy to apply. But even in simple examples we can dig deeper and discover possible ambiguities. For example, suppose you receive an email about a recent survey of your organisation's canteen facilities which discovered that most of the staff "were in favour". What exactly does that mean? What sort of facility did they want? And how often would they use it? This general "approval" might mask very strong differences in terms of what particular groups of staff want from a canteen. Of course, this detail may be in the attached report, but the email should highlight key findings. At the moment, this does not give a very clear pointer to any management action. So, always consider what the written communication aims to achieve when you apply the criteria.

Tone criteria

Even if the content is good, business writing can fail to achieve its objectives if its tone offends or upsets readers. We have already argued that communication always conveys two simultaneous messages – information and relationship. We can examine the style of professional writing to see if it establishes or reinforces an appropriate relationship. This is especially important because everything you write can be interpreted as writing on behalf of your organisation (or your part of the organisation in an internal communication). Any attitudes you express are assumed to be those of the organisation. Be aware of the image your organisation wishes to project and write accordingly.

For a simple illustration, compare the following sentences from letters to customers and decide which organisation is projecting the most suitable "professional" and positive image:

- "If this does not sort out your gripes give me a ring".
- "If this does not solve your problems, communicate with the undersigned at your earliest convenience".
- "If this does not solve the problem, please telephone, email or text me as soon as possible at..."

Of course, different relations that exist in organisations mean you must be sensitive to the requirements of these situations. Therefore, you do not use the same tone when writing to a customer who has not paid his account for six months as you would to a potential customer. There are, however, certain tonal requirements that almost invariably apply to written communication. Written communication constitutes a permanent record – this means that writers should:

- adopt a professional tone, appropriate to the status of the receiver.
- be sensitive to the existence of different business practices.
- be sensitive to cultural differences.

The last two points are particularly important in international business where there is always the danger of unintentionally giving offence. A common example would be the use of American conventions in messages for British readers – phrases like "have a nice day" are often seen as insincere and formulaic.

If we are searching for a business style which satisfies these criteria of content and tone, can Plain English provide the answer?

The rise of Plain English

Criticisms of official and business writing are nothing new. Equally long-standing are pleas for plain and understandable writing – in the *Oxford Guide to Plain English* (2020), Martin Cutts notes pleas going back to the 16th century. He offers a detailed history so here we simply highlight some major landmarks in the rise of Plain English in the United Kingdom.

Earlier in the 20th century, there were several attempts to simplify the language of government, including the very influential book by Sir Ernest Gowers – *Plain Words* (later revised and extended into *The Complete Plain Words*,1987).

Another influential article, still quoted in modern guidebooks, came from George Orwell in 1946 ("Politics and the English language"). See Box 7.2 for discussion of some of the broader implications of his approach. His six elementary rules are a useful summary of early Plain English thinking which had lasting influence:

(i) Never use a metaphor, simile, or other figure of speech which you are used to seeing in print.
(ii) Never use a long word where a short one will do.
(iii) If it is possible to cut a word out, always cut it out.
(iv) Never use the passive where you can use the active.
(v) Never use a foreign phrase, a scientific word, or a jargon word if you can think of an everyday English equivalent.
(vi) Break any of these rules sooner than say anything outright barbarous.

One major issue which prompted the more recent rise of Plain English in the UK was the poor quality of official forms and government publications. The Plain English Campaign was formed as a pressure group to tackle this.

Plain English is now encouraged for all documentation in UK government circles (https://www.gov.uk/guidance/content-design/writing-for-gov-uk). Plain English is mandatory for gov.uk. One of the parts most people pick up on is the plain English (or words to avoid) list found at that link.

There is a lot of common ground between these sets of principles, which is also reflected in more recent and current texts. We explore the most important recommendations in more detail later in this chapter.

BOX 7.2

The politics of language style

George Orwell was not simply interested in improving the quality of official documents. One of his main concerns was the way that totalitarian states used "corrupt" forms of language to disguise the true intentions behind political dogma. One of the key weapons used by the state in his classic novel, *1984*, is the language Newspeak. This language systematically destroys the link between words and meanings and is used to make the dogma of the ruling party both meaningless and indisputable at the same time. Orwell argued for clear and transparent language to prevent specific linguistic features being used to confuse and dominate.

Another important aspect of Orwell's thinking is also very relevant to modern thinking on plain English – the notion that plain language will be "automatically transparent". This assumes that there is a fixed code whereby a word corresponds to a fixed meaning. This is not our view. As we showed in Chapter 3, language is a fuzzy code where flexibility is the norm. Although plain English may assist understanding, it can *never* guarantee it.

Developments in plain language

One major difference between modern Plain English recommendations and previous writers such as Gowers is the attention paid to the organisation, design, and layout of documents – good writing is not just about "getting the words right". We also follow this philosophy and look at organisation and layout in the next chapter.

BOX 7.3

This organisation has rules

Some organisations publish very definite rules to control their staff's writing. Many official UK publications endorse ideas we discuss in this chapter. For example, the link above related to government documents and use of plain English. Others would be:

- the National Institute for Health and Care Excellence in the UK publish information to support the creation of written information for the general public, and for specialists in the medical field. https://www.nice.org.uk/corporate/ecd2/chapter/rules-of-clear-writing

- similarly, the UK Law Society publish a "Ten Rules of Written Communications for Business" guide which suggests how to create clear information and writing on complex legal terms for businesses and organisations. https://www.lawsociety.org.uk/Topics/In-house/Features/10-rules-of-written-communication-for-business

What is your organisation's approach or "rule book"' (implicit or explicit)? And how is this expressed and enforced?

Current agreement on plain language

If you read a selection of recent and current texts on professional or business communication, then you may be struck by the consensus that emerges over recommended language style. Table 7.1 illustrates this agreement – and also suggests some differences in emphasis - listing eight major characteristics of plain language style and showing how they are summarised in three recent texts: one of the best recent British summaries of the Plain English approach by Martin Cutts, and two American texts.

We recommend the book by Cutts as the best single source on plain language. He offers "twelve main guidelines" – the ones listed above plus:

- "Organise your material so readers can see the important information early and navigate the document easily"
- "Use good verbs to express the actions in your sentences"
- "Use vertical lists to break up complicated text"
- "Use good grammar"
- "Check your material before the readers do"

You can evaluate your writing against these 12 characteristics (Cutts, 2020).

Another option we can safely recommend on modern PCs/Macs is the use of dictation to prepare documents. Speech recognition software has been available for some time, but earlier versions demanded significant dedication and patience to use them effectively. Now it achieves impressive accuracy levels and is well worth considering. It will enable you to see if a more conversational approach improves your documents (as well as helping to cut down keyboard time and attendant health risks from excessive typing).

But is Plain English always the answer?

A range of studies and examples make a persuasive argument in favour of Plain English/Plain Language (e.g. the 50 studies summarised by Kimble, 2012). But Plain English has also had its critics. For example, Robyn Penman argued that we need to consider the context when we write, and we cannot rely on universal principles of plain or simple English. He reviewed the evidence that Plain English revisions do not always work – such as an Australian study which compared versions of a tax form and found that the revised version was "virtually as demanding for the taxpayer as the old form" (Penman, 1993, page 128).

We agree with Penman's main point – that we need to design *appropriate* documents – but current Plain English practice is more flexible than Penman implies. So, we still think that *all* professional writers should consider the recommendations coming from Plain English sources. Unless you have clear contrary evidence, they are the "safest bet", especially if you have a general or mixed audience. For the rest of this book, we shall talk of "plain language" to refer to this approach – using the simplest and clearest expression which is appropriate for the audience.

A recent research contribution may give us further clues as to how we decide on the most appropriate language style for any given situation. Julie Baker looked at the comparison between traditional legal language and plain legal language using the concept of "cognitive fluency" which:

> *relates to the level of confidence a person has regarding his or her understanding of an object or piece of information. Simply put, a reader more quickly and easily processes fluent communications.*
>
> (2011, page 12)

She concludes that "plain language is, in fact, the right way to write, as it is:

> *"fluent"and thereby inspires feelings of ease, confidence, and trust in readers (whereas legalese is "disfluent", engendering feelings of dislike and mistrust). …however, …there are times when the legal writer's analytical or persuasive goals may be served by more difficult, less fluent language.*
>
> (Pages 1–2)

While this may be difficult to translate into specific recommendations for a given situation, it is worthwhile thinking in terms of the levels of cognitive fluency *which you are assuming* in the readers of the documents you are writing – how much effort will they have to put in to understand what you are saying?

It is also worth remembering that even simple language may not tell the whole story. Martin Cutts, one of the co-founders of the UK Plain English Campaign, now runs the Plain Language Commission, and makes the point that:

> *corporate language should be not only plain in style but also plain in intention and in content.*
>
> (Cutts, 2020)

There is one further word of caution we need to emphasise – changing language styles in an organisation does not just change the language. Language use reflects important aspects of organisational culture as we saw in Part 1 of this book. There may also be specific implications for organisation relationships as the study in Box 7.4 illustrates.

BOX 7.4

Where Plain English disrupted the organisation structure

Jim Suchan studied how Report Assessors (RAs) in a government agency made decisions based on information in written reports from subordinates (with whom they had no direct contact). The RAs felt the reports were badly organised and difficult to read but they had various strategies to "make sense of all the garbled stuff in these reports" (Suchan, 1998, page 312). Despite these criticisms, they did not suggest that their subordinates should change their writing style – it was accepted as part of the job. The RAs had "become very skilful in the manoeuvring through the reports to find the information they needed to make a decision. They were proud of that skill: it differentiated them from others".

A few reports were rewritten using techniques such as headings and subheadings, bulleted lists, active verbs, shorter paragraphs etc. However, these revised reports did not lead to better decisions. They were disliked and described as "abnormal discourse". The new report style was seen as deskilling the RAs and "usurping their authority". Rumours circulating in the organisation about possible cutbacks and restructuring were an obvious factor in these perceptions.

This study shows that we cannot simply impose a new language style on an organisation without considering broader impact and implications.

Applying plain language strategies

In this final section, we suggest plain language strategies which you should always consider in your own writing:

Hit the right point on the "word scales"

You need to use appropriate words in a specific situation. Some organisations have tried to control word choices by introducing simplified English. Unfortunately, this can bring other problems. Assuming you have free choice, consider where your words fit on the following four scales:

Abstract – concrete

The main problem with abstract terminology is its vagueness. It often needs a concrete example to clarify it. Although a statement like "Inflation is affecting our administration costs" may be true, it is vague. The statement could include a concrete example, like "Inflation is affecting our administration costs – costs of printing and stationery have risen by just over 7% per year each year since 2020".

Generic – specific

"Vehicle" is a generic term, as it covers a variety of things. There is a range from generic to specific, as in: vehicle – motor vehicle – motor car – Toyota car – 1998 Toyota Corolla – 1998 green, 1.6 L Toyota Corolla – and so on. Professional and business writing tends to be too generic.

Formal – colloquial

"The company is in financial difficulties" is more formal, while "The company is going down the drain" is more colloquial. It is very important to pitch your writing at the point on this scale which is appropriate to your audience.

Emotive – referential

Emotive words convey both facts and attitudes or dispositions. Referential terms convey facts rather than attitudes. Therefore: "The shop floor was covered with sawdust" is essentially factual, whereas "The shop floor was filthy" conveys the writer's attitude.

Avoid jargon and technical slang

Jargon is technical language, which is usually unintelligible to a wider audience. A term like "discounted cash flow" would be unacceptable jargon to a general audience if no explanation was given. Technical slang covers slang terms that are used in technical conversation: expressions such as "the bottom line".

Avoid cliches

Cliches are expressions which once may have been fresh and insightful but have become stale through constant use. Our latest list is on the website.

Avoid piled-up nouns

Nouns are often "piled-up", so it is difficult to disentangle the meaning, as in: "staff induction emergency training procedures". Apart from the difficulty of disentangling the meaning there is always the danger of ambiguity. In this example it is not clear whether we are dealing with emergency-training procedures (how to train people to deal with an emergency), or emergency training-procedures (how to organise the training if there is some sort of crisis).

Simplify sentence structure

Simple straightforward structures make for easy reading. The most common structure is to start the sentence with the subject, e.g. *The company* increased its profits by *25%* compared with the last financial year.

A common alternative structure is an adverbial opening such as:

In the last financial year, the company increased its profits by 25%.

Adverbial beginnings are particularly useful when you wish to link the sentence to something that has gone before, as in:

However, unfavourable trading conditions may not continue after the first quarter.

It requires considerable skill to structure long sentences. Modern word-processing software has built-in spelling and grammar checks which will identify "poor" or overlong sentences. But these checks can give some strange results as we illustrate in Box 7.5.

BOX 7.5

Grammar checkers may not know what you mean!

You can try the following exercise yourself – you need a reasonably long text which you have written yourself.

Table 7.5 below gives examples of corrections to sentences and phrases which are recommended by the free version of Grammarly (https://app.grammarly.com) when we asked it to analyse this chapter. It spotted several typos and offered some simplifications which we found helpful, but it also made some suggestions which we rejected as they did not make a useful difference – see a few examples in Table 7.2.

This shows that you should approach these automatic devices with some caution. Their recommendations can fail if they rely on the over-strict interpretation of grammatical rules, if they misinterpret the context, or if they *automatically* follow supposed "good practice" (like avoiding the passive at all costs). We also found problems where Grammarly wanted to get rid of some necessary quotation marks and change words in direct quotes. There can also be problems with different cultural norms – see Box 7.6.

Table 7.2 Disagreements with Grammarly

	Original phrase or sentence	What Grammarly recommends	Did we accept the recommendation?
1	This puts the emphasis on the means of measurement.	This emphasises the means of measurement.	No. We wanted to emphasise "the emphasis".
2	So the criteria must always be applied in relation to what the written communication needs to achieve.	So the criteria must always be applied about what the written communication needs to achieve.	No But we agreed that our sentence was not very clear, so we rewrote it.
3	which has had lasting influence.	Which has had a lasting influence.	No We do not think that the "a" makes any difference.

After revising the chapter using Grammarly suggestions, we then asked the Editor in Microsoft Word to check the chapter. It made over 60 grammar suggestions – mainly about use of commas – and spotted a few typos which Grammarly had missed. Responding to these suggestions lifted our "score" from 89% to 100% and we stopped checking! This demonstrates that you cannot expect complete agreement between different checkers – you do need to review their suggestions before you finish any document.

Use the appropriate balance of active and passive sentences

A common misconception is that the passive form is the "preferred"' business style for official documents. Active sentences are usually preferred in Plain Language. In practice, you need a sensible *mix* of active and passive.

The criterion for choosing between active and passive should be emphasis. Consider the following sentences:

(1) *The company* gave each employee a bonus.
(2) *Each employee* was given a bonus by the company.

In (1) the emphasis is on "the company"; in (2) the emphasis is on "each employee". Both sentences are perfectly clear. Your choice depends on whether you wish to emphasise "the company" or "each employee".

Use clear and simple punctuation

Punctuation is an important code – it can change the meaning or emphasis within a sentence:

Consider the difference between these two simple examples:

a) Insert the ID card into the slot, with the label on the top right.
b) Insert the ID card into the slot with the label on the top right.

In (a) the punctuation tells you that the label is part of the ID card; in (b) the punctuation tells you that the label relates to the slot. In more complicated instructions, possible ambiguities of this sort could be very dangerous. You could punctuate the following to give very different meanings:

> *"Send replacement motherboard if the system fails again we will need to shut it down".*

But how do we decide which punctuation to use and when to use it? Here the situation becomes more complicated. You can find very different interpretations of how and when to use some punctuation marks so we suggest you follow the advice of Martin Cutts:

> *Only about a dozen marks need to be mastered and the guidelines are fairly simple*
>
> (Cutts, op cit, page 98)

There have been changes in taste and style but there are several useful and entertaining guides to punctuation, including one best-seller from Lynne Truss (2003 and 2008). This illustrates how sensitive many of us are to the punctuation we see around us.

Another good example of this sensitivity is the Apostrophe Protection Society whose website shows both how to use them properly and how many organisations fail to do so – http://www.apostrophe.org.uk. At the very least, you should:

- make sure you are familiar with the conventional uses of the main punctuation marks.
- use these main punctuation marks consistently.
- recognise that punctuation marks are important signals to the reader about when to pause and which parts of the sentence go together.

One strategy is to use a limited set of punctuation marks. We do not agree with some advice which suggests that you only really need to use the full stop and the comma. But we could write virtually every type of official document using only the punctuation marks discussed in one of the well-known British advice books – *The Economist Style Guide* (12th edition published in 2018) – where you can find specific advice on apostrophes, brackets, colons, commas, dashes, full stops, quotation marks, question marks, and semi-colons, and a useful discussion of different uses in American and British English.

This raises the question of which grammar/punctuation guide to use – there are many on the market and they do not always agree on specific points:

> *Generations of schoolchildren were taught grammar as an arbitrary set of dos and don'ts laid down by people who knew, or thought they knew, best. Nowadays, grammar might be more helpfully defined as the set of rules followed by speakers of a language.*
>
> (Marsh and Dodson, 2010, page 7)

The problem is that different users may follow different rules, depending on their background, and some guidebooks on the market still offer "rules" which are suspect or arbitrary. We suggest you stick with established texts on Plain Language which are based on research and/or practical application (such as work by Martin Cutts, or David Crystal, 2015, or the useful chapter on grammar and punctuation by March and Dodson, 2010). And you need to pay special attention to these issues when you write online (Darics, 2016) – more on this on the website.

A(void texts which adopt a more dogmatic stance. For example, we cannot recommend *Gwynne's Grammar* (2013) although this recently sold well in the UK. This book claims that grammar is a "science" but then offers no method for its scientific investigation! Look for reviews of this text on the web and you will find very different opinions, reflecting the strong feelings that many people have about what counts as good or acceptable grammar.

As additional help, most modern word processing packages offer ways of checking your writing. This chapter was prepared in Word which:

- automatically puts a capital letter after every full stop – at the beginning of every sentence.
- highlights incorrect or unknown spellings.
- suggests when our sentences "fail" its in-built grammar checker.

However, do not be tempted to rely too heavily on these automatic systems – they only offer very general guidance which can be misleading (see Box 7.6).

BOX 7.6

Why doesn't my word processor know I'm English?

Another problem with computerised grammar-checkers is that they may be insensitive to cultural variations. Microsoft Word continually criticises us as we do not follow one of the rules laid down by one of the main *American* authorities on written style – the *Chicago Manual of Style*. According to this manual, you should use the word "that" to introduce a restrictive clause and the word "which" to introduce a non-restrictive clause. For example, the Manual approves of the following sentences:

a) The book that Nigel gave me was no good.
b) The book, which Nigel gave me, was no good.

In example (a), the clause is restrictive because I'm talking only about the specific book which Nigel gave me and not any of the other books which I own. In example (b), the clause is non-restrictive as the fact that Nigel gave me the book is simply added as extra information – the clause is not used to identify which book we are talking about.

UK English speakers often do not make this distinction, although it does crop up in some well-known guides to "good English" used in Britain. This is an interesting example of a stylistic rule which makes little or no difference to communication. This reinforces the point made by Deborah Cameron:

> *statements about 'good writing' are not self-evident truths about language but value judgements upon it.*

Her book on popular attitudes towards language should be required reading for anyone who advises others on how to write good English (Cameron, 1995, 2012).

Readability

Readability formulae claim to predict how easy or difficult it is to read a particular text. These usually combine some measure of sentence length with some measure of average word length. Examples include the Fog index and the Flesch formula which is supplied as an automatic feature in many word processors.

Readability formulae can give a useful check – they can be used to revise texts to make them easier to understand. However, the results must be interpreted with caution as they ignore some critical points (James Hartley, 1994):

- some short sentences can be difficult to understand.
- short technical abbreviations may be very difficult to understand.
- some long words are very familiar (e.g. communication).
- the formulae ignore any graphics or visual aids which can help readers to understand.
- the formulae ignore the impact of any layout, such as headings and subheadings.

- the formulae ignore the readers' past experience and knowledge.
- the formulae ignore the readers' motivation.

James Hartley has also shown that you can increase the readability of text according

to the scales and make it *more* difficult to understand. Our favourite example of a short text which would pass a readability test but which is difficult to understand is the following notice, stuck by the elevator doors in a large multi-storey American office block:

Please
Walk up one floor
Walk down two floors
To improve elevator service

If you take the notice at face value and walk up one floor, you discover the same notice by the elevator doors on the next floor (in fact, on every floor). The writer managed to construct a very tortuous way of advising users not to take the elevator for very short journeys! For more examples of this type of problem (and how to fix them), see Chapanis (1988). Another of our favourites in the same vein is the following notice on a fence in the middle of a large national park in the UK:

The land within is outside open land.

SUMMARY OF KEY POINTS

- professional writing often fails to communicate because of poor expression.
- we need to evaluate our writing using both content and tone criteria, bearing in mind the demands of the situation.
- Plain English/Plain Language has made a significant impact on official writing. We now have a wealth of guidance plus good and bad examples thanks to the work of organisations like the Plain English Campaign and the Plain Language Commission. But we need to consider research studies which suggest that this approach is not always as straightforward as might first appear.
- "Plain language" should be considered as a personal and company strategy, remembering that this argues for an *appropriate* style of language and *not* the same simple style for every document. Also, it is not just about using the right words – we also need to examine organisation and layout and consider the needs of users/audiences.
- we should follow standard conventions on punctuation while remembering that the rules are both flexible and changing
- readability tests and grammar-checkers offer some useful information but should always be interpreted carefully.

References

Baker, J. A. (2011) And the Winner Is: How Principles of Cognitive Science Resolve the Plain Language Debate, *University of Missouri-Kansas City Law Review*, Forthcoming Suffolk University Law School Research Paper No. 11-33. At: https://papers.ssrn.com/sol3/papers.cfm?abstract_id=1915300

Bovee, C. and Thill, J. (2013) *Business Communication Essentials*. London: Pearson.

Cameron, D. (1995) *Verbal Hygeine*. London: Routledge.

Chapanis, A. (1988) 'Words, words, words' revised. *International Review of Ergonomics* 2: 1–30.

Cutts, M. (2020) *Oxford Guide to Plain English*, 5th edition. Oxford: Oxford University Press.

Darics, E. (2016) *Writing Online: A Guide to Effective Digital Communication at Work*, 1st edition. New York: New York Business Expert Press (Corporate communication collection).

Gowers, E. (1987) *The Complete Plain Words*, 3rd edition. Harmondsworth: Penguin.

Gwynne, N.M. (2013) *Gwynne's Grammar: The Ultimate Introduction to Grammar and the Writing of Good English*. Incorporating also Strunk's Guide to Style. London: Ebury Press.

Hartley, J. (1994) *Designing Instructional Text* (3rd edition) London: Routledge

Horton, W. (1997) *Secrets of User Seductive Documents: Wooing and Winning the Reluctant Reader*. Arlington, VA: Society for Technical Communication.

Kimble, J. (2012) *Writing for Dollars, Writing to Please: The case for plain language in business, government, and law*. Durham, NC: Carolina Academic Press.

Kirkman, J. (1992) *Good Style: Writing for Science and Technology*. London: E and F N Spon.

Luntz, F.I. (2007) *Words That Work: It's Not What You Say, It's What People Hear*. New York: Hyperion.

Marsh, D.R. and Dodson, A. (2010) *Guardian Style*, 3rd edition. London: Guardian Books.

Penman, R. (1993) Unspeakable acts and other deeds: A critique of plain legal language. *Information Design Journal*, 7(2): 121–131.

Poole, S. (2007) *Unspeak: Words are Weapons*, 2nd edition. London: Abacus.

Suchan, J. (1998) The effect of high impact rating on decision making within the public sector bureaucracy. *Journal of Business Communication*, 35(3): 299–327.

Timm, T. and Bienvenu, P.R. (2011) *Straight Talk*. London: Routledge.

Truss, L. (2003) *Eats, Shoots and Leaves: The zero tolerance approach to punctuation*. London: Profile Books.

CHAPTER 8

Effective design and visual aids

Introduction

It is worth emphasising how quickly the process of producing business documents has been transformed through technology.

One obvious change is the way that we can all now incorporate visual elements into documents such as graphics, charts, tables and diagrams which were either impossible or impractical without specialist technical help only a few years ago. It is also much easier to prepare and distribute documents online although that can generate further complications. The way we read online documents is different to reading on paper. This means that clear design of documents is even more important than previously.

Because of these technological developments and the associated changes in office structures, *all* professional writers now need to understand basic principles of document design. We also need to know when and how to construct simple and effective visual aids – and these are the main themes of this chapter.

OBJECTIVES

This chapter will:

- explain why effective document design and layout is such an important part of effective professional writing.
- explain why and how we should make documents accessible to all readers.
- review the main design features which we need to consider when we produce professional documents.
- summarise main features of typography which professional writers need to know about, e.g. fonts, size, space, and alignment.
- demonstrate how page layout can show the reader how the document is structured.

DOI: 10.4324/9781003297550-11

- analyse why and when you need to incorporate a visual aid into a business document.
- review main types of visual aids used in documents and highlight their main advantages and disadvantages.
- demonstrate the major dangers of inappropriate construction of graphs and charts and show how you can avoid misrepresentation.
- identify how to avoid bias in the use of visual aids, and how to support equality, diversity, and inclusion.
- introduce the changing uses of presentation software to produce documents.

Why is effective design and layout now such an important aspect of effective writing?

Our answer to this question reflects the views of those responsible for the development of technical writing:

> *No matter how brilliant or important the content, if it is not formatted in a way that enhances readability, it will likely not receive the attention it deserves*
>
> (Suzan Last, 2019)

Psychological research supports the designers' view that the "look" of a document influences how it is read (Vora, 2019; Knaflick, 2015, Hartley, 1994). But despite the importance of good design, many organisations are still content to treat the development of documents, reports, and forms of communication as secondary considerations to the content. A consequence of this is that the reader won't understand either the content or the purpose of that communication. If the purpose is to persuade, motivate, or initiate an action then these things are more likely to happen when the style of the document is designed alongside the content of the communication. See Box 8.1 for a brief discussion of these problems.

BOX 8.1

The PC/laptop/Mac etc is not a typewriter – changing conventions

Although the typewriter is now obsolete, some interesting habits from traditional typing still survive in modern word-processing. For example, leaving two spaces after a full stop (period) made sense on an old mechanical typewriter where all the characters take up the same amount of space (monospaced). The two spaces helped to separate the sentences. But word-processors use typefaces where each character is proportionally spaced – for example, the letter "i" takes up less space than the letter "m". So you do not need more than one space to separate sentences. Other features in many printed documents we have seen in organisations are also a legacy of typing, such as the use of underlining. Professional printing avoids underlining and uses italics or bold for emphasis.

Making documents accessible to all readers

Designing documents to achieve their objectives and to make them fully accessible means taking full advantage of word-processing features, such as styles and templates. These improve the look of the document, and they are *essential* for accessibility. For example, if a partially sighted person reads the document using the read-aloud feature then the headings are described as such. If these features are not used, then the read-aloud programme cannot structure the reading in a way that the partially sighted person can understand. It's also useful for those colleagues who can listen to these documents whilst travelling rather than read them on the screen or in print.

Changing the style characteristics of "Heading1" takes a few seconds – from that point, every Heading 1 in the document uses the same format. Changing every heading individually in a long document can take some time.

You can quickly work out whether a document has been efficiently produced by looking at the styles associated with headings and subheadings (you can also use the outliner facility to check this). If the headings/subheadings are simply the "normal" style with extra formatting then you have uncovered an example of using the PC/laptop/Mac/Chromebook in the same way that typewriters work. This shows serious lack of concern for the range of readers who may need to read the document.

For both ethical and professional reasons, we need to make all our documents accessible to all readers, i.e. anyone can "read" it, including those who are sight impaired, or dyslexic, or have other issues such as dyscalculia etc. In the UK, since 2018, all public sector bodies have had to make all aspects of a website or mobile app accessible. That includes documents that may be read online – and covers internal and external communication. While the legislation does not formally apply to other organisations, it does set both a valuable precedent and good practice which we should all follow (https://www.legislation.gov.uk/uksi/2018/852/contents/made).

What are the main design features of business documents?

Every business document has a characteristic layout – ranging from the simple layout of an internal briefing paper to the glossy multicolour annual report from a large company. Only the latter may have received much attention from professional designers but all documents have been put together with *some* attention to their design. And the design is important no matter how humble the document.

A well-designed document has three main advantages over a poorly designed one:

- it makes a good impression on the reader.
  It suggests a professional and competent approach. So it can enhance the credibility of the person who prepared the document. In this way, it improves the chances of its message being accepted.
- the content/information is easier to understand.
- the reader is in a better position to respond appropriately, by assimilating the information or responding to the questions raised, or taking necessary actions.

Conversely, poorly presented material can put the reader off and create a poor image. A simple example from our professional experience would be coursework assignments which students have to complete at college or university. A well-prepared word-processed assignment is likely to gain more marks, *not* because the tutor is consciously awarding marks for presentation, but because the word-processed assignment is easier and quicker to read and looks as if it has been carefully prepared. Conversely, the poorly word-processed assignment – no page numbers, no headings or subheadings, poor use of visual aids etc. – can lose marks. At the very least, it gives the impression of having been "knocked together" at the last minute. This may seem unfair but being able to write for the audience of your writing is an important skill to develop – and that includes writing for tutors at college/university! Reports, emails, and memos in organisations create similar impressions on the reader, depending on the way they look.

Also remember that a document may have several different readers. If it is a report, then the person who asked for it is likely to read the whole report. There will then be secondary readers who only want to read the summary or specific sections relevant to them. Each of these readers need to be able to navigate their way through the report easily and to understand and respond to either the whole document or those individual sections.

There is no excuse for poorly formatted documents. Software now enables us to produce most of the characteristics of professional typesetting. As a result, readers have come to expect documents which satisfy longstanding criteria used by graphic designers (Lichty, 1989):

- proportion – where all the elements of the page are clearly in proportion to each other.
- balance – where there is a clear sense of balance in the design of each page.
- contrast – where contrasting parts of the design are used to focus the reader's interest on the page.
- rhythm – where the reader's attention is drawn smoothly down the page without distraction.
- unity – where the various components of the page fit together to give a coherent impression.

What do business writers need to know about typography?

Modern software offers writers a wide variety of typefaces, or fonts (a typeface is a collection of fonts). When these were first made available it resulted in documents with many different fonts included. This resulted in messy and confusing documents, with little to guide the reader through what had been written. Whilst the choice of a typeface or font is largely subjective, the impact on the reader and its accessibility need to be considered at the design stage rather than after the text has been written.

There are a few technical aspects of fonts, typefaces, and page layout which are worth knowing so you can make sensible choices. You also have to understand some technical terms with rather odd names – much of the terminology has been carried forward from the days when printing was a mechanical process using letters made from "hot metal". We outline these terms below before returning to the issue of which type is "best" for particular business documents.

Type families

A font is a specific style and size of a typeface, for example **'this font is 12 point Times New Roman Bold.'** You may find these terms are used interchangeably (although the distinction is important for designers and typographers). Any single typeface can appear in different styles, which make up its "family". For example, Arial can appear as Arial, Arial Black, or Arial Narrow.

Especially given changes in requirements for accessibility, it is important to know which fonts/typefaces are easier to read. An easy distinction to remember is the difference between those typefaces that have extra decoration attached to letters (serif) and those that do not (sans-serif). To illustrate this, look at the following sentences in different fonts.

This sentence is written in Times New Roman
This sentence is written in Arial.

For many readers, the sentence written in Arial is easier to access.

A further important type style is italic – this is not a separate typeface but a sloping version of the basic font. It has several main uses:

- to emphasise a particular word or phrase.
- to show the name of a book (see the reference list in this book and in most textbooks)
- to indicate technical terms or foreign words.
- to indicate a quotation.

Type size

Type size is usually measured in "points", one point being approximately 1/72nd of an inch. However, this does *not* mean that different typefaces which are the same point size will look the same. The points measurement is taken from the top of a capital letter to the bottom of a lower case letter which extends below the baseline. But when we look at a typeface we are more inclined to notice its "x-height" – the distance from the baseline to the top of a lower case letter like x. The example below shows the difference between two fonts having the same point size but different x-heights.

This is Times Roman in 12 point.
This is Arial in 12 point.

Despite these differences, we can make reasonable generalisations. Eleven or twelve point is common for body text, with larger sizes usually used for headings. Eight or ten point is often used for less important information as well as the "small print" which you are always advised to read before signing a document.

Consider your audience before you finally decide on the type size. Bearing in mind earlier comments around accessibility, we recommend a font size of at least 12 for printed documents. If a document is viewed onscreen, then the reader can adjust the size of the screen to suit their needs.

Space between lines

This is called leading after the old printing practice of putting extra slices of lead between lines of metal type to increase spacing. It is measured in points so that 10 on 12 point Times Roman means a 10 point font with two extra points of leading. A rough rule of thumb is to use leading which is about 20% of the font size and this is what current software tends to do as the default on body text.

You can see the difference by comparing the last paragraph (with zero leading) to this one where the setting is 1.2. In the next paragraph we have increased it to double the normal setting. Increasing the leading does not necessarily make the text easier to read beyond a certain point.

You can see the difference in this paragraph where we have put the leading to 2.0. Increasing the leading does not necessarily make the text easier to read beyond a certain point.

Alignment

You can align your printing on the left-hand side and/or the right-hand side of the paper. Traditionally, professionally typeset material has been aligned on both sides. In the past, this often left uneven gaps between some words as the control of the space between letters (letterspacing) was not very sophisticated (from a distance, you can see "rivers" of white space winding down the page). Although this control of spacing has improved, we recommend that word-processed documents leave a ragged right margin, as there is some evidence that this improves readability.

Categories of typefaces

There are thousands of different typefaces and there are official classification systems. For practical everyday purposes, a simpler classification will do and five main categories are used:

- Serif.
  The endings of the letter shapes are decorated in a way which harks back to the way that letters were carved out of stone in Roman times. Famous examples of serif type are Times Roman which was designed as a readable and economical typeface for *The Times* newspaper in London. The modern equivalent is the widely available Times New Roman.
- Sans-serif.
  The letters are without (sans) serifs. Examples here are Helvetica and Arial which are recommended where the readership is unknown and may have dyslexia or be partially sighted.
- Script.
  The typeface imitates the letterforms of handwriting.
- Display.
  The typeface has been designed for use in displays such as advertising or posters.
- Symbols.
  The alphabet is replaced by symbols. As an example of the practical application of a symbol font like Wingdings, we often use the "r" symbol when we create a document which needs a tick box. You can resize the symbols in exactly the same way you can resize conventional letters.

And which typeface is best?

This is an almost impossible question to answer. The best one will depend on the context and the audience.

For printed documents, the traditional view was to use serif typefaces for body text and sans serif for headings. Many graphic designers had very definite views. For example, McLean stated that one of the "rules" of legibility for continuous reading was that "Sans-serif type is intrinsically less legible than serifed type" ((McLean, 1980, page 44). However, thanks to the increased understanding of neurodiversity and the barriers that serif text can pose to dyslexics (e.g. British Dyslexia Association, 2022), our opinions have shifted. But traditions still prevail – at the time of writing, academic literature is usually presented using serif typefaces and online resources will be sans serif.

Many organisations have now adopted sans serif typefaces as standard (even without any considerations of neurodiversity). They do not seem to have suffered as a result. We can (and do) get used to a particular typeface over time. Any intrinsic advantages or disadvantages may be less important than some designers have argued. Where you have a choice of typeface, this should depend on several factors:

- the known or potential needs of the reader.
- the purpose of the document.
- what the readers are used to and what they might expect.
- how the document might be used. For example, some fonts are not suitable for repeated photocopying or faxing as some of the letter shapes are too thin.

Page layout and document structure

Document design and page layout should emphasise the structure of the document. This can be done in several ways, including the use of headings, numbering, and layout.

The use of headings and subheadings

Word-processing software like Microsoft Word or Apple Pages gives you preset styles which you can reformat to your own taste and which provide an easily identifiable hierarchy of headings:

- Main Heading (Heading 1).
- Subheading (Heading 2).
- Sub-Subheading (Heading 3).

These guide the reader through the text, identifying the major topic under discussion and the various elements that make up that topic, and the relationships between the elements.

Clear numbering

Alongside the use of the variety of headings, the decimal numbering system is used because it adds to the visual impact when identifying a hierarchy of headings.

1. Main Heading
1.1 Subheading
1.1.1. Sub-sub-heading

We recommend using no more than three levels for most professional documents. Excessive numbering and subdivision fragments the document, making it difficult to read.

You can also use space on the page to further emphasise the hierarchy of headings, as below. One disadvantage that this uses a lot of space on the page.

1. Main Heading in 14 point Arial bold

The text under the main heading is in 12 point Times New Roman and will be set out like this on the page so that it lines up…

1.1 Subheading in 12 point Arial italic bold

The text under the subheading is in 12 point Times New Roman and will be set out like this on the page so that it lines up…

1.1.1. Sub-sub-heading in 12 point Times New Roman bold

The text under the sub-sub-heading is in 12 point Times New Roman and will be set out like this on the page so that it lines up…

Table 8.1 shows how the three levels of heading have been formatted in this book:

This shows how:

- different typefaces distinguish main headings from body text.
- spacing emphasises the hierarchy of headings and subheadings.

Although these applications of spacing and numbering may seem fairly obvious, they are often ignored or not understood. For example, when James Hartley asked his undergraduate students (experienced in word-processing) to use space and typographic cues to improve the readability of a short text, they were often inconsistent or failed to use the full variety of cues.

Table 8.1 Levels of heading

	Typeface	Size	Characters	Spacing
Heading 1	BELL GOTHIC	11 pt	Black,	Before 19.5 pt
			Capitalised	After 6.5 pt
Heading 2	Bell Gothic	11 pt	Black	Before 19.5 pt
				After 6.5 pt
Heading 3	*Bell Gothic Light*	11 pt	Italic	Before 19.5 pt
				After 6.5 pt
Body text	Perpetua	11 pt	Normal	Standard line
				spacing

Using lists with bullet points

Lists are a simple way of presenting information to make information more readable. For example, sometimes a sentence becomes long because several items are governed by the main verb, e.g. When leaving at the end of the day make sure that: all the windows are closed; the back and side doors are locked; the burglar alarms are set; and all the lights are switched off, except the one at the front door.

This sentence can be made more readable just by listing the items:

When leaving at the end of the day please make sure that:

- all windows are closed.
- the back and side doors are locked.
- the burglar alarms are set.
- all lights are switched off, except the one at the front door.

You can also change the style, to focus on what the reader has to do:

When you leave at the end of the day, please make sure that you:

- close all the windows.
- lock the back and side door.
- set the burglar alarms.
- switch off all the lights, except the one at the front door.

Layout and design

Good page layout contributes to ease of reading. Text together with images should be presented in a way that there is a sense of balance on a page. For example, those items that are placed at the top or on the right of a page can easily dominate and make a page seem unbalanced – and less easy to read.

Both Google Docs and Microsoft Word provide a range of layout options, including margin width, paragraph style, paragraph spacing, number of columns etc. It is well worth the time to investigate the options available – they can help you to be more efficient in your production of documents as well as enhancing their accessibility. However, each organisation will have its house style, or style dictated by the profession, that needs to be adhered to. Your opportunities for creativity may be limited – but it is always worth questioning whether the document design support its purpose. Your readership should always be your top consideration.

When and how do you need to incorporate a visual aid into a business document?

The range of visual aids used in professional documents has grown rapidly as a result of increased access to both software and information. Tables, charts, and graphs may continue to dominate the presentation of numerical data in formal documents, but flowcharts, icons, presentations, photographs, infographics, and maps are increasingly useful.

One of the most respected academic writers on the presentation of statistical evidence and information design, Edward R. Tufte, argued that good graphics should "*reveal* data" (Tufte, 2006). We extend this idea to *all* the visual aids which you use in a document. They should not simply display data but they should *reveal* its importance and meaning. They should present information which clearly supports the argument expressed in the text.

Using Vora's (2019) and Knaflic's (2015) concept of data storytelling, the visuals have to connect at different levels with the audience as well as present information. Vora (2019) suggests the impact of storytelling is fourfold:

- release of dopamine improves understanding and retention by improving the brain's attentiveness.
- the audience will link their own experiences to points made in the story (neural coupling).
- patterns in a story appeal to the logical reasoning in the brain.
- an emotional connection can move the information into the long-term memory which can influence decision-making and action.

For a simple illustration of the way that a visual aid can reinforce or start telling a story, consider Figures 8.2 and 8.3. There is no obvious explanation for the

Figure 8.1 Impact of Storytelling

dip in performance in August. A label with short explanation (e.g. department restructuring) could give readers clues to explain the change.

Deciding which visual aids to use

The following table illustrates main types of visual aid linked to the information that is being conveyed and their relative advantages. Whatever form of visual representation you use, you must ensure that the audience of the document can interpret the information appropriately. This means taking into account whether or not they are specialists in the subject area, and the purpose of the data presentation.

We now have access to all these methods to improve the visual quality of documents. For example, Microsoft Word offers tables, pictures, shapes, icons, 3D models, SmartArt, *charts*, and screenshots/screen clippings which you can add to the document (as well as choices for word art and document design). In addition, websites such as Canva.com offer professional-looking infographics for online and paper-based use.

Presentation software, such as PowerPoint and Google Slides, has also experienced a shift in the way that it is used. PowerPoint is still primarily used in face-to-face or online meetings to complement what is being said. However, because of the benefits of the quality of presentation – particularly around data – that were widely recognised during pandemic lockdowns, the PowerPoint presentation is now often used as a "pseudo-document". The traditional report that may have been produced for a meeting is replaced by the PowerPoint presentation with all the necessary data included and key points suitably highlighted.

Tables, charts, and graphs

Vora (2019) and Knaflic (2015) use the concept of data storytelling to underpin the potential of data presentation. Effective data presentation should enable good decision-making, either because the data shows that a particular set of actions is working (or not) or because the data raises questions that need to be pursued.

Table 8.2 Visual representations of information (adapted from Peterson, 2019)

Information to Convey	Visual Type	Advantages
Numbers, percentages, categories	Tables, charts, graphs	Data can be summarised Easier to access by non-specialists Can show trends and correlations between data sets
Processes	Flow charts, diagrams, mindmaps relationships between items, e.g. organisational charts, schema	Information can be communicated more efficiently than text
Geographic data	Maps	Provides an indication of area, distance between locations, particular characteristics of a specific location
Chronological or prioritised lists	Number lists, or timeline	Provides a clear representation of sequence or level of significance
Non-chronological lists	Bulleted lists	Easier to read than a body of text
Significance of the information, or type of information	Icons	Easy to recognise and respond to

Consider the following example of three representations of sales and profits data for two departments across a calendar year.

Before you read on, look at Table 8.3 and Figures 8.2 and 8.3 and answer the following questions:

- what is the main message the writer is trying to get across?
- which of these figures presents the data most effectively from your point of view?
- who would need this information and what questions would they be likely to ask?

Our interpretation

Both departments overall have the same overall sales and profits but what is the relationship between these two variables? Table 8.3 provides the data, but it is difficult to see the pattern across the year, or the relative profitability of the two departments. The writer is making the reader do all the work!

Table 8.3 Sales and profit data (tables)

	Department A		Department B	
Month	*Sales (£)*	*Profits (£)*	*Sales (£)*	*Profits (£)*
January	914	100	746	100
February	814	80	677	80
March	874	130	1274	130
April	877	90	711	90
May	926	110	781	110
June	810	140	884	140
July	613	60	608	60
August	310	40	539	40
September	913	120	815	120
October	726	70	642	70
November	474	50	573	50
December	600	85	580	55

(Datasets adapted from Tufte, 1983, page 13–14)

Figures 8.2 and 8.3 are both commonly used and provide a clearer insight into the pattern of sales over the year indicating the variations between months. This could support planning for the following year. For Department A the chart may be indicating when more should be spent on marketing (July and November) to even out sales per month – or it may be that staff are more likely to take holidays in July and August and therefore less available to make those sales!

A scattergram shows the association between two variables. Figure 8.4 shows the association between sales and profitability. For Department A data the association between sales and profitability is inconsistent, where sales of 800 units can yield either £80 or £140 of profit. The reasons for this may be well known by management, but if they are not then they need to investigate this further. In contrast, there appears to be a more consistent correlation between sales and profitability for Department B – although there are signs of diminishing returns at about 1000 units of sales. It may be that management feel that there continues to be a benefit to the organisation to have sales above 1000 units, or it may look to find ways to address that growing disadvantage of increased sales.

Whatever the correct interpretation, the important general lesson is that writers should clarify their main points and should make sure that these points come across clearly in the accompanying text.

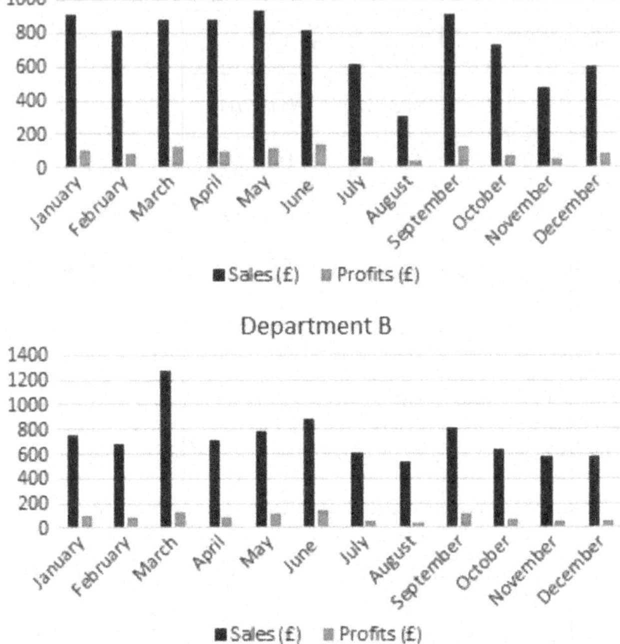

Figure 8.2 Sales and profits data (bar charts)

Avoiding bias and misrepresentation in tables and charts

Graphs and charts can be used to deceive, to present the best picture possible or to hide unwanted news. Sometimes the line between honest emphasis and deceit is not always clear. In the final analysis, the author's or the professional illustrator's professional integrity is the best guide. The following are some of the methods that can, intentionally or unintentionally deceive an audience.

Suppressing the zero

The zero on a graph is sometimes suppressed to save space or to emphasise a small but significant change. In Figure 8.5 there is no indication on the graph that the zero has been suppressed. The graph suggests that sales are rising much more steeply than if the full range was included, as in Figure 8.6.

Mixing the scales

Often two- or three-dimensional presentations are used in pictographs, but the scale used is linear. Spreadsheets like Microsoft Excel offer you a range of 3-D presentations, but this can lead to distortion. The data in Figure 8.7 is turned into three-dimensional cylinders in Figure 8.8 to suggest that the difference between

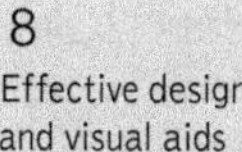

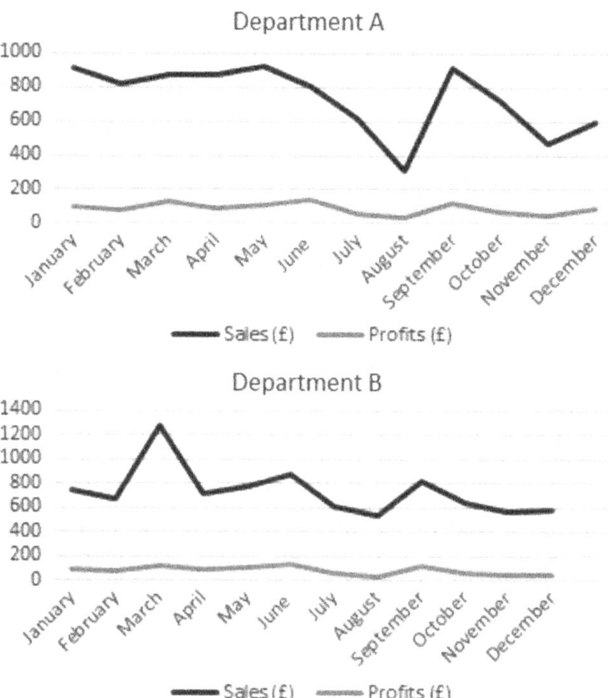

Figure 8.3 Sales and profits data (line charts)

sales is much bigger than it actually is. Tufte suggests that you can quantify the distortion by working out what he calls the "lie factor" which is:

$$\frac{\text{Size of effect shown in graphic}}{\text{Size of effect in data}}$$

This formula is taken from Tufte, 1983, Chapter 2, which also contains many more examples of distorted graphics.

Unjustified line fitting

Where the data shows a considerable scatter writers can be tempted to fit a line or curve which supports their favoured hypothesis. Even using sophisticated curve-fitting methods, the result will not necessarily be the best representation of the data. Ideally, any relationship derived from the data should be used to plan and test further observations. This is, however, not always possible. Figure 8.9 shows that you can fit both a straight line (AB) and a curve (CD) to the data.

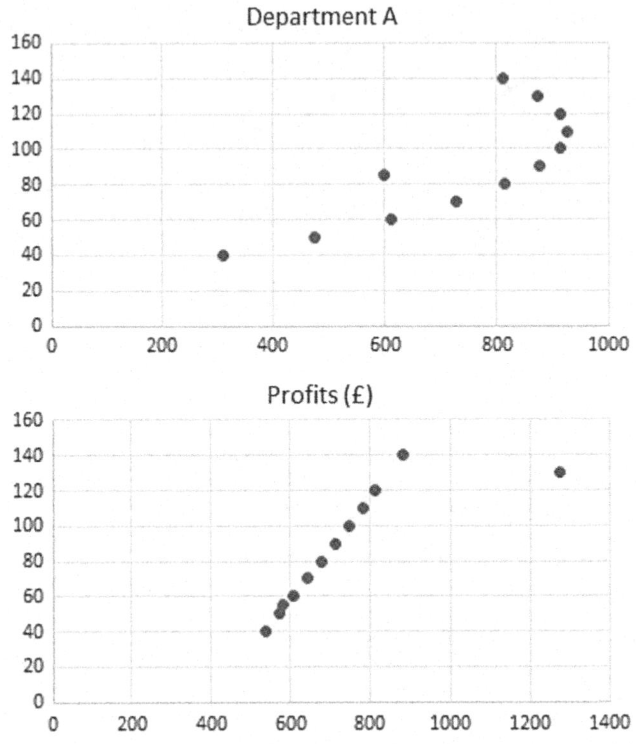

Figure 8.4 Sales and profits data (scattergrams)

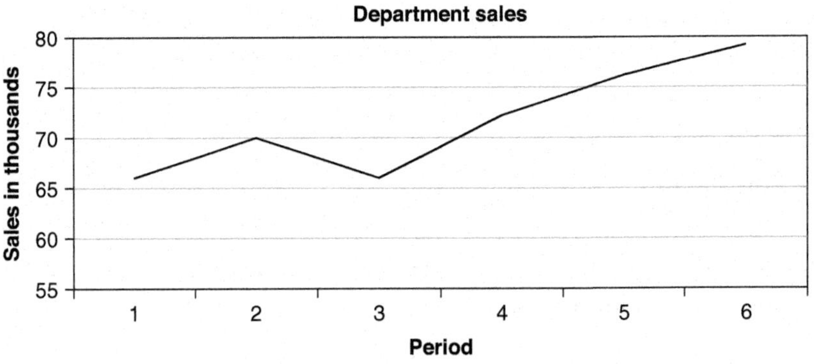

Figure 8.5 Line graph with suppressed zero: the effect is to exaggerate the change

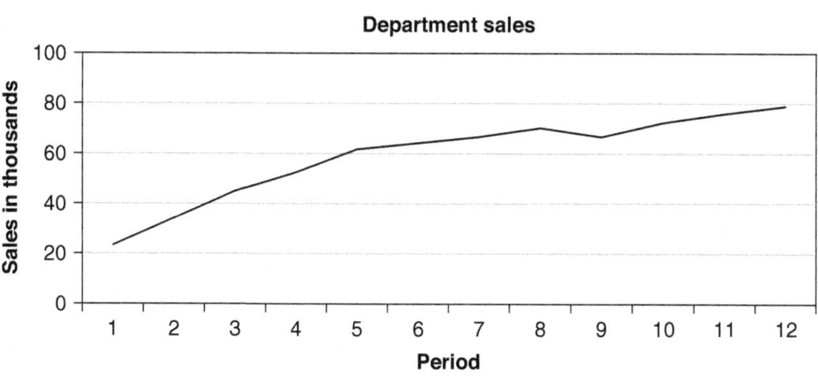

Figure 8.6 Line graph without suppressed zero

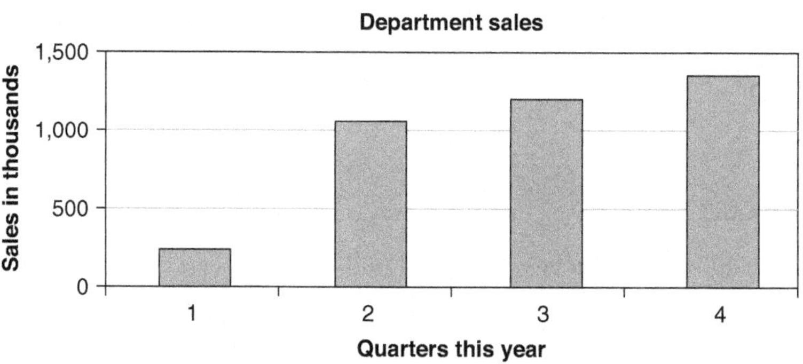

Figure 8.7 Sales data expressed as a bar chart

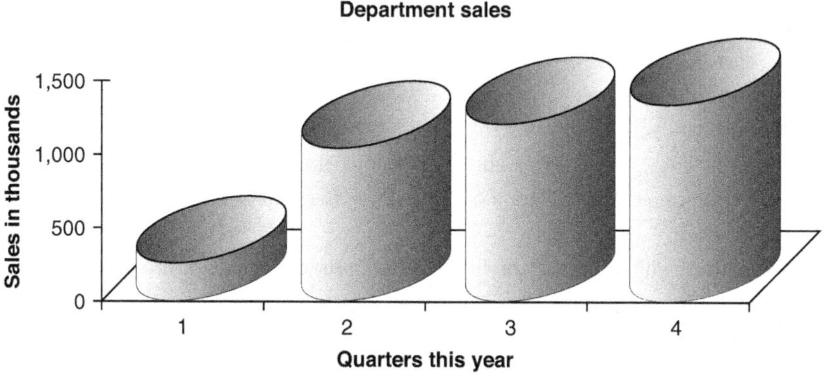

Figure 8.8 Sales data in 3-D cylinders: the effect is to exaggerate the difference

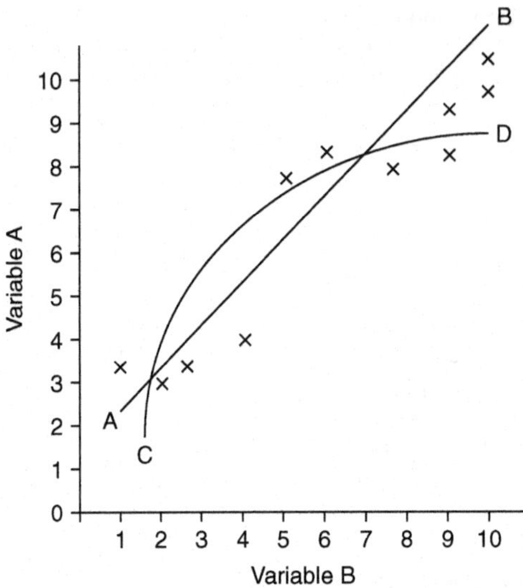

Figure 8.9 Fitting a line

BOX 8.2

Using graphs and charts – practical guidelines

If you intend to produce your own graphs, we suggest the following practical guidelines.

- keep the graph simple. Remember the purpose and the audience; provide no more detail than your purpose requires and your audience needs.
- place titles either above or below the graph but be consistent throughout.
- ensure that your title accurately reflects the contents of the graphic. Words like "Graph of..." or "Diagram of..." are unnecessary as this should be apparent. An explanatory note below the title can help the reader.
- see that your graph has some logic behind its presentation, e.g. largest to smallest, most important to least important, by provinces, or by time sequence. Use the ordering of information to emphasise the point you wish to make.
- make the illustration attractive. It should provide a welcome break from the written word and not be a distraction or puzzle.
- use specific devices to help your reader and to emphasise important points. Examples of such devices are: colour, arrows, heavy lines, distinctive plotting points, annotation, and keys.
- avoid bias in presenting information.

- make sure that axes are clearly labelled and that units are unambiguous and consistent.
- wherever possible, use horizontal labelling in preference to vertical labelling.
- where possible, label line graphs directly rather than using a key, but do use a key if the graph becomes cluttered.
- do not place a graphic before its first reference in the text but place it as soon as practicable thereafter.
- do not just repeat information from graphs in the text but rather use the text for comment, explanation or interpretation.
- for scales use multiples or submultiples of 2, 5, or 10.

Tables

With small amounts of numerical information, simple tables can be constructed within Microsoft Word or Google Docs etc. This sort of table can be incorporated into the main text if removing it from the text would result in a loss of meaning of the information.

Where you have more extensive datasets, spreadsheets such as Microsoft Excel, Google Sheets, or industry-specific software, offer increased flexibility in both the management and the presentation of the data. Specialists who work with large datasets may be comfortable using and reading spreadsheets. However, others who are less expert will usually require the data to be presented in more visual ways.

Where a formal table is needed in a document, the following characteristics need to be taken into account:

- it appears in the text in a convenient position after its first mention in the text.
- it has an identifying number.
- it has a clear and informative title.
- the data is arranged in some rational order.
- columns should have clear descriptive headings.
- where appropriate, the units of measurement should be stated.
- important data should be emphasised by its position in the table.

When including data it is worth considering whether or not to include the full table in the body of the text, or as an appendix. If there is more than one audience for the data, it may be that the key elements are provided in the body of the text for non-specialists with full datasets available as an appendices for specialists.

Unfortunately, many complex formal tables you will find in business documents are not well organised. We can still find examples of the misuse of tables, as criticised by Ehrenberg (1977). He offered the four principles for presenting data in tables which are still relevant and useful:

- round off numbers so that readers can make comparisons quickly and easily.
- include averages for each set of data so that readers can quickly work out the spread of values.
- organise your table so the reader compares the columns. Figures in columns are easier to compare than figures in rows.
- order rows in columns by size with larger numbers placed at the top. Again this helps the reader compare the data.

BOX 8.3: USING EHRENBERG'S PRINCIPLES

Consider the following table comparing the composition of the workforce in the ABC Corporation over the last few decades. All figures are in thousands employed:

Table 8.4 Trend table which makes the reader do all the work

	1980	1990	2000	2010
Total	201.66	342.54	410.44	567.21
Males	150.64	278.50	323.22	441.16
Females	51.02	64.04	87.22	126.05

After revising the table using Ehrenberg's principles, it is much easier to see patterns in the data.

Table 8.5 Trend table which tries to analyse the data

	Males	Females	Total
2010	441	126	567
2000	323	87	410
1990	278	64	342
1980	151	51	202
Average	298	82	380

Of course, we always need to question the purpose of a table like this. If the real purpose is to investigate any gender bias in ABC's employment practices, then this should be the focus of the table:

Table 8.6 Trend table which highlights the key statistic

	Total	**Female numbers**	**Females as % of workforce**
2010	567	126	22
2000	410	87	21
1990	342	64	19
1970	202	51	25
Average	380	82	22

Flowcharts, diagrams, schema

As we reimagine the presentation of numerical data through the concept of storytelling, we must also consider other forms of data presentation to enhance accessibility and impact. Figure 8.10 explains the recruitment and selection process as a flowchart. While this could be produced in bullet points, or sentences/paragraphs, the image makes information easier to follow and clarifies the sequence of actions needed after the decision to recruit new staff.

New and online software is having impact on the range of documents. Figure 8.11 is an infographic for students on a Postgraduate Certificate in HE. Previously presented as text within a handbook. This revision is easier to read and emotionally more engaging. Students are more likely to retain the information (remembering the impact of data storytelling in Figure 8.1, after Vora, 2019).

We are now seeing growing use of AI-powered image software (e.g. DALL-E, Midjourney), where images are generated by text prompts. This software is developing very rapidly – see the website for more updates.

Maps

The traditional view of maps is that it provides geographic information and apart from planning purposes would rarely be used. However, there are business reasons for the use of maps, such as identifying where and how marketing budgets should be spent. For example, a postcode review of the client list of a small gym in the UK revealed that the majority of members came from PR9, divided into four areas (see Table 8.7).

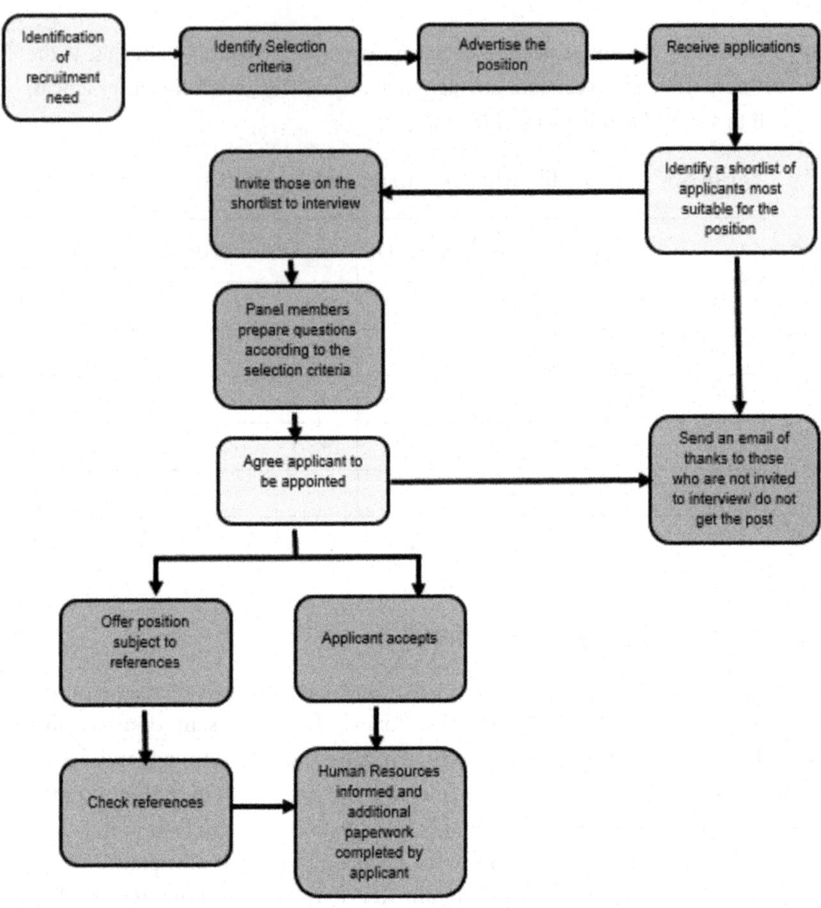

Figure 8.10 Recruitment and Selection process

Using www.streetlist.co.uk, the representation of PR9 7 (Figure 8.12) was much easier for the management team to work with when considering a marketing strategy.

Icons

Icons are often used in text to draw attention to the various elements within the text. For example, throughout this book icons have been used to draw attention to key sections within chapters, as in Table 8.8.

Checking the audience and purpose

Your choice of data presentation depends upon both your audience and the intended purpose of the document. As data analysis and interpretation is not widely taught in our education systems the simpler and more pictorial the device the better. Of

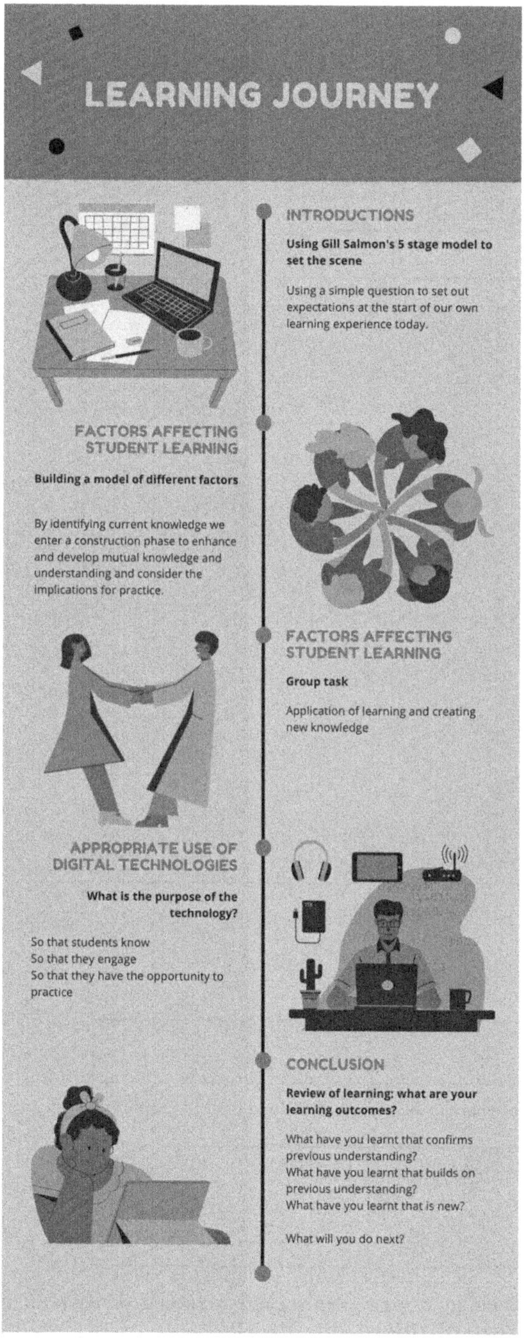

LEARNING JOURNEY

INTRODUCTIONS

Using Gill Salmon's 5 stage model to set the scene

Using a simple question to set out expectations at the start of our own learning experience today.

FACTORS AFFECTING STUDENT LEARNING

Building a model of different factors

By identifying current knowledge we enter a construction phase to enhance and develop mutual knowledge and understanding and consider the implications for practice.

FACTORS AFFECTING STUDENT LEARNING

Group task

Application of learning and creating new knowledge

APPROPRIATE USE OF DIGITAL TECHNOLOGIES

What is the purpose of the technology?

So that students know
So that they engage
So that they have the opportunity to practice

CONCLUSION

Review of learning: what are your learning outcomes?

What have you learnt that confirms previous understanding?
What have you learnt that builds on previous understanding?
What have you learnt that is new?

What will you do next?

Figure 8.11 PG Certificate in HE Learning Journey

Table 8.7 Geographical spread of members within one postcode district

PR9 0	10
PR9 7	45
PR9 8	20
PR9 9	35

Figure 8.12 Map of PR9

Table 8.8 Use of icons

Icon	Purpose
	Key image highlights the key points at the end of each chapter
	Book image used to highlight the boxes

course, many professions such as engineers, economists and architects do have their own technical language and conventions which can be used where appropriate.

In general, you have more information available than can be used in the visual aid, so the selection and processing of information is essential. Where the information is numerical, you need to use a form which matches the purpose and the needs of the audience. You can then decide the content of the message using the content criteria we have already discussed in this book:

- accuracy.
- brevity.
- clarity.
- emphasis.

Equality, Diversity, and Inclusion

As well as recognising the advantages of presenting numbers, processes etc. in visual formats, we need to check to what other messages are included that may undermine the message. For example, many illustrations in documents continue to propagate stereotypes – even if this is unintended.

We all carry inherent bias, even if that is over which football team we support – and recognising these will help us to consider what overt and subliminal messages we send in our work. Graphics which treat any part of the audience without respect for their essential human dignity are unacceptable. This is particularly the case where humour is used to make a point. A more subtle form of incorrect attitude to audience is stereotyping, for example where managers are portrayed as white and male and workers as black.

Presentations

Whilst traditional style documents continue to be the norm in many business contexts, such as the Annual Reports and Accounts, instruction manuals, committee documents, investment reports etc. there are opportunities to present data more clearly using presentation software, such as PowerPoint and canva.c om in these same contexts. In Chapter 13, we look at this in more detail.

SUMMARY OF KEY POINTS

- understanding the audience and purpose of the document lies at the heart of good document design.
- psychological research supports designers' views that the "look" of a document influences how it is read. But despite the importance of good design, many organisations use traditional and dated conventions.
- a well-designed document is accessible to all potential readers, is easy to understand and will enable good decision-making – as well as presenting the author as professional and competent.

- writers should consider basic technical aspects of typefaces and page layout so they can make sensible design choices, such as using page layout to emphasise the structure of the document.
- good visual aids should enhance engagement with the data. It is important to highlight the main points you wish to make in whatever visual aid you decide to use.
- there are three main types of visual aids you can use in documents – visual representations of numerical data (including tables, charts, and graphs), process presentations like diagrams, flow charts etc. and pictorial presentations like photographs and maps. These sit alongside bullet points and number lists which also alter the visual presentation of material.
- graphic devices (graphs and charts) can be used to deceive. You must recognise the potential for misrepresentation and avoid it in your own documents.
- new forms of data visualisation, such as infographics and presentations are changing the way documents are being developed and in some cases replacing traditional documents in professional and business processes.

References

British Dyslexia Association 2022 Dyslexia friendly style guide Available from British Dyslexia Association (bdadyslexia.org.uk)

Ehrenberg, A.S.C. (1977) Rudiments of numeracy. *Journal of the Royal Statistical Society A* 140: 227–297.

Hartley, J. (1994) *Designing Instructional Text*, 3rd edition. London: Kogan Page.

Knaflic, C.N. (2015) *Storytelling with Data: A Data Visualization Guide for Business Professionals.* Hoboken, NJ: Wiley.

Last, S. (2019) *Technical Writing Essentials.* University of Victoria. British Columbia. Canada. Available from https://onlineacademiccommunity.uvic.ca/scholarlycommunications/2019/08/07/technical-writing-essentials/

Lichty, T. (1989) *Design Principles for Desktop Publishers.* Glenview, IL: Scott, Foresman.

Peterson, K. (2019) Document design – Technical and professional writing genres. In Beilfuss, M., Bettes, S. and Peterson, K. (eds) *Technical and Professional Writing Genres. A Study in Theory and Practice.* https://open.library.okstate.edu/technicalandprofessionalwriting/.

Tufte, E.R. (1983) *The Visual Display of Quantitative Information.* Cheshire, CT: Graphics Press.

Tufte, E.R. (2006) *Beautiful Evidence.* Cheshire, CT: Graphics Press.

Vora, S. (2019) *The Power of Data Storytelling.* Thousand Oaks, CA: Sage Publications India Pvt.

CHAPTER 9

Effective documents

Introduction

This chapter discusses the range and type of documents we need in organisations, both now and in the immediate future, and considers the ways in which we engage in the online world.

Whilst there are different demands on the writer in print and online documents, there are key principles which apply to all contexts, including:

- knowing your audience.
- knowing your topic/subject matter.
- having a clear rationale for each document.

We begin by summarising principles of effective communication from the previous three chapters – structure, style, and design – organised in checklists you can use with your own documents.

We then apply these principles to common professional documents, ranging from the informal to the official, and from the individual to the corporate. Many print documents have well-established conventions that can be adapted and transferred between organisations. In the online world, expectations continue to be in flux. These expectations vary considerably, both in the range of media used across any single organisation and in the ways technology is embraced in the development and use of documents.

This is part of the larger debate about the future of work post-pandemic which we introduced in Chapter 4 and return to in Chapter 15. The nature of documents and professional communication will be influenced by the ways that organisations resolve the balance between working in the office or at home/virtually.

DOI: 10.4324/9781003297550-12

OBJECTIVES

This chapter will:

- summarise main principles which we need to consider when preparing all professional and business documents.
- apply these principles to main forms of professional and business documents.
- identify particular principles to consider when writing online.

Underpinning principles

To identify principles that help us prepare effective professional and business documents, we start by highlighting key points from the last three chapters, suggesting key questions you can apply to your own documents, and adding a few comments from our experience.

Planning and structure
Style
Layout and visual aids

Table 9.1 Planning and organisation

Principle	Key question	Our comments
Planning	Do you have a clear plan?	This does not mean that you have to write in a rigid sequence of steps. Plans should be flexible and regularly reviewed.
Objectives	Do you have clear objectives for the document?	Phrasing your objectives helps you decide what information you need to provide.
Audience	Have you considered the particular needs of your audiences?	A specific document can have several different audiences. Can you satisfy all of them?
Organisation	Have you organised the information in a way which makes sense to the audience?	Your audience will find the information easier to understand and remember if it is clearly organised. Remember the three basic principles: chunking, ordering, and signposting.
Structure	Does the document structure support your objectives?	Your audiences need to recognise what you are trying to achieve.

Table 9.2 Quality of communication

Principle	Key question	Our comments
Expression	Does your document express the appropriate tone for the audience and context?	We need to evaluate writing using both content and tone criteria.
"Plain language"	Have you used clear, plain language?	This argues for an *appropriate* style of language and *not* the same simple style for every document. We can use plain language approaches to evaluate and improve our expression.
Punctuation	Does the punctuation help your audience to understand what you mean?	Follow standard conventions on punctuation while remembering that the rules are both flexible and changing

Table 9.3 Design

Principle	Key question	Our comments
Overall image	What "image" does your document convey?	The "look" of a document influences how it is read.
Accessibility	Is your document fully accessible?	Every document must be accessible to all readers.
Good design	Is your document well-designed?	A well-designed document has three main advantages: it makes a good impression on the reader by: • suggesting a professional and competent approach. • making the content or information easier to understand. • enabling the reader to respond appropriately.
Page layout and design	Does the page layout and use of typefaces convey a	You should understand basic aspects of typefaces and page layout/design and use them to make sensible design choices.
Visual aids	Do your visual aids convey clear messages?	Good visual aids should support the purpose of the document. If it is data, then the form of presentation should enable good decisions to be made. Graphics can be used to deceive. Avoid misrepresentation in your documents.

Other general considerations:

You are the organisation!

Whenever you write to another person, you are representing not only yourself but your organisation or your part of it. If you create a poor impression then both you and the organisation suffers.

Format, image, and house style

Professional documents project your image. Large organisations usually employ professional designers to design their corporate stationery. The current trend is towards simple stationery, but you may have to work within a certain format dictated by the house style.

Legal and statutory requirements

There are certain legal requirements which obviously vary from country to country. For example, in South Africa, letters *must* carry the company's registration number and the names of its directors. How this information appears depends on the image that the organisation is trying to project.

Document designs reflect organisational structures and culture

Susan Katz's suggestion continues to hold true:

> *every organization, and every department within an organization has its own conception of what makes 'good writing.'*
>
> *(Katz, 1998, page 109)*

She found that some managers very carefully coached new staff in their writing, explaining the importance and purpose of documents, providing models of good practice, and commenting on drafts and outlines. Some managers were less diligent. Support and training can be very uneven as these four different examples illustrate:

> *"My own introduction to business writing was 'ghost writing' letters for senior partners in the organisation – where each partner had a distinctive style of their own".*

> *"As Roger's new manager, I wanted to give him the best performance appraisal I could. I'd received some negative feedback on his reports for one committee. When I tried to discuss that with him, he reacted very strongly – 'I've been doing those reports for two*

years now, ever since I came here, and nobody have ever commented on them before.'" Unfortunately. I discovered afterwards that this was true. No-one had raised issues with Roger – they had just grumbled to themselves".

"As Chris undertook a new role as secretary for some of the governance committees of the organisation, he was mentored by a more experienced committee secretary known for their good practice. This provided a smooth introduction to the demands of the role and minimised potential mistakes".

"Being responsible for the induction of new professionals to the business, Jordan had to respond to complaints regarding the style of emails being sent by a new colleague which had been considered too abrupt. This was a shock to the new colleague who had intended the emails to be clear rather than rude. Jordan was aware that other organisations delivered 'netiquette' training for staff which included policy on the writing of emails so there was a common understanding of good practice".

Changing the design of documents can also change relationships between staff and their perceptions of their roles. So, we cannot assume that making documents easier to read and understand will *automatically* make the organisation more effective, as we said earlier.

Increasing reader engagement

At the height of the pandemic, much was written about the quality of communication both within businesses and between businesses and external stakeholders in response to the continual state of change.

Key lessons have been learnt – emphasising the need for clarity, credibility and empathy to maintain engagement and motivation (Mayfield and Mayfield, 2022). Continual change meant that professional communication had to be agile to ensure that messages would be heard and responded to appropriately. More importantly, clarity, credibility, and empathy do not exist independently. Where a message is delivered clearly, and the author has credibility, then this is in itself empathetic because it generates a sense of security for the recipient.

As we think back to messages around mask-wearing/social distancing etc., we can reflect on our own feelings of security during this time. During the first lockdown in the UK, the message to stay at home was widely adopted reflecting the clarity of the message, the credibility of the experts delivering the message, and the sense of empathy engendered by the sense of "being in this together". However, credibility and empathy was undermined by news of lockdown parties at the heart of government and it is questionable whether there would be such uniformity in response should the need arise again.

In turn, we can see the impact on our productivity and activity when we recognise that communication is not just about words on a page. Against this backdrop, the next section provides guidance on some of the key documents that are produced by organisations to maximise their effectiveness.

Different types of documents

There is no simple answer to the question of which are the most important documents for a business, although there are plenty of websites that will define a list of documents that "every business" needs.

For example, Agile CRM (www.agilecrm.com) identifies five types of documents – email, business letters, business reports, transactional documents, financial reports, and documents (3 Jan 2020).

The list of over 20 documents provided by Indeed (www.uk.indeed.com) includes contracts, internal regulations (bylaws), employment agreements, business plans, financial documents, business reports, minutes, etc.

We focus on those documents that you are likely to encounter in most organisations, especially early in your career, and which reflect our own professional experience.

Email

Despite the growing use of instant messaging systems such as Teams or Slack, constructing an effective email is still a key requirement in most organisations. Ejim (2022) suggests it "plays an essential role in business communication". But we are concerned that many users do not fully appreciate its importance as an "official" document, even though it can become a legal document in some circumstances.

Reflecting its 1970s origins, email continues to be viewed as a simple communication system, albeit with significant sophistication for the passing of information and integration with other systems. Perhaps due to its perceived simplicity, most users receive little formal training or education in its best use. For example, we have colleagues who are exasperated by what they see as a "lack of courtesy" in student emails. Some students fail to recognise the expectations of staff who use email as a semi-formal system within higher education institutions. They write using textspeak, or occasionally write nothing at all and just send an attachment. There are some useful guides on both university and college websites but we are not sure how well they are used (e.g. University of North Carolina).

One main issue is the number of emails that we may have to deal with. Email is so easily accessible on a range of devices that some people find themselves continually overloaded by work queries. We return to these issues below.

Content, structure, and layout

Emails include a space for the sender, the receiver and the title, with date and timing of sending automatically supplied. The title of the email is very important and needs to reflect the aim or goal of the email. It should engage the recipient to increase the chances of getting the intended response.

The key requirement is to simplify the message so that its intent is clear to the recipient, and they know what their next steps are. The email is not the place for a long report or extensive piece of writing, although in some circumstances there may be an attachment to provide further information.

While some of the formalities often expected for other communications are missing, we still recommend courtesy in the opening and closing of an email. The opening can range from traditional formal openings of "Dear…" to "Hello…" and "Hi…" etc. with the use of a name, with similar considerations at the close. Increasingly, electronic/business signatures are used to end an email. These can be personalised (e.g. by adding a graphic that looks like your normal written signature), but in larger organisations there will be a house style that determines its look. This may include the use of a particular logo, name, title, and key elements of the role. Beyond this, the contents and style of an email will reflect the culture of the organisation or sector and – to a greater extent than in other documents – the personality of the author.

Currently layout is more restricted than for word-processed documents, but this is continuously developing so there is now a choice of fonts, bullet points etc. Hyperlinks can be inserted and a range of attachments can be incorporated. In addition, emoticons can be added – whether they should be used is debatable and depends on both the context and your relationship with the recipient.

These developments in email have meant that simplifying the content has become easier, e.g. by the judicious use of bullet points or numbers. Other tips for streamlining the message include:

- removing repetition.
- avoiding adverbs, such as *really, extremely*, and *very*.
- stating facts, rather than qualifying them with terms such as "I think" or "I feel".
- embedding images – not attaching them.
- cropping images so that only necessary detail is showing.

(Adapted from Kelly Stephanie, 2019, 123,126)

Tone: hitting the right note in an email

Email is often used in a way that blurs the distinction between talking, texting, and writing. However, emails are permanent, can be used as legal records, and once sent are no longer under the control of the author. For these reasons, the tone of an email can be as important as the subject. As a result, we disagree with one aspect of Kelly's guidance – we would use "I think" or "I feel" more often in emails to soften a message.

Another way of creating engagement is to note the context of the recipient of the email, e.g. by acknowledging the fact that a colleague is particularly busy when sending a request for something to be done within a certain timeframe. Recognising that there is a person at the other end of the email could be considered as an aspect of emotional intelligence and is more likely to lead to a successful outcome. There are situations where emotions should not be entertained, such as when a message is emotive or reflects private relationships between colleagues. Such messages can damage reputations and relationships – as well as being on permanent record.

Many organisations routinely monitor email use. This is partly due to legal reasons. Another reason is because of concerns about staff "wasting time" on personal concerns. One of our colleagues was fired from a temporary job when his employer noted that he used his company email to follow up another job advert.

As we said earlier, knowing your audience, the purpose of the email, and the culture(s) of the organisation or sector will make the difference between whether or not an email is received well and acted upon. For example, within some parts of the legal profession, formality of communication has continued to be the norm, even in emails.

Reflecting on how well you know your audience can also prevent the confusion or loss of reputation that may arise as a result of false assumptions of what the recipient understands or expects, such as with the use of abbreviations, colloquialisms, poor phrasing or typos (i.e. misspelt words), or clumsy phrasing.

BOX 9.1 HITTING THE RIGHT NOTE IN AN EMAIL

Imagine you are the owner of a small software company and you receive an email from one of the industry's most well-known and pioneering characters with the following subject line "Get together?"

Do you:

1. email back immediately to suggest a meeting?
2. ring him up or text him immediately?
3. email him to say you are busy at the moment and will get back to him?

And what style would you use in your message?

a) formal and very "business-like"?
b) formal but not too 'business-like?
c) casual and chatty?

If you look up the detailed correspondence between Mark Zuckerberg of Facebook and WhatsApp then you might be surprised at the casual tone of the messages – 3 and c in the above lists – especially when you realise that this led to a $19 billion dollar business deal. But the style was right for the context and established the right framework for the relationship.

BOX 9.2 EMAIL FATIGUE

The combination of the volume of email that hits our inboxes, together with the ability to access email on multiple devices, has led to increasing levels of stress – "email fatigue" (Mittal, 2022) – that sense of being overwhelmed by both the number of emails and the amount of information that we are expected to manage.

The benefits of email are widely recognised, such as increased information sharing across different locations and asynchronously. However, there are also disadvantages, such as the disruption to workflow, decreased engagement during tasks, and the blurring of work and non-work boundaries. The combination of these factors has led to an increase in employee fatigue and burnout and has led some countries to legislate for employers to uphold their employees' rights to disconnect from the workplace (e.g. in France, Germany and Spain) (Steffensen et al., 2022).

Managing work boundaries

The issue of boundaries between work and non-work is more complex than it might first appear, particularly with the increased flexibility that came with working from home during Covid. While some individuals used this to manage their own time and emailed at times convenient to them, there was unintended impact on colleagues who felt that they needed to mimic the availability at either end of the normal working day – or on changing clients' expectations of responses in the early morning or evenings.

There are some practical solutions (or at least things you can do to minimise the problems). You need to choose solutions which suit your working practice:

- some time management texts recommend only answering emails at particular points in the day, say at the beginning and end, so that you do not get continually distracted during the day.
- how often do you read any given email? Can you commit to only reading emails once and deciding what to do with them there and then?

- using some form of filtering which automatically sorts incoming email and eliminates particular forms of message.
- schedule your emails to be sent only during normal working hours irrespective of when you choose to write them.

Spam, hacking, abuse

As well as the increase in genuine messages, there has been the growth of spam and hacking. Every organisation needs appropriate protection and filtering in the system. Even then, you are likely to receive daily messages which are suspect but which can look surprisingly authentic. It is always worth taking a few precautions:

- never open an attachment unless you are confident that the email is genuine.
- check the sender's address even if the message looks authentic.

As long ago as the 1990s it was recognised that emails could harbour abuse. For example, Hargie et al. (1999, page 182) reported one survey where over half of email users claimed to have "received abusive e-mails…which irreparably damaged working relationships". Over half of these came from their managers and were much more likely to be written by men than women (five times more likely, according to this study). Much of the debate around the causes of this type of abuse continues and is not only about the use of email but across all types of social media. There is no clear answer to this. However, the solution is for us to ensure that we are not the perpetrators of that abuse and to support those who experience and report it.

What is your individual style?

Individuals do develop their own style of writing emails. This covers such things as how you express politeness, how you use short sentences and abbreviations, and your use of what linguists call metalanguage, where you use language to comment on itself as in the phrase "*can I ask* when the minutes will be distributed?"

Your style should be appropriate to your audience. Reviewing our own use of email, we noticed how our style varies from very conversational with close colleagues to a more impersonal style in messages which may reach a large group. You also need to consider your organisational culture. See Box 8.1. for an interesting example of matching your style to the other person.

Reports

A report is an official or formal statement, often made after research or an investigation and usually made to your immediate line manager, or to a working group

Table 9.4 Audience analysis

Your audience	Definition
The primary audience	As a report aims to achieve action, these are people who have the authority to act on the recommendations. This may be a single person, such as a general manager, or a group, such as a committee or even the board of directors. Key parts of the report (especially the executive summary, conclusions, and recommendations) should be targeted specifically at this primary audience.
The secondary audience	Few decision-makers act entirely on their own; they seek advice from departments and specialists. This group of advisers is the secondary audience, which often has limited or special interests.
The tertiary audience	If the recommendations of a report are approved, then it may be distributed to further readers who have to implement the recommendations. They will need details which were not necessary for decision making, so make sure these are covered in the appendices.
And other readers	There may be a fourth category of reader who, for policy reasons, "need to know" (often senior staff in other parts of the organisation). Or there may be people at a later date who find the report useful for similar investigations.

or committee. The audience(s) may be either internal or external to the organisation, or, on rare occasions, both. The audience may not share the writer's expertise.

Analysing the audiences

The structure and content of any report must meet the needs of up to four distinct categories of audience, as outlined in Table 9.4.

Executive Summary

The purpose of this is to allow readers to engage with the main points quickly and decide if they need to read the rest of the report, or specific sections. Its role is to state the objective(s), the findings or supporting evidence, and the next steps. Getting this section right is crucial for the report to achieve its aim.

Types of report

Whilst you can find a wide range of "types of report" on the internet, these three main categories cover most of the variation you will find in practice:

- form reports.
- short reports.
- long formal reports and proposals.

Form reports – forms and questionnaires

These share important features, which are to:

- compile specific information from a variety of respondents.
- collect information which can then be collated, analysed, and interpreted.

Form reports are regular and standardised, such as production reports, sales reports, accident reports, progress reports, etc. There are definite advantages in having standardised forms for these:

- the same information is in the same place each time.
- we can check that all the required information is submitted.

Forms and form reports are increasingly online so that the information is fed directly into the organisation's information systems. This can also lead to direct action if the system is set up for it.

Designing forms and questionnaires requires high levels of skill. It is all too easy to create ambiguous or misleading questions and collect data which is effectively useless.

Short reports

These are internal reports, usually less than five pages, which do not require all the formalities of long reports. They often have simple subsections, such as:

- introduction.
- investigation.
- conclusion.

Descriptive reports of this sort are usually intended to supply information, rather than recommend specific action. In terms of effective style and structure, we echo what is said about memos, emails, and letters, emphasising the importance of informative headings and subheadings to guide the reader through the text.

Long formal reports and proposals

Long reports deal with a complex investigation or issue, often addressed to a number of different audiences. To cater for different audiences and to provide a logical structure, reports are subdivided into sections with distinct functions.

A complete investigation (from problem definition through to recommendations) requires a logical sequence of actions, which are reflected in this sectional structure.

Proposals might be for a new company or departmental initiative. These have a similar format to reports but use some sections differently.

Objectives

Writing a report is easier if you have a clear objective, i.e. identifying the purpose and expressing this clearly at the start of the document. For example, we suggest two parts to the opening sentence(s):

- the first part ("the aim of this report is to…") expresses the report's immediate aim.
- the second part ("so that…") looks to the future. What benefit, payoff, or actions do you see as a result of the report?

Having a clear view of the objective is especially important with complicated reports which involve a lot of preparation. Not only does this make it clearer for the audience, it is a useful way of confirming that it meets the needs of the person or organisation that commissioned the report.

Structure and report sections

One large consulting company we know adopts a "pyramid reporting" approach as a way of engaging its clients with both the detail and the "big picture" aspects of its reports. It borrows a format from the world of journalism, where the headline presents the big picture – and the reason for reading on – the introductory paragraph provides the purpose of the article as a succinct summary and the remainder of the article provides the detail.

The most typical report structure is an expansion of the begin-middle-end structure we have come across before, as in the following table. See our website for a more detailed description of each section and other links to useful guidance on the web.

Not all reports will contain all these sections – how they are subdivided depends on the contents and the audience requirements. Table 9.5 gives a few variations to meet specific needs. The important principle is to choose a structure which supports your objectives and which readers will follow easily. For example, many writers advocate the SPQR approach:

S = the situation (this company is the leading producer of grommits)
P = the problem or problems which have arisen (sales of grommits are falling)
Q = the question which arises in the reader's mind (how can we restore grommit sales?)

Table 9.5 Typical outline report structure

	Report structure	**Report sections**
Begin	Introduction	• title page. • synopsis or summary. • contents list. • introduction.
Middle	Main Body	• methods of investigation. • results. • discussion of results.
End	Conclusions and Recommendations	• conclusions. • recommendations.
		• appendices.

Table 9.6 Examples of different specific report structures

Report which summarises the results of an investigation to arrive at a conclusion: "the new manufacturing process does/does not meet Health and Safety standards"	**Report which investigates three possible solutions to a specified problem and recommends the best course of action**	**Proposal which recommends that the department or organisation adopts new working practices (e.g. adopts new computer system)**

• Title page
• Title
• Summary
• Contents list
• Introduction
• Investigation, which comprises
  • method of information gathering
  • results
  • discussion
• Conclusion
• Appendices (e.g. detailed test results)
	• Title page
	• Title
	• Summary
	• Contents list
	• Introduction (which specifies the problem)
	• Solution 1
	  • advantages
	  • disadvantages
	• Solution 2
	  • advantages
	  • disadvantages
	• Solution 3
	  • advantages
	  • disadvantages
	• Conclusion
	• Recommendations
	• Appendices
		• Title page
		• Title
		• Summary
		• Contents list
		• Introduction
		• Analysis of present working practices
		  • problem 1
		  • problem 2
		  • and so on
		• How a new system would deal with these problems
		  • advantages
		  • disadvantages
		• Conclusion and Recommendation
		• Appendices

R = response (solutions and recommendations, which may of course challenge assumptions behind the original question. For example, it may be impossible to revive grommit sales as this technology is in long-term decline – what should the organisation do about this?)

Whatever the final structure in terms of headings and subheadings, it is essential that this reflects *the structure of your argument*. As we said in Chapter 8, visual aids can be used to present or support an argument as well as improving engagement.

Report style

All the general issues of language style we have discussed previously are relevant, but there are two issues which are worth emphasising:

Style and organisational structure

A particular language style can reflect deep-rooted organisational attitudes which may be difficult to change. For example, some traditional conventions of formal reports, like avoiding the first person and using the passive voice, were justified by the claim that this writing style was more "accurate" or "objective". Some organisations still insist on some of these conventions.

However, adopting this strategy can lead to tortuous expressions which can be vague or misleading. The best practical solution is to make your reports compatible with the organisational house style and avoid any sentence constructions which can confuse. Further suggestions include using specific and concrete terms rather than general and abstract terms. For example, "the function of allocation and distribution of revenue will be performed by the Business Development Department" is improved by simplifying the statement to "the Business Development Department will *allocate* and *distribute* the revenue".

Letters

Business letters have a long history. Their main advantages are that they provide a permanent record of what is said and can be referred to easily. On the other hand, letters are relatively expensive – they have to be composed carefully, and feedback may be slow or non-existent. For these reasons, the use of letters has been overtaken by email. However, there are still individuals (external to business) who do not use email and there are situations when hard copy written documentation is needed, for example where an individual needs proof of address for identification purposes.

Standard and circular letters

There are situations where a letter is written and sent by email to a closed group of recipients, particularly common within the public sector. This includes the advice given to schools throughout the lockdowns – when schools were still open. A circular letter also refers to flyers promoting social events. The logic of a circular letter is that everyone receives exactly the same information and at much the same time. In practice, this may have unanticipated consequences. For example, consider the following message in a circular letter from the relatively new general manager of a large multi-site organisation:

> *From September to December this year, we shall be holding consultations with all staff on the Greenfield site to consider proposals to amalgamate the departments on that site.*

Many staff on the Greenfield site received this news by word of mouth. But the meaning of the grapevine message was more definite than the written message: "The new general manager has decided to amalgamate the departments on that site". This interpretation was strongly justified by its advocates. They pointed to several clues to management's "real intentions":

- the way that the circular had been announced, out of the blue, and just before the annual holiday period.
- the fact that the current department managers were completely unprepared for it.
- the "fact" that the new general manager obviously wanted to establish her authority.

The important principle here is that a message which is designed to reach and mean the same for everyone (like circular letters) must take account of the context and anticipate different interpretations. In the last example, some of the problems could have been avoided, at least in part, by briefing department managers *and* by issuing the circular after the holiday period.

But is a printed circular the best method for this sort of message?

Would an email have been greeted with more or less suspicion?

That depends on the history and culture of the organisation. For example, in a large distributed organisation, why not organise a webinar led by the senior manager making the announcement with opportunities for staff to raise questions and receive immediate answers?

Style in individual letters

We can write individual letters of various types, including: making/answering enquiries; appointing an employee; submitting or accepting a quotation, and so on. We can highlight main principles and issues with an example where the tone is particularly important: responding to a complaint.

Chunking in letters

If you follow chunking principles from previous chapters then each paragraph has a specific theme. We can think of business letters in terms of the basic begin-middle-end structure, as recommended by many trainers and teachers (Table 9.7).

Deciding on the tone

As well as making sure that the content was accurate, is the tone appropriate? For example, we would recommend a "positive and neutral" tone for a letter of complaint to another person/organisation.

One issue with any letter of complaint is the possible assumption that the other person is directly to blame. As accusations usually put the other person on the defensive, they are not a good strategy to resolve the problem, especially in the first letter (and even less in person!). It is much safer to assume that your audience is someone who wishes to provide a good service, but that something has gone wrong.

Layout conventions in letters

Conventions have changed – for example, most organisations now use the block format of presentation:

- everything starts at the left-hand margin, except possibly the company letterheading/logo at the top of the page.
- the right margin is either justified or ragged (we recommend the latter for word-processed documents).
- punctuation is kept to a minimum with only the necessary full stops (periods) and commas.

You can see these rules applied in many templates now offered in word-processing software.

Table 9.7 Chunking in letters

Begin	Explain why you are writing
Middle	Explain the detailed information
End	Explain what action you are going to take

Memos

Memos continue to be important in many organisations. They are recognised as a way of raising the importance of the message, act in a way that is similar to a press release, although for an internal audience. They have a particular format – provided by the organisation – which reflects their formality. The typical memo will be focussed on one topic and will be brief but may reference a report or other sources of further information.

According to Indeed, the job-finding website, memos are effective when:

- the purpose of the memo is highlighted in the introductory paragraph.
- the message is concise, and the language is positive throughout.
- the subject line communicates the message of the memo.
- the body paragraph and conclusion are used to break down the information. (Indeed, 2022)

Fax

A fax is the scanned copy of a document that is then transmitted by telecommunications links. Nowadays, online faxing is increasingly common. Dedicated fax machines are now obsolete (or heading that way) in many places (e.g. recent changes to telecommunications policy in the UK).

Once extremely common, the use of fax decreased steadily after the introduction of email. However, fax still has some possible advantages over email:

- messages can be sent to incomplete addresses – only the name of the business needs to be known.
- fax is traditionally sent using phone lines, not through the internet. Even when the internet goes down or you are out of range, fax can still be transmitted.
- fax provides confirmation that the recipient has received the message and can be used as evidence if needed (and it won't get lost in spam).
- it is considered to be more secure than email and is therefore commonly used by legal services, medical providers etc.

Messages specially written for fax share many of the characteristics we discussed for email, although abuse does not seem to be an issue. They are short (often less than one page, not counting the cover sheet with the contact information); they mainly supply or request information; and they are written in a more conversational style than traditional business letters.

Writing online

Writing online (and distinct from digital marketing) has become an essential expectation for the professional, reflecting the blurring of the lines between writing internally and writing to engage a wider range of stakeholders in a more immediate and conversational way. According to Jameson (2014) there are four types of potential and actual audiences of online communication:

- the intended audience.
- the addressed audience who are mentioned in postings.
- the "empirical audience" who actually read the postings (which may or may not include the intended audience).
- the potential audience of the future who may access the communication due to its electronic permanence.

Depending on your organisational context, you might be expected to write for a range of media, such as:

- managing social media with external partners, such as Twitter, Instagram, Facebook, Google, Snapchat, Flickr etc.
- writing blog posts for the organisation or your own professional development.
- setting up and/or managing an online discussion group or forums
- contributing to a wiki, for either internal or external use.
- managing internal communications through social media.

To successfully manage communication across such a wide range of contexts, understanding the audiences and using appropriate language is essential, as the reputational risks, both for the professional and the organisation, are significant. Understanding the audience will include an awareness of the level of familiarity between the conversation partners, their conversation history, and the organisational culture.

Effective communication in the online world

Business documents such as reports, letters, and e-mail have established conventions that can be relatively easy to adopt and use. However, in the online world, the rules of engagement are still in a state of flux and potentially carry greater reputational risks. The effectiveness of online engagement depends on hitting the right tone as well as being factually correct – and the right tone may not be one of deference, or formalised courtesy. The Twitter relationship marketing campaigns of Tesco Mobile, Old Spice, Taco Bell, amongst others have eschewed traditional customer service approaches with “snarky” interactions with online audiences. For example, Tesco Mobile’s “letter of apology” (2021) on behalf of rival networks for changing the prices mid-contract hit the headlines in the world of public relations as a positive example to follow – but is also notoriously difficult to emulate.

Communication in the online world provides several advantages due to its flexibility. One is the ability to share across online platforms so that messages have a much broader reach than traditional business communication. For example, images and text in WhatsApp can be shared on Facebook; blogs can be shared on Twitter, LinkedIn, and email; marketing posts can be shared on Facebook and Instagram etc. Alongside these opportunities to share, you can include adapted hyperlinks to other sources within the text so that audiences can access the full story behind the post.

As positive engagement is key in the online world, Darics (2016) makes the following recommendations for creating the right tone and facilitating interactivity online:

- discourse markers, which words that reflect engagement e.g. *OK*, *I mean*, *You know.*
- interjections, such as *wow*, *OMG*, *aww*, *hey.*
- direct addresses and imperatives, such as *Check this out*, *on closer inspection you will see…*
- Questions, which are aimed to stimulate *Can you believe that? Would you stay here again?*
- Answers to hypothetical questions, such as *and yes, I always use an oven thermometer.*
- Questions and answers, like simulated dialogues such as *Would you toss whole strawberries into a £40 blender? No.*

These textual markers can be added to with the use of speech-like features, such as:

- enthusiasm markers, for example !!!, ALL CAPS, elongated letters – sooooo.
- backchannel signals.
- emoticons (adapted from Darics, 2016).

The problem with some of these recommendations is that they imply a “super-friendly” relationship which some customers might resent or find annoying. We always suggest that you test messages like this with members of your target audience.

To maximise the reach of online writing, tags can be used, such as hashtags where # is used alongside key words to make the post or blog easy to find by the provided search engines within the application. Another way of extending the reach is by adding specific individuals' online handles so that they are notified of the post and can respond.

It is worth noting that this use of language is very different to what would be used for reports, letters and email etc. and some of our colleagues consider these interactions to be "unprofessional". The existence of contrasting opinions reflects the newness of online communication and its current state of flux within the business world. In Chapter 16 we look further into navigating this complex world which blurs the boundaries between the professional and personal worlds of the individual.

How to write a blog

Blogs are a more extended form of writing online to enhance professional standing. They are written for many different purposes: to create communities formed around professional interests, lifestyle and/ or life stages, or themes within a subject area – or to develop student academic writing – and are extensively used in the United States, Canada, and the UK.

The approach is often more informal than other forms of document writing, whilst not being casual. The structure reflects the pyramid reporting style mentioned in report writing, with a title that will draw the reader in, and an opening paragraph that describes the purpose and the remainder providing the detail in a clearly structured way, and with a conclusion to pull the whole piece together. With blogs, we expect images will be incorporated into the text to support both engagement and recall of information.

If you wish to explore blogging for yourself, there are plenty of sources to help you, including:

- sites which can support the development of your own personal blog pages, such as www.wix.com, www.squarespace.com, and www.masterclass.com, often aiming to draw you in to subscribe to the website and/or buy their templates.
- examples of popular blogs across different categories.
- online courses in blogging, from organisations such as www.udemy.com

Alternatively you may choose to start writing within an already established online community which may be within a professional association, or for the organisation/department that you work for or, perhaps for an online platform such as LinkedIn. Or it could be something as prosaic as being required to write regular blog posts on behalf of your organisation.

The most successful blogs are those that connect at some deep level with their audience. This can be due to the passion for the subject which is evident

Table 9.8 Questions to consider before you blog

Question	Comment
What is the *purpose* for the blog?	What do you want to achieve from the blog?
Who is your ideal *audience*?	Is this everyone who might read the blog, or a subset of that audience?
What *value* do you want to offer?	For the average reader there needs to be a sense of immediate value, i.e. that the material can be applied right away without purchasing your product/service
How do you want to *engage* with your audience?	Examples may be to connect via social media, to respond to a poll, or to download a free giveaway

in their cutting-edge knowledge or due to their deeply personal experiences, the blog by Dame Deborah James "Bowelbabe" being a prime example of this latter style of blog writing (Dawson, 2007). If either of these describes you, then the motivation for creating and sustaining a blog series may already be in place. Even if this doesn't describe you, it may still be the case that you will find yourself responsible for the development of a blog. Whatever your context, the questions in Table 9.8 will need to be addressed before putting pen to paper – or text to screen.

Where an online community already exists, such as with a professional association or LinkedIn, or an employer, then reviewing the structure, tone, and content of pre-existing blogs will support your development. This will include the straightforward aspects of length, use of headings and subheadings, font etc.

If you are not driven by personal passion, then identifying content for regular posts may be something of a challenge. One way to address this would be to identify keywords within a particular field and begin to develop a blog series based on those keywords. For example, if your audience was small businesses then keywords would probably include profit and turnover. As a result, it would be likely that a blog describing the difference between profit and turnover would be useful for small business owners (especially as so many business owners and students struggle to understand the distinction).

If you write blog posts in your private rather than professional sphere then take care that one aspect of your identity does not undermine the other. For example, a medical practitioner could not prescribe a course of treatment and then blog about the inadequacies of that treatment. If that were the case, then the credibility of the medical practitioner and the treatment would both be open to question. That is not to say that the medical practitioner cannot raise questions around the efficacy of treatments with the purpose of improving patient care. The issue would be about where those questions are raised and how steps are put in place to investigate improvements in practice. Similarly, undermining your employer or specific individuals within the organisation would generally be considered inappropriate.

Any and every example of business writing should present your professional voice, including blogs. An advantage of blogs over other forms of online writing is the control that you have as author to fashion the content before exposing it to the online world, without requiring instant engagement.

SUMMARY OF KEY POINTS

- writing online and print documents can require different skills but general principles apply to *all* business and professional documents whether print or online: deciding on appropriate objectives, meeting audience needs, organising the message, writing in an appropriate style, and using layout and design to support your message.
- effective professional and business correspondence must meet both content and tone criteria. Written messages can be interpreted in different ways depending on the context in which they are received.
- the design of documents reflects aspects of organisational structure and culture.
- email has become ubiquitous in business and strategies need to be developed to manage the number of emails and quantity of information.
- each type of business document can be analysed in terms of structure, style, and layout, and it is important to understand both the conventions which readers will expect and the potential problems caused by limitations of the system.
- you need to adapt the structure and style of your documents to the specific situation, as for example with the different ways of structuring long reports. Relying on a standardised approach will not usually be successful.
- communication in the online world provides opportunities for interactivity and immediacy to reach a wider audience but can require careful negotiation to support the development of a professional profile.
- blog writing offers a way of developing your professional profile or the profile of your business/employer with fewer risks than other forms of online engagement.

References

Darics, E. (2016) *Writing Online: A Guide to Effective Digital Communication at Work*, First edition. New York: New York Business Expert Press (Corporate communication collection).

Dawson, K.M. (2007) Blog overload. *Chronicle of Higher Education* 53(22): 2.

Ejim, E. (2022) *What Is the Role of Email in Business Communication?* https://www.smartcapitalmind.com/what-is-the-role-of-email-in-business-communication.htm.

Hargie, O.D.W., Dickson, D. and Tourish, D. (1999) *Auditing Organizational Communication: A Handbook of Research, Theory and Practice.* London: Routledge.

Henwood, D. (2020) *Business Writing for Innovators and Change-Makers.* (First, Ser. Corporate communication collection). Business Expert Press.

Katz, S. (1998) Part 1: Learning to write in organizations: What newcomers learn about writing on the job. *IEEE Transactions on Professional Communication* 42(2): 105–115.

Mayfield, J. and Mayfield, M. (2022) Business communication lessons in agility: Introduction to the special issue on the COVID-19 pandemic. *International Journal of Business Communication* 59(2): 163–173. doi:10.1177/23294884221077813.

Mittal, N. (2022) *How to Manage Email Fatigue to Keep Your Subscribers Engaged.* https://www.mailmodo.com/guides/email-fatigue/.

Steffensen, D.S., McAllister, C.P. and Perrewé, P.L. (2022) "You've got mail": A daily investigation of email demands on job tension and work-family conflict. *Journal of Business Psychology* 37: 325–338.

Stephanie, K. (editors) (2019) *Computer-Mediated Communication for Business; Theory to Practice.* Newcastle Upon Tyne: Cambridge Scholars.

PART 3

Effective interpersonal and group communication

CHAPTER 10

Effective interpersonal communication

Defining interpersonal skills in an information age

Introduction

Various methods have been proposed over the years to develop our interpersonal skills. For example, in the 1990s, many organisations were influenced by best-selling books on "emotional intelligence" (EI) which emphasised self-awareness and the importance of handling relationships:

> *a new competitive reality is putting emotional intelligence at a premium in the workplace and in the marketplace.*
>
> (Goleman, 1996, page 149)

You can still find EI in many current training courses in interpersonal skills, alongside more recent trends such as the increasing focus on EDI (equality, diversity, and inclusion) and employee wellbeing, increasing use of online resources, and the need to manage virtual teams (Symonds Research, 2022). Other training systems such as Neurolinguistic Programming (NLP) are much more controversial as we see later.

This chapter reviews research and theory which suggests that effective communication depends on interpersonal skills which *include* personal awareness and understanding, and which can be adapted successfully to both face-to-face and online settings.

We examine what effective interpersonal communication involves, highlight the main characteristics of essential skills, and show how these skills can be used together in everyday situations. We also warn against the "over-mechanical" use of certain techniques and highlight the growing role of new technologies in the way that we both create and receive impressions of others.

Our overall conclusion suggests that we cannot simply rely on skills and technique to arrive at effective interpersonal communication. We need to become "mindwise" as suggested by Nicholas Epley –

DOI: 10.4324/9781003297550-14

The secret to understanding each other better seems to come not through an increased ability to read body language or improved perspective taking but, rather, through the hard relational work of putting people in a position where they can tell you their minds openly and honestly.

(Epley, 2014, page 183)

OBJECTIVES

This chapter will:

- explain what effective interpersonal communication involves.
- identify and explain the most important interpersonal skills.
- comment upon popular models of interpersonal skills and communication training.
- identify important implications of this analysis for your behaviour towards others at work.
- suggest ways you can use technology to enhance your interpersonal effectiveness.

What does effective interpersonal communication involve?

One answer to this question is that we need "good" interpersonal skills so we can respond or react to the other person or persons in ways which appear "natural", and which are "effective". This suggests that we have accurately assessed what the other person is trying to communicate, and this depends upon how we perceive that other person.

But what if our perception is misleading?

Suppose that you worked behind the counter in an English bank and were confronted by a male customer who handed over a cheque and said "give me the money" with no change in intonation over these four words. Would you interpret this behaviour as "rude"? Many native English speakers would – to them it sounds too abrupt or even aggressive. The most common "polite" English expression would be to say this phrase with a slight rise in intonation on the last word (assuming that the person does not have a strong regional accent where different rules might apply).

If you interpreted the flat intonation as rude, would you deal with this customer in a correspondingly abrupt way? Or perhaps you would not give him quite the same positive greeting you would give to other customers?

Suppose your customer came from a Middle Eastern country and is using the pattern of intonation seen as polite in his native culture. Would you be sufficiently aware of this cultural difference to avoid an inappropriate reaction?

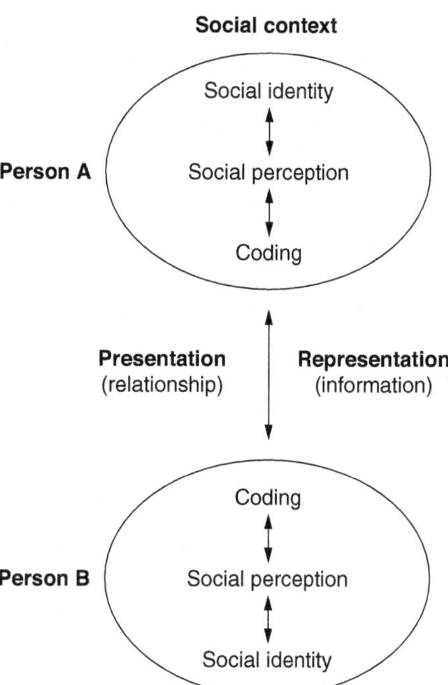

Figure 10.1 Hartley's model of interpersonal communication

The process of interpersonal communication is complex – unless you understand some basic features of this process, you can easily behave in ways which the other person will not accept or appreciate. For example, consider the model of interpersonal communication in Figure 10.1 (from Hartley, 1999) This suggests that there are a number of fundamental processes:

- social perception – how person A interprets the behaviour and characteristics of person B.
- social identity – how person A sees him or herself in terms of their role and status. We communicate in ways which support this sense of social identity.
- coding – how A and B choose to express themselves. Do we use slang or jargon or technical words? What nonverbal signals do we use?
- the dual nature of "the message" which always includes both information and relationship aspects. When we communicate, we pass on information to the other person(s), and we simultaneously set up or reinforce a particular relationship with that person.
- the influence of the social context.

We also need to emphasise the potential ambiguity which is inevitable in our everyday communication – which effective communicators anticipate and avoid. The more you investigate these processes, the more you realise that effective interpersonal communication demands both social understanding – recognising the processes – and social skills – being able to use the behaviours and techniques. We shall look at fundamental behaviours and techniques before we return to this question of how they all "fit together".

This model was developed in a pre-digital age, but we can still apply it, provided that we also consider the range of technologies now available to enhance or replace face-to-face interaction. And we need to consider how we use those technologies to both support our face-to-face encounters and to replace any missing cues, as in our discussion of "digital body language".

What do we mean by interpersonal skills?

Suppose you have been asked to nominate someone you know to lead a discussion group. Who would you choose? What do they do to make you think of them? What makes them good at getting people to talk? Do they make you feel that they really are listening and interested in what you are saying? How do they do this? How do they encourage you to contribute? What are the specific behaviours which make them successful? How and when do they smile, nod, invite you to speak, gesture etc? If you do this analysis in detail, then you will be doing a social skills analysis – you will define some of the social skills possessed by that individual.

This detailed approach to our social behaviour was pioneered in Britain by Michael Argyle in the 1970s. He developed the analogy between a motor or physical skill (like playing tennis or riding a bike) and a social skill like having a conversation with someone. He suggested that they had the following features in common (Argyle, 1994):

Goals

You need to decide what you want to achieve. If you talk to someone, are you trying to persuade them, sell them something, make friends or what? Of course, my goals may differ from yours and this could lead to problems or conflict.

Perception

You need to perceive what is going on around you and you need to do this accurately to achieve your goals.

Translation

In order to perform effectively you have to "translate" your idea of what you want to achieve into the correct action.

Responses

Even if you have the correct idea of what you need to do, can you physically do it?

Feedback

If you talk to someone, can you work out how interested they are? Can you recognise when they are getting bored or irritated? Can you accurately interpret the feedback you receive? For example, suppose you express your point of view, and they lean back and cross their arms. What does this signal mean? Does it mean agreement or disagreement? If you think it means disagreement, then do you try to restate what you think more clearly or in a different way? This example illustrates that there are several problems in reacting to feedback:

- did you notice the signals? You might have been concentrating so hard on expressing yourself clearly that you did not notice the other person's NVC.
- did you interpret the signals correctly?
- were you able to respond effectively?

There are other important analogies between physical and interpersonal skills:

- we have to learn how to perform effectively. We can always learn something new and/or some improvement.
- we can benefit from good coaching and tuition.
- as we learn any skill, our actions become more fluent and better-timed. We become less aware of what we are doing – the action becomes sub-conscious. The same process can apply to interpersonal skills. For example, if you have to learn interviewing skills, your first interviews are likely to be hesitant and nervous until you gain some confidence. After some successful experience, you will no longer have to concentrate so hard as the behaviours have become more "automatic".
- we can let our skills "lapse" by failing to practise. This is the downside of the previous point. As with a motor skill such as driving a car, we can become lazy and careless – we can fall into "bad habits".

One influential and more recent development of this approach comes from Owen Hargie (2022). While endorsing Argyle's main ideas, he developed a more elaborate model – see Figure 10.2. This incorporates the following important ideas:

- the social context is an important influence on our behaviour. The skills that are effective in one context may not work in another.
- we gain feedback from our own actions as well as the other person's reactions. We are continually aware of our own behaviour and feelings, and this can help us decide what to do next.

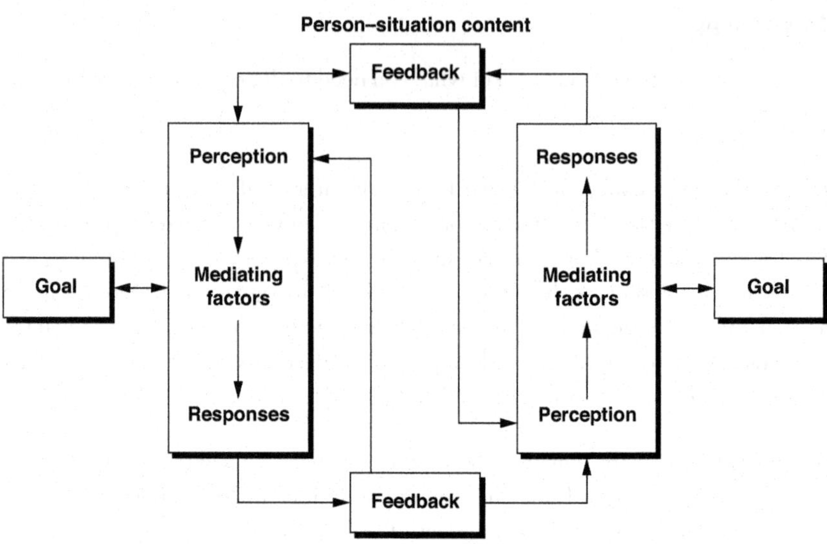

Figure 10.2 Hargie's model of social skills

- we are influenced by our emotions as well as by our thoughts, and so the term "mediating factors" is used instead of "translation".

It is important to emphasise that these authors do *not* think that social skills are just the same as motor skills. We have already highlighted some important differences – the fact that other people may have different goals, the importance of feelings – and there is another more complex problem:

Metaperception

As well as directly perceiving our own behaviour and the behaviour of others, we can also reflect on how those other people are perceiving us. This has been called "meta-perception" and is an important factor in determining how people react to one another. For example, if we are having a conversation and I get the impression that you think I am being too "chatty" then I might become more reserved to counteract this impression. If my initial impression is wrong, then I will probably confuse you or even offend you with my sudden and unexplained change in behaviour.

What are the most important interpersonal skills?

As well as developing the model described above, Owen Hargie has produced what is probably the most comprehensive textbook on interpersonal skills (the most recent edition is Hargie, 2022). This includes the following topics – the phrases in brackets below are Hargie's:

- nonverbal communication (NVC) ("communication without words").
- reinforcing ("rewarding others").
- questioning ("finding out about others").
- reflecting ("showing understanding for others").
- listening ("paying attention to others").
- explaining ("getting your message across").
- self-disclosure ("telling others about yourself").
- opening and closing ("set induction and closure").
- assertiveness ("standing up for yourself").
- persuasion ("using your influence").
- negotiating ("working things out together").
- working with others ("participating in and leading small groups").

In an earlier edition of this text, Hargie included a specific chapter on humour and laughter.

We shall summarise the essential features of some of these to illustrate the importance of this analysis and approach.

Nonverbal communication

We have already suggested some of the important features of non-verbal communication (NVC for short) in Chapter 3 of this book, notably that:

- there are a wide range of NVC signals, including facial expression, gaze, gestures, posture, bodily contact, spatial behaviour, clothes and appearance, non-verbal vocalisations (paralanguage), and smell.
- we usually react to the combination of these signals. For example, we may decide that someone is lying to use because they fidget, *and* avoid eye contact, *and* hesitate when they talk etc.
- these signals are ambiguous. For example, the indicators of someone lying are very close to the signals of nerves and anxiety. This problem of ambiguity is very important if you are considering adopting particular NVC strategies.
- there are significant cultural differences in the meaning of nonverbal signals.
- when verbal and nonverbal signals seem to contradict each other, we are usually more inclined to believe the nonverbal "message".

Bearing these points in mind, we can suggest some recommendations for the skilled use of NVC in workplace situations:

Use a combination of signals to show what you mean

For example, some texts suggest that managers should be very careful to choose the right seating position when they want to have a discussion with one of their staff. The usual recommendation is to avoid the direct frontal position as this implies confrontation and to talk “at an angle” – across the corner of the desk rather than directly facing the other person across the desk. This will help to establish an atmosphere, but other cues are also important. To achieve cooperation, you also need to use appropriate eye contact and gestures. Just sitting at the “correct” angle will not help the manager who continues to belittle his staff verbally and nonverbally in other ways, perhaps by constantly interrupting them! These other signals will create the lasting impression in the staff.

Make sure that your verbal and nonverbal messages are "in harmony"

The boss who tells you he is listening to you while looking at his smartphone will not be believed!

Make sure your NVC is appropriate to the culture and the context

The English manager who uses his “native” pattern of eye gaze when dealing with Arabian colleagues may well be seen as “shifty-eyed” and perhaps untrustworthy because he does not engage in sufficient eye contact.

Avoid NVC which has a popular interpretation which you do not want

Many popular books on NVC claim that particular signals definitely pass on a specific message. Even if this is not always true, what if the other person believes that it is? Will they read a specific message from the way you cross your arms?

Develop your awareness of your own NVC and its likely impact

Perhaps the most important way of developing your NVC skills is through awareness of your own behaviour. Does your NVC always reflect what you want it to mean? You can only develop this awareness by reflecting on your own behaviour and by getting feedback from others who are prepared to give you an honest response. If you decide to change your behaviour, then you also need to monitor the effect of change. You need to behave in a way which comes across as “natural” for you rather than relying on “textbook techniques”.

Look out for micro-expressions

We introduced the concept of micro-expressions in Chapter 2 – very fleeting nonverbal expressions which are supposed to reveal the true emotional state. As we suggested earlier, there is some still some doubt about this, but they can offer an additional clue to someone's feelings. And you should look out for any impressions you may be creating along these lines.

BOX 10.1: THE CASE FOR "DIGITAL BODY LANGUAGE"?

In her consultancy work with clients, helping them to collaborate more effectively at work, Erica Dhawan noticed increasing concerns with "miscommunication in the workplace". This stemmed from misunderstandings because the participants:

> *didn't know what empathy meant anymore in a world where digital communication had made once-clear signals, cues, and norms almost unintelligible.*

She concluded that "the digital world required a new kind of body language" and developed the following "four laws" as the practical steps to avoid future problems (Dhawan, 2021).

- "value visibly".
- "communicate carefully".
- "collaborate confidently".
- "trust totally".

These "laws" suggest a mix of behaviours and approaches which should ensure that online interactions are as "rich" in social cues as their face-to-face equivalent.

Reinforcing

When you use reinforcing behaviours, you use behaviours which encourage the other person to carry on or repeat whatever they happen to be doing. Various experiments have shown how people respond to quite small expressions of praise, encouragement, and support, including head nods, grunts and the "uh-huh". For a quick demonstration of the power of these simple cues, ask a friend to listen to you talking for a couple of minutes without showing any signs of support or agreement. First of all, they may find it very difficult if not impossible to do. Secondly, you will find it very disconcerting to speak what is effectively a "blank wall". And this brings us on to the importance of listening, which we talk about later.

Questioning

If you have attended a series of job interviews, you will know that some professional interviewers are much better than others at extracting information from you. This will be due in part to their question technique – whether they are asking the right sort of question at the right time. For example, texts on interviewing technique usually distinguish between open and closed questions.

An open question allows the person to answer in whatever way they like, e.g. what do you think of the government's economic policy? A closed question asks for specific information or a yes/no response, e.g. do you agree with the government's economic policy? Open questions encourage people to talk and expand; closed questions encourage short answers. Inexperienced interviewers often ask too many closed questions and do not get the detailed answers which they really want. We say more on this in the next chapter.

Reflecting

This is a skill often used by counsellors and other people who have to conduct very personal interviews and who want the other person to talk in some detail about their own feelings and attitudes. Even the most open-ended questions can sometimes suggest the way that the other person should construct their answer. Reflections are more neutral – they feedback to the speaker some aspect of what they have just said. This invites them to elaborate or extend what they have been saying.

You can reflect in different ways and achieve different results. This will depend on whether you are interested in the factual statements that the other person has made or their feelings about what they are saying. Textbooks often distinguish at least three different forms of reflection:

- identifying a keyword or phrase which will encourage the speaker to say more.
- summarising what you have heard in your own words.
- identifying the feelings which seem to lie behind what the speaker is saying.

This last form of reflection is perhaps the most difficult and most skilful – you have to sense the underlying emotion accurately and read between the lines.

However, these different strategies focus on rather different aspects of the other person's communication – the first two relate to concentrate on what has been said; the third concentrates on how it was said, trying to interpret the non-verbal accompaniment.

Listening

It is worth emphasising the importance of listening as it is often taken for granted. Perhaps because we do it so much, it can be dismissed as a "natural" behaviour

which we have all learned. But educators concerned with the development of interpersonal skills usually give it central importance:

Developing your skills as a listener involves two major steps:

- recognising (and eliminating) any barriers which prevent you listening with full attention.
- adopting and practising behaviours which help you listen (and which convince the other person that you are giving them your full attention).

Examples of important common barriers include being distracted by personal stereotypes or other perceptual biases, such as listening selectively for what you expect to hear.

Detailed analysis of the skills which are used by people who are recognised as "good listeners" shows that they use a variety of techniques. For example, Bolton (1986) found three clusters of skills:

- attending skills, where you show the other person that you are attending to them. NVC can be especially important here.
- following skills, where the listener uses technique which encourage the speaker to give a full account of what they want to say. Reinforcing behaviour can be very important here, or what Bolton calls "minimal prompts" like "mmm", "uh-uh", "yes", "and", etc.
- reflecting skills, which we talk about in more detail below.

So, typical recommendations to support active or positive listening include (Hartley, 1999):

- being receptive to the other person – showing that you are prepared to listen and accept what they are saying (of course, this does not mean that you automatically agree with it). Nonverbal signals are obviously important here and you need to avoid any signs of tension or impatience.
- maintaining attention – using eye contact, head nods, and appropriate facial expression.
- removing distractions.
- delaying evaluation of what you have heard until you fully understand it.

As well as reviewing the research evidence on this topic (e.g. Hargie, 2022, Chapter 7), it is useful to read accounts of from professionals whose effectiveness depends on their skills. For example, Kathryn Mannix's medical career has focused on working with people with incurable, advanced illnesses. She offers suggestions on "style and skills (which) can be used when the occasion for conversations is particularly challenging" and talks of "tender conversations" (Mannix, 2021, page 4).

Perhaps her most important message is her focus on fundamental principles which we need to apply in our own style, as in:

> *To offer somebody help or support, we must start from where the person is, and understand the situation from their perspective. That sounds so simple, and yet it can be difficult to do.*
>
> (Mannix, 2021, page 15)

Opening and closing

This refers to the ways in which we establish the beginnings and endings of a particular interaction. For example, sales staff often receive very detailed training on how to start the interaction with the customer. Often this involves making conversation to establish the sales representative as more friendly and helpful than "just a salesperson". But this can rebound if the customer sees this as insincere.

Consider all the different possible ways of starting a conversation with someone – some ways will be much more appropriate than others in particular circumstances.

The choice of opening can be very important in more formal situations such as an interview where the opening can establish either a positive or negative atmosphere and we shall give some examples in the next chapter.

Self-disclosure

When you communicate with other people you can tell them various things about yourself (or you can decide not to). Sidney Jourard coined the term "self-disclosure" – the process of sharing information about ourselves with other people (Jourard, 1971). When you self-disclose, you provide some information to the other person about yourself: how you are feeling; what your background is; what your attitudes and values are, and so on. Jourard was interested in how people came to reveal aspects of themselves to others and what this meant for the way that they developed relationships with others.

Self-disclosure and relationships

You need to self-disclose to develop a relationship with another person. And this raises several practical issues:

- what do you tell them? What sort of information do you pass on? When is it "safe" to reveal your personal feelings?
- how quickly do you reveal yourself? There are important social and cultural differences here. For example, in the USA, you are often expected to say a lot about yourself very early in a relationship. In the UK, a more leisurely pace is the norm.

In business, we have to develop good relationships with other people in the organisation. And so self-disclosure is an important issue. How far can we (or should we) keep these relationships on a strictly formal basis and not self-disclose? If you develop a very close and open relationship with a group of staff and are then promoted to be their supervisor, can you maintain the relationship at the same level?

Assertiveness

Over the last five decades, assertiveness training has been one of the most popular ways of developing social skills. As well as training courses and workshops, many popular books on business communication use assertiveness principles even if they do not use the term. And some of these have endorsed it very strongly, even claiming it can "change your life" (See Hartley, 1999, Chapter 12).

What do we mean by assertive communication?

The following quotes summarise essential points:

> *The aim of assertive behaviour is to satisfy the needs and wants of both parties involved in the situation.*
>
> (Back and Back, 2005, page 2)

Anne Dickson wrote one of the classic texts on assertiveness 40 years ago. She describes her updated version as follows:

> *the single unifying focus of every chapter of this book is: how to communicate effectively without the use of aggression.*
>
> (Dickson, 2022, page xi)

Following on from this, she suggests that:

> *Assertive communication is counter-cultural: it is not what we witness as the normal form of direct communication, which tends to be aggressive and competitive with a focus on one individual being right and the other wrong. The values at the heart of the assertive skills I teach are equality, care and honesty.*
>
> (Dickson, op cit, page xii)

What are the different styles of behaviour?

Books on assertive behaviour usually define three styles of behaviour: assertion, aggression, and submission (or non-assertion). These are often expressed as a continuum with assertion in the middle.

Aggression --------------- Assertion ------------- Submission

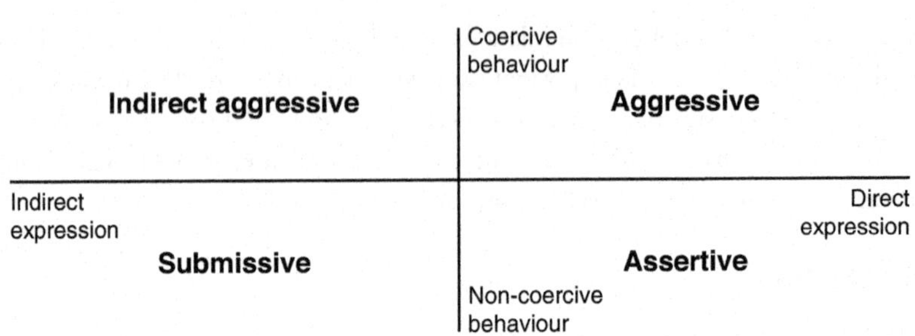

Figure 10.3 Styles of behaviour Source: Hartley, 1999, p. 196

But a better way of comparing styles of behaviour is to look out the two underlying dimensions:

- from indirect expression through to direct expression.
- from coercive behaviour through to non-coercive behaviour.

This gives Figure 10.3 above. The fourth style is where you express aggression in an indirect way without direct confrontation. For another useful discussion of this approach, see Hargie (2022) pages 332ff.

Most texts concentrate on the three main styles, and so will we in this chapter (descriptions taken from Hartley, 1999).

Aggressive behaviour

This includes some form of threat which undermines the rights of the other person. It is about winning, regardless of the other person's feelings. The verbal and non-verbal accompaniment to aggressive behaviour includes loud and abusive talk, interruptions, and glaring or staring eye contact.

Submissive behaviour

This behaviour gives in to the demands of others by avoiding conflict and accepting being put upon. Verbal and nonverbal accompaniments include apologetic and hesitant speech, soft speech, nervous gestures, and a reluctance to express opinions. Submissive individuals will be seen as weak and easily manipulated. They will certainly not inspire confidence in others.

The verbal and nonverbal behaviours associated with these styles have been demonstrated quite clearly in research studies as well as from observation of everyday life.

Assertive behaviour

The characteristics are open and clear expression, firm and fluent conversation, and quick spontaneous answers. The nonverbal components include medium levels of eye contact; appropriate facial expressions; smooth gestures; relaxed but upright body posture; and appropriate paralinguistics.

Using assertive behaviour

There are various ways of categorising assertive behaviour. For example, Ken and Kate Back define six main types of assertive behaviour which can be divided into two levels, and this is summarised in Box 10.2. The practical implications of this are that you should normally start by using a low-level assertion. If this is not successful, then you try a high-level assertion. Other texts concentrate on what they regard as the main assertive techniques. To illustrate the approach, we can quote a typical example from Linehan and Egan (1983). They offer the "broken record" technique as a way of resisting influence. This technique simply involves repeating your initial request or response, without being side-tracked, until the other person accepts it.

BOX 10.2: DIFFERENT TYPES OF ASSERTIVE BEHAVIOUR

Ken and Kate Back define six main types of assertive behaviour which can be divided into two levels, listed below (Back and Back, 2005, Chapter 7). The practical implications of this are that you should normally start by using a low-level assertion. If this is not successful, then you try a high-level assertion. The three types at the lower level are:

- basic assertion (a straightforward statement of what you need, want, believe, or feel).
- responsive assertion (where you check what the other person needs or is feeling, by asking them in a straightforward way).
- empathetic assertion (where you make a point of recognising the other person's point of view or feelings, before you state what you want).

The three high-level types are:

- discrepancy assertion (where you point out the discrepancy between what you have agreed previously on what seems to be happening or is about to happen).
- negative feelings assertion (where you point out the effect that the other person's behaviour is having upon you).
- consequence (the strongest form of assertion – where you tell the other person what will happen to them if they do not change their behaviour.)

They suggest that you should "*use the minimum degree of assertion for achieving your aim*" (page 91, their emphasis). If you do not then you may be seen as aggressive, and you will have fewer options if the other person does not wish to co-operate.

Does assertiveness always work?

Most texts on assertiveness emphasise the possible benefits of this style of behaviour. But there are also potential problems:

- assertive behaviour may be "misread".
  It may be *seen* as aggressive, especially when the person is behaving differently from the way they have acted in the past.
- people have different definitions of assertiveness.
  For example, untrained women stress the importance of consideration for others, whereas untrained men seem to see assertiveness in terms of power and influence.
- there are issues of gender roles.
  Male assertion and female assertion can have different consequences and so reliance on the same techniques may actually work out differently.
- there are situational factors to consider.
  Certain types of assertiveness may well work better in some situations than others.
- there are cultural differences to consider.
  Behaviour which is culturally acceptable in the USA and Western Europe may not be accepted in cultures which place very different values upon humility and submission.

One final issue comes from work by Daniel Ames (2009) whose studies suggest that both under-assertiveness and over-assertiveness contribute to ineffective leadership and/or management. He found that under-assertive leadership leads to "failure to deliver on task objectives" whereas over-assertive leaders are:

> *jeopardising their relationships with others. Getting assertiveness 'right' appears to be a prevalent challenge for leaders.*
>
> (op cit, page 129)

Popular theories to improve your communication

Specific theories of interpersonal communication which are often used on training courses may not feature in mainstream social science texts. They may have achieved wide popular acceptance but have often been dismissed and/or neglected by professional and academic social scientists. To illustrate why this may have happened, we can use one main idea from Neurolinguistic Programming (NLP) – and highlight some important issues. There is more detail on this on the website.

Neurolinguistic Programming (NLP)

You can find NLP ideas in several popular management and communication texts, as well as being widely used in training. A typical claim from NLP trainers is that you only need three things to communicate well:

- a clear idea of the outcome you want.
- flexible behaviour.
  You need to find the behaviour which will work in the specific situation.
- the ability to recognise the responses you are getting from other people.
  If you can do this, then you will be able to "home in" on the behaviour which achieves the response you want from the other person.
  They also emphasise the importance of nonverbal communication.

Representational systems

One fundamental idea from NLP is that we think using three main representational systems:

- visual, where you see visual images as you think.
- auditory, where you hear sounds inside your head.
- kinaesthetic, where you think in terms of feelings.

According to this theory, you can increase rapport with someone by "getting to know the thinking preference of the person you are communicating with and changing your behaviour to literally make more sense to them" (Bandler and Grinder, page 88). For example, if you are talking to a visual person then you should use language which corresponds with that representational system. You should say things like "I see what you mean" or "that looks fine to me". By using this technique, "*sometimes almost miraculously*, rapport increases as you share their experience" (Adler and Heather, 1999, page 62, our italics).

For this to work, you have to be confident which representation system the other person is using. And that leads to another important idea – that there are reliable ways to recognise somebody's representational system.

The snag with this analysis is that it has not been supported by systematic research.

For example, you can find many critical accounts of NLP listed on the Wikipedia page.

Can we believe this (and any other) popular theory?

NLP contains some interesting propositions and ideas. But we suggest that you approach it (and other popular systems you may come across) with some scepticism. We have important concerns about NLP and similar approaches:

- it has suffered by being over-simplified and applied too "mechanically".
- it has been "over-sold". We believe some of the claims for their success are exaggerated.
- probably because of the "over-selling", it has not attracted the interest of independent researchers. As a result, there is little independent evidence to show that it really works over a wide range of circumstances.
- it seems to ignore cultural differences. And this is a general issue for all skills approaches (see Box 10.3 below).

So, one way of looking at any popular analysis of human communication is to ask questions based on these concerns:

- what are the ideas based upon?
  (do they come from well-organised studies or from systematic observation or what?)
- are the ideas critically examined?
  (what are the recognised limitations to the ideas?)
- are they applied in a way which recognises the specific social context?
  (is any account taken of social and cultural differences?)
- who are the gurus or advocates?
  (and what is their expertise based upon in terms of experience, training etc.?)

BOX 10.3 ATTENDING TO CULTURE

So much of the research into interpersonal communication (and so many of the advice texts) is based on American and European examples that it is easy to forget the potential complications of cross-cultural communication. For example:

- patterns of self-disclosure and relationship development are very different in cultures with strong politeness norms and where the saving of face is critical, like Malaysia.
- NVC has strong cultural variations.
- assertive behaviour is seen very differently in cultures which do not share the individualistic values of the US and UK.

The role of new technology in interpersonal communication

We now live in the age of "perpetual contact" thanks to the ubiquity of smartphones and social media. There are three aspects of this which are especially important to this chapter. We can:

- enhance our relationships with others by careful use of social media.
- use these media to gain initial impressions of others.
- check our own public face through these media and try to limit any misleading messages.

We shall explore these issues in more detail in the next chapter.

Becoming "mindwise" and putting the skills together

Earlier in this chapter, we argued that social skills depend upon social understanding. You need to *understand* how and why people are behaving as they do in order to select the appropriate way to behave. We are very suspicious of communication skills training which does not emphasise the need for social understanding and research to accompany the practice of techniques. We are not alone in this concern – Deborah Cameron surveyed a range of communication skills courses and training materials and found "consistent disregard for those bodies of knowledge that derive from the empirical investigation of naturally occurring talk" (Cameron, 2000, page 51).

We need to become "mindwise" (Epley, 2014) and recognise that the major barriers to understanding other people include our own often misplaced confidence in our abilities to understand the way that we come across to other people and to interpret their behaviours and feelings, what Epley calls the "illusion of insight" (op cit, page 11). For example, think of your current partner and/or a close friend and give yourself a percentage rating on the following questions, where 100% means "completely" and 0% means not at all?

a) how high is your partner's sense of self-worth (self-esteem)?
b) how confident are you in this judgement?

Following the typical pattern of research on this topic, we would expect you to be reasonably (but *not* perfectly) accurate on Question (a) and to be significantly over-confident on Question (b). Your degree of confidence in your judgement is likely to be up to twice as strong as your actual accuracy and this does not depend on the length of time you have known the other person. If anything, we seem to become more confident but not more accurate in our judgements over time. And the same pattern of results appears when you ask people to make judgments about others' verbal and nonverbal behaviour.

Epley describes a number of cognitive and social processes which explain these results. Particularly important for this book is his analysis of how we interpret others behaviour and three important traps we can fall into:

Projecting from our own mind

We tend to be too self-centred in our social judgments and that can include overestimating our own contributions to a group effort and feeling more self-conscious about our own behaviour than is warranted (often called the spotlight effect). We assume that other people interpret the world in much the same way as we do and so we can seriously underestimate the degree of ambiguity in certain messages.

Basing our judgements on stereotypes

If we rely on a stereotype when making judgement about others (e.g., age, gender) then we can be misled. For example, Epley refers to the common stereotype that "women are more emotional than men" (op cit, page 125). Physiological studies of reactions to emotional scenes demonstrate that men and women have much the same emotional reaction, but social and cultural factors come into play when we look at how men and women express (or do not express) their reactions. So, we will be misled if we rely on a stereotype which does not distinguish between feeling (the invisible internal reaction) and expressing feeling (the outward behaviour which is influenced by a range of social and cultural factors).

Inferring someone's intentions just from the way they act

Attribution theory tells us that we are likely to be more sensitive to contextual influences when we try to explain our own behaviour than when we try to explain others – "I failed the test because the environment was so hot and uncomfortable; he failed it because he is not very bright".

So, we cannot just rely on skills

As a result, Epley suggest that we cannot and should not expect to fully understand others by relying just on our own "skills". Our observations and interpretations of others' body language may be limited or misleading and we may have real problems in trying to put ourselves in their position (what he calls perspective-taking which has been a key component of many self-help books on communication since the classic text by Dale Carnegie – Principle 8 of *How to Win Friends and Influence People*).

Epley describes several studies where conscious attempts at perspective-taking, e.g., in negotiation, made things worse as it led to people acting on inaccurate conclusions. Being "mindwise" is about "Knowing the shortcomings of your social sense" which will then "push you to be more open in sharing what's in your own mind with others, but also more open to listening to others" (op cit, page 187).

One practical way of thinking about this is to approach face-to-face communication as a process with a series of stages in a way that allows a genuine exchange of perspectives, as in Table 10.1.

The table emphasises the planning and preparation which you can undertake before an important face-to-face communication. At first sight this might seem a very deliberate or perhaps even a manipulative approach to human relationships. But we are not advocating that you lose all spontaneity and plan *every* encounter in minute detail. The following points were made by Peter Honey many years ago and are still relevant:

- "on many occasions we need consciously to *organise* our behaviour".
- "one of the hallmarks of an interactively skilled person is that they frequently declare their objectives openly and explicitly".
- "if you have got objectives, your behaviour should be in step with them" (Honey, 1988, page 18ff).

Honey was very critical of people whose behaviour is "out of step" with their declared objectives, such as the manager who invites staff to contribute ideas and suggestions and then seems to relish pointing out the defects of every idea but his own. He also commented that planning is not just something we do before an event or activity:

> *On-going planning requires us to size up the situation as we are in it*
>
> (Honey, 1988, page 22)

This point highlights a potential criticism of our approach which implies that we walk into a situation with a single predetermined plan and then simply try to achieve it. Taking the situation described in Table 10.1, what would you do if you received a very negative reaction from X when you asked for help/advice? Suppose X's response was "I'm surprised you don't know that. Aren't you properly qualified for this job?" You need to respond to this not very subtle attack before you can proceed toward your objective. What do you say?

You could respond in a way which allows X to reinforce their negative image of you. For example, if you responded by asserting how well-qualified you were then this could allow X to say "well, you're so well-qualified that you obviously don't need my help". You have just made the relationship worse – X is even more

Table 10.1 Interpersonal communication as a staged process

Stage	Content	Points to watch	Example
Decide the general goal	What do you want to achieve overall?		You are a new member of the organisation and have been sent to join a new project team. One of the older members of the team seems to be deliberately uncooperative with you. You want to develop a better relationship with this colleague.
Consider the context	What's happened in the past? Who are the participants? What is the setting? Are there any hidden agendas because of the history? What do your audience need or expect to happen?	What do you know about the history of this group and about X. Suppose you find out from other members that X is generally suspicious of 'new, young, know-it-all's who want to come in and take over.' So, is this the pattern of behaviour which X is expecting of you? If so, how can you modify this stereotype?	
Plan	Decide on the objectives Decide on the structure	Make your objectives realistic and achievable. Make sure your structure leads up to your objective	Your objective is to show X that you value and respect his opinion. You find something which X is very familiar with and you are not: perhaps some aspect of the history of the project or some complex company procedure which is new to you. You plan to ask their help by asking them to explain it.

Act	Use the relevant skills	What are the most important skills in this situation? e.g. listening, questioning etc. How do you make contact with X? Do you drop in on them or attempt to set up a meeting? What message do you send to X to start the conversation? Do you make contact online? Would an email or a text be appropriate?	You need to choose the right moment so that X feels that the request is genuine, and you need to make sure that you listen carefully and don't say anything which X could interpret as criticism.
Follow-up	What can you do to make sure your communication has been effective?	What can you do to reinforce what you have achieved?	Have you followed up the request so that you can check how X has responded? If X's response is positive, how can you build on that to create a better long-lasting relationship? If X's response is negative, is there anything else you can do to create a better long-lasting relationship?

convinced that you are the "know-it-all" who is just trying to show off your superiority.

So, the key to effective interpersonal communication is the flexibility to respond to the other person in order to maintain the original objective. Perhaps asking X for advice is too indirect an approach. Should you adopt a more direct approach and explain how you see the problem to X: "I feel that we've not managed to sort out how we work together, and I'd like to talk about it". Would this achieve the first step?

We cannot provide a definitive answer to this example because so much depends on the context. What is X feels that all is well, and you have misinterpreted his NVC? In this case, a very direct approach might make X feel defensive. And this reflects one of the most important points in this chapter – communicating effectively with other people is *not* just applying special techniques or behaviours which "always work". A fundamental issue is how we perceive the other person and recognise their needs – and this is also an important theme of the next chapter.

SUMMARY OF KEY POINTS

- the process of interpersonal communication can be complex – unless you understand some basic features of this process, you can easily behave in ways which the other person does not accept or appreciate.
- you can analyse social interaction as skilled behaviour – it has many of the characteristics of other skills, including the importance of goals and feedback. But it is also important to emphasise that social skills are not just the same as motor skills. There are important differences, including the fact that other people may have different goals, and the importance of personal feelings.
- there are several important interpersonal skills, including nonverbal communication (NVC), listening, self-disclosure, and assertiveness.
- many authors stress the advantages of assertiveness without highlighting potential problems. For example, assertive behaviour may be *seen* as aggressive; there are issues of gender roles; and there are important cultural differences to consider.
- there are several "popular" models of effective communication which are virtually ignored by social science researchers but are often used in business and management training. We commented briefly on Neurolinguistic Programming. It does offer some interesting ideas, but we also raise some important concerns. For example, it has been over-simplified and applied too "mechanically", and often seems to ignore cultural differences.

- major barriers to understanding other people include our own often misplaced confidence in our abilities to understand the way we come across other people and to interpret their behaviour and feelings. We need to engage with others in ways that allow a genuine exchange of perspectives.
- you can approach face-to-face communication as a process with a series of stages, from deciding the goal through planning and on to action. But this must be seen flexibly – effective communication must be based on flexible behaviour which is appropriate to the specific context.

References

Adler, H. and Heather, N. (1999) *NLP in 21 Days: A Complete Introduction and Training Programme.* London: Piatkus.

Ames, D.R. (2009) Pushing up to a point: Assertiveness and effectiveness in leadership and interpersonal dynamics. In Brief, A. and Staw, B. (eds) *Research in Organizational Behavior*, Vol. 29, 111–133.

Argyle, M. (1994) *The Psychology of Interpersonal Behaviour*, 5th edition. Harmondsworth: Penguin.

Back, K. and Back, K. (2005) *Assertiveness at Work: A Practical Guide to Handling Awkward Situations.* London: McGraw-Hill.

Bolton, R. (1986) *People Skills: How to Research Yourself, Listen to Others, and Resolve Conflicts.* Sydney: Prentice Hall.

Cameron, D. (2000) *Good to Talk.* London: Sage.

Dhawan, E. (2021) *Digital Body Language: How to Build Trust and Connection No Matter the Distance.* London: HarperCollins.

Dickson, A. (2022) *A Woman in Your Own Right: The Art of Assertive, Clear and Honest Communication*, 2nd edition. Richmond: Duckworth.

Epley, N. (2014) *Mindwise: How We Understand What Others Think, Believe, Feel and Want.* London: Allen Lane.

Goleman, D. (1996) *Emotional Intelligence.* London: Bloomsbury.

Hargie, O. (2022) *Skilled Interpersonal Communication*, 5th edition. London: Routledge.

Hartley, P. (1999) *Interpersonal Communication.* 2nd edition. London Routledge.

Honey, P. (1988) *Face to Face: A practical guide to interactive skills.* 2nd edition. Aldershot: Ashgate.

Jourards, S. (1971) *The Transparent Self*, revised edition. New York: Van Nostrand Reinhold.

Linehan, M. and Egan, K. (1983) *Asserting Yourself.* London: Century.

Mannix, K. (2021) *Listen: How to Find the Words for Tender Conversations.* London: HarperCollins.

Symonds Research. (2022) *Challenges and Solutions for Successfully Managing Virtual Teams in the Workplace or When Teaching Online.* https://symondsresearch.com/challenges-virtual-teams/.

CHAPTER 11

How do interpersonal skills work in practice?

Introduction

The previous chapter emphasised that effective communication depends on personal awareness, interpersonal skills, and the context in which people operate. We also argued that all these factors are open to interpretation – your view of the context may not be the same as mine. If that is the case, then we have the opportunity for serious misunderstanding.

If we have an inaccurate perception of ourselves or of the other person, then we may apply the wrong approach or techniques. In all practical situations, we need to establish a dialogue which allows the participants to understand each other.

This chapter applies these ideas to common face-to-face situations of two very different types:

- the more casual, unscheduled, or informal interactions and exchanges of information which go on all the time – conversations and discussions in the office, shopfloor, or service area, or online outside the scheduled formal meetings.
- the more formal interactions which are often subject to company rules, regulations, and procedures, such as interviews. The last few years have seen enormous change here. Organisations had to adjust when everything moved online during the pandemic; some have made significant changes to their practice as a result.

In all these situations, we can look at how the participants are working together (or not!) to achieve some understanding which will have an impact on the effectiveness of the organisation. As well as highlighting specific skills which we described in the last chapter, we need to examine the way that participants understand or make sense of the events which unfold, and this is a main theme of the case study which starts the chapter.

DOI: 10.4324/9781003297550-15

OBJECTIVES

This chapter will:

- apply principles developed in Chapter 10 to common face-to-face situations in organisations.
- analyse a case study which shows how misunderstanding, and "miscommunication" can quickly and easily develop through conversations and discussion in the organisation unless the participants take deliberate steps to avoid this.
- use the examples of selection and appraisal interviews to illustrate how communication influences the outcomes of interactions.

Conversations in the office – the case of the missing service engineer

The following case study is based on real events which we and colleagues have experienced over the years, suitably anonymised to protect the guilty!

The situation

As General Manager of ABC Computer Services. Kai Brown receives an urgent text from XYZ, an important customer in Durban, who has a "major fault in their computer system" and demands an immediate visit from a service engineer immediately. Kai tries to contact Sam Smith, Service Manager, at once but finds they are out visiting PRQ Engineering, another important customer. PRQ are based in a remote location where mobile reception is unreliable and Kai cannot immediately contact Sam.

Deciding that the Durban problem is urgent, Kai goes to the service department and finds engineer, Chris Anker. They have the following conversation:

KB: "Have you any really urgent work on hand?"
CA: "Well, I'm sorting out a few updates for the new system we've sent to PRQ. Sam Smith is expecting me to have them done by tomorrow".
KB: "But is it really urgent?"
CA: "Well, I don't know...I don't suppose so".
KB: "Good – you can sort out the Durban problem first".

Kai suggests that Chris should fly to Durban on an afternoon flight and start work at XYZ first thing next morning. Chris has to leave the office immediately but continues the conversation before leaving.

CA: "I had better leave a message for Sam Smith".
KB: "Don't worry, I will let Sam know what is happening so we can re-schedule your work for the next few days!"

Kai returns to their office and phones XYZ to confirm that Chris Anker will be there first thing in the morning. Kai then calls Alex Botham, their personal assistant, leaves several messages and instructions, answers some queries, and ends the call as follows.

KB: "Oh, by the way, let Sam Smith know that Chris Anker will probably be in Durban for a few days working on XYZ's computer problems!"

Sam Smith returns just after 2 pm and finds that Chris Anker is not in the office. Knowing from his e-calendar that Chris is scheduled to be in the office for the rest of the day, Sam sends an email, instructing Chris to drop everything and go to clear up an urgent problem at PRQ engineering first thing in the morning.

Sam then leaves the office at 3.30 pm to meet another customer. Sam does not return that day and goes home to work on a technical report, turning off their smartphone to avoid interruptions.

After working through the other jobs from Kai by around 3.45 pm, Alex Botham sends an email to Sam Smith, saying that Chris Anker will probably be in Durban for a few days on the XYZ job.

The next day

Sam Smith arrives in the office at 8 am, notes that Chris Anker is not there, and assumes that Chris has gone to PRQ Engineering. Sam has an urgent technical report to finish so does not check email (Sam usually does this first thing).

About 9.30 am, Sam receives an irate phone call from PRQ Engineering – the promised service engineer has not arrived, so they are threatening to cancel the lucrative service contract.

At first, no one else in the office knows anything about Chris Anker's whereabouts. As a last resort, Sam checks email to find the message from Alex Botham: "Kai has asked me to let you know that Chris Anker will probably be in Durban at XYZ for a few days". Sam is both puzzled and annoyed by the brief message.

About five minutes later, Sam Smith storms into Kai Brown's office and says:

"How do you expect me to run an efficient service department, when you send my staff around the country without letting me know? We will probably lose the PRQ Engineering contract because Chris Anker did not report there this morning as I promised".

What do you think of communication at ABC?

Before reading on, consider the following questions:

- what are the most important problems of interpersonal communication illustrated in this case study?
- what are the key factors (both process and meaning) which have created these problems?
- who was responsible for the problems?
- how could the participants have behaved differently to avoid these problems? (both short-term and long-term.)
- does this case study simply illustrate poor interpersonal communication? Or do you recognise any broader issues?

Our analysis

There are many ways to analyse this incident – we focus on the interpersonal issues. But perhaps there are broader problems in the organisation and this conflict is simply a symptom. For example, we have not mentioned the physical surroundings – researchers have suggested that this can have important influences, as we suggest in Box 11.1.

We have also not provided any information on the social identities of the characters in our scenario. For example, you might like to guess the gender of each character – what were the images you created in your imagination as you read the case? We return to this issue later.

Moving back to the interpersonal difficulties, we have picked out the following problems. Each one suggests that the participants are not paying much attention to the impact of their communication – they could do with some urgent training in listening, NVC etc. For each problem, we also suggest an important practical principle which has been ignored:

The request from Kai Brown

Consider the way Kai communicates to Chris Anker. If your boss asks you "Have you any really urgent work on hand?", this implies that a request is about to follow which *is really* urgent. How is Chris supposed to respond? What does "really urgent" actually mean? Why did Kai not start on a more neutral note and ask what jobs Chris was undertaking?

And the principle: other people will always try to interpret the *intention* behind what you are saying. This can be a particular problem when status differences are involved.

Kai's reassuring message to Chris

When Chris says, "I'd better leave a message for Sam Smith", Kai says "Don't worry, I will let Sam know what is happening". Kai does not do this in a way which guarantees the communication happens – leaving a message for Sam but making no real attempt to ensure either that Sam has received it – or that the full urgency of the situation is explained.

And the principle: if you give a commitment and a reassuring message, you should always make sure that you act on it in the way that you have implied.

Kai's message to Sam

Kai does not contact Sam directly but leaves it to Alex Botham. But note the way Kai does this: "Oh, by the way, let Sam Smith know that Chris Anker will probably be in Durban for a few days working on XYZ's computer problems!" There are several hints in this sentence that the message is not very important – "by the way" and "probably". Alex gives it low priority and leaves it till later.

And the principle: if you delegate a job then you need to *explicitly* communicate its urgency or priority. Otherwise, the other person will assume the priority from the way you pass it on. In this case, the casual way the message was expressed signalled "low priority".

Sam's attempt to contact Chris

Finding no one in the office, Sam emails Chris to "drop everything" – if the demand is so urgent, is an email sufficient to explain what needs to happen? Surely not. Sam makes no further attempt to check that the message has been received and understood.

And the principle: always try to receive feedback on messages you send, especially if they are important or urgent.

Sam's confrontation with Kai

Imagine you are Kai.

How would you respond to Sam's opening comment: "How do you expect me to run an efficient service department, when you send my staff round the country without letting me know?"

This immediately puts Kai on the defensive, both in the tone and the specific accusation – it is aggressive rather than assertive. Kai will almost certainly respond to the accusation and the conversation will turn to argument over who told what to whom, rather than resolving the immediate crisis.

Your perception might have been influenced by the way we said Sam "storms in" – if we had simply said "Sam arrives at..." then this frames the interaction very differently.

And the principle: the way that you open a conversation establishes the tone and the agenda. If you "say" you want a fight, do not be surprised if you get one.

Resolving the issues

As with so many problems in organisational communication, this crisis could have been avoided if the participants had communicated more carefully. And everyone contributed to the crisis. Even Alex who simply passed on the message can be criticised – failing to establish whether the message was important or urgent.

The most significant outcome in our case study is the conflict which has now emerged between Kai and Sam. Of course, we have not explored their history – this may be one symptom of a long-standing personal dispute – Kai does not make a very serious attempt to consult Sam. Or it may be a symptom of confused or sloppy management style.

If we assume that there is no personal animosity between them, what could Sam have said? He could have presented the *problem* to Kai:

> *"We have a crisis – we both assigned Chris Anker to urgent jobs with different customers. We may lose an important customer if we do not respond promptly".*

This form of expression sets out the problem, assumes joint responsibility, does not assign blame, and suggests what needs to happen – it is *assertive* rather than aggressive. Deciding what went wrong, and how it should be resolved long-term, is best left till the crisis is over.

BOX 11.1 HOW IMPORTANT ARE THE PHYSICAL SURROUNDINGS IN THE WAYS WE COMMUNICATE?

The idea that our physical surroundings influence how we communicate persuaded many organisations to move to open plan offices. But the outcomes can be more complex. Moving to open plan *may* give more opportunities for conversations and *may* lead to *perceptions* of improved communication. But we cannot guarantee positive outcomes. In fact, the evidence points in the opposite direction – open plan offices have negative effects on both communication and staff wellbeing.

Research studies report consistent difficulties in having certain types of conversations, such as very confidential ones, in open plan spaces.

As we have discovered many times, communication cannot be determined by a simple change. What have been called "gathering places" may be more significant than the individual's workspace – places where staff typically congregate or meet during their daily routines, by vending machines, photocopiers, in canteens etc. Organisations should ensure these places are conveniently situated to encourage communication.

Another aspect of physical space which is relevant to this chapter is the way that staff can manipulate office layouts. For example, Sundstrom quotes the executive who arranged his office so visitors had to sit opposite him, and directly in the light, so it was easier to study their faces.

One common issue which runs through all these conversations is the way that the participants build up ideas about what an incident means and then translate this into action which may be counterproductive in the long term.

One every useful way of analysing this process is described by Linda Ellinor and Glenna Gerrard, building on work by Chris Argyris and Peter Senge (Ellinor and Gerrard, 1998, page 82ff). They talk about the way we interpret data, make assumptions, draw conclusions, and then act on the basis of those conclusions. Other people use a different "ladder of inference" and arrive at different conclusions from the same event. Figure 11.1 below shows the steps in the left-hand column. If you start from the bottom and work up, then you can see how two people (A and B) can arrive at very different conclusions and actions from the same starting point. The logic of Person A is taken from Ellinor and Gerrard.

	Person A	*Person B*
Take action	I won't give Sally any key tasks	I must see Sally for a counselling interview
Adopt beliefs	Good team players follow the rules and attend meetings on time	Staff who are on top of their job are able to explain problems to the team
Draw conclusions	Sally is not a good team player	Sally is under pressure at the moment
Make assumptions	Sally does not think this meeting is important	Sally must be worried about something if she didn't explain
Add meaning (personal and cultural)	Being late is not acceptable	People should explain if they cannot attend on time
Select data (personal and cultural)	Sally came to the meeting late. She didn't say why	Sally came to the meeting late. She didn't say why

Figure 11.1 The ladder of inference

Thinking about difference

What was your image of the participants in the case study? Were they all male, or all female, or a mix and who occupied which roles? For example, was the secretary male or female? Was the service engineer male or female?, etc.

Another useful question would be to consider the racial background of the actors in the story – many of the names could be considered to be white and Anglo-Saxon but Asian and Dutch names were also used within the narrative. Would this make a difference to the interactions and sense of self-image, self-esteem and, possibly, entitlement?

You probably assumed we set the location as Durban in South Africa. We did not specify this. According to https://geotargit.com, there are five places called Durban across three countries. This adds further layers of complexity – what if African surnames such as Obadan or Inyang had been used? Would other undercurrents be at play in the various interactions within the story?

As one colleague commented:

> *Having worked with an Indian/African Muslim woman in England I have seen how people make various assumptions which play out in the conversations and discussions that she has.*

In your context, there may be legislation which aims to prevent individuals from suffering from discrimination on the grounds of disability, age, sex, sexual orientation, marriage or civil partnership, religion or belief, or gender reassignment (e.g. in England this is covered by the Equality Act 2010, www.acas.ork.uk). Despite this legislation, these factors continue to make a difference in the workplace and in everyday interactions. Understanding and addressing our own conscious and unconscious biases by getting to know the people that we work with can make all the difference in terms of effective communication in the workplace.

Supportive communication

Another way of looking at conversations is to ask whether they are supportive or defensive. Several of the conversations in the case study put the other person "on the spot", as in Kai's initial request to Chris. This was manipulative and did not encourage Chris to respond openly.

Andrews and Herschel (1996) summarised developments in our ideas of supportive communication. They suggested five important characteristics which are still relevant (pages 103–106):

1. it focuses on the problem, not on the person. Contrast what Sam said to Kai in the case study above with our suggestion.

2. it is based on "congruence" where what we communicate is really based on what we think and feel. In other words, we are not trying to mask what we say – the critical comment delivered with a smile is an example of incongruent behaviour which puts the other person on the defensive.
3. it is descriptive rather than evaluative. Again, compare what Sam said to Kai with what we recommend.
4. it is "conjunctive" – in other words, it flows from what has already been discussed and does not interrupt or cut across others.
5. it "validates" individuals – in other words, it gives the impression that "whatever the difference in official organisational rank, she or he considers the other individual of equal worth as a person" (pages 105/106). Box 11.1 gives an example which shows how brief comments can have a very destructive impact.

They also suggest these principles may be especially important in communications between superiors and subordinates given some of the research which suggests that:

> *superiors believe they communicate with subordinates more effectively than they actually do.*
>
> (page 110)

Managing difficult conversations

Another useful approach comes from the Harvard Negotiation Project – *Difficult Conversations* by Stone, Patton, and Heen (2020). This proposes a common underlying structure to every difficult conversation we have to have, either at work or home. They suggest that:

> *no matter what the subject, our thoughts and feelings fall into the same three categories, or 'conversations.' And in each of these conversations we make predictable errors that distort our thoughts and feelings and get us into trouble.*
>
> (page 7)

These three categories that we have to address and hopefully resolve are:

- what happened?
  We need to agree on what actually happened which led up to the conversation.
- feelings.
  What do we do with the various feelings (often ones of anger and hurt) which we are experiencing?

- identity.
  What does this situation mean for us in terms of our self-image and self-esteem?
- managing difficult conversations: "requires learning to operate effectively in each of the three realms" (op cit, page 8).

BOX 11.2 HOW TO DESTROY A RELATIONSHIP IN ONE EASY SENTENCE

The dangers of the careless or thoughtless comment sentence is illustrated in the following example. Non-supportive communication can have a powerful and lasting impact:

> *the meeting had been quite productive, but we had got to a point where we seemed to be a bit stuck, and no way forward was emerging. I proposed a possible solution. The senior manager in the meeting immediately responded – 'you obviously have not been listening to me. That solution is not appropriate because... ' I felt quite shocked and humiliated by this retort. I had been listening very carefully indeed – we just didn't agree on the way forward. I never trusted that manager again.*

When organisations provide the script...

Many modern organisations train their employees to follow a 'script' in particular situations, e.g., in sales or telephone conversations with customers, as the following examples illustrate:

- the "have a nice day" from the restaurant as you leave.
- the "come again soon" plus "'cheery wave" which restaurant staff were forced to deliver every time.
- the designer clothes shop whose sales staff are forbidden to describe clothes as "lovely" or "nice" (among the right words are "exquisite" and "glamorous").
- the supermarket whose staff must smile and make eye contact with all customers and are graded on these behaviours as part of performance appraisal. (examples from Cameron, 2000, page 57)

The problem with all such scripts is that they assume the same behaviour means the same thing to all receivers and they assume that everyone can deliver the same script in a completely uniform way. Both these assumptions are suspect. We argue throughout this book that communication is sensitive to context and is inherently ambiguous. And skilled behaviour is flexible. In the long term, organisations who believe that "good communication" simply equals a "standard script" may find they have very disgruntled employees.

Communication and interviews

We broadly agree with the definition of an interview from Maureen Guirdham (1995):

> *In an interview, two people meet, face to face, to accomplish a known purpose by talking together. An interview is different from either a negotiation or a problem-solving meeting because it is one-sided – as the words 'interviewer' and 'interviewee' suggest.*
>
> (Guirdham, 1995, page 180)

But we do have caveats – this definition ignores the possibility that there might be more than one interviewer in some situations (e.g., the selection panel) and that the interview may be online. But it does highlight the explicit "known purpose" which is recognised by both sides and the different roles involved. She goes on to discuss the obligations that this places on the interviewers. They are in control and must not only take responsibility to achieve the purpose but also to treat the interviewee fairly and honestly. As we shall see in some later examples, interviewers sometimes ignore this last responsibility and "play games" which cannot be justified.

The purpose of the interview can also be complex. For example, the main purpose of a selection interview is to select the right person for the particular job. But this is not the only goal which the interviewers have to work towards – they must also realise that they are "representing the organisation" to candidates. Candidates will use the interviewers' behaviour and competence as information about "what the organisation is really like" and "what it might be like to work here". There is the well-known tale of the organisation which decided that the best test for managerial candidates was a series of short, aggressive, and stressful interviews. The candidate who performed best in these – staying calm, sticking to his arguments under pressure – was offered the job. He immediately refused it and walked out, commenting that "if this is how you treat your prospective employees then I do not want to work for you".

There are many different types of interviews with different purposes which mean that interviewers have to adopt a different approach and use different skills. For example, the typical selection interview demands good questioning technique; the counselling interview places more emphasis on reflecting and listening techniques. To illustrate these differences, we shall examine two types in more detail: the selection interview and the performance appraisal interview.

Communication in the selection interview

In theory, the selection process is a process of logical steps:

- job description, where the nature and demands of the job are thoroughly reviewed and analysed.
- person specification, where the job demands are translated into the skills and personal characteristics which the person will need to do the job well.
- advertising the vacancy, so that everyone who might meet the specification has the opportunity to apply.
- sorting and short-listing applications, to select candidates who fully satisfy the person specification.
- the selection event itself, which will normally include an interview (see Box 12.3 for some data on how this differs across cultures), but which increasingly includes other tests such as psychometric tests or group tasks.

In practice, this process can be both difficult and time-consuming. For example, the job demands may be changing and there may be some argument as to how this should be decided. There may also be argument about which of the characteristics in the person specification are the most important. The choice of selection methods may also be controversial. For example, there is debate about the value of psychometric tests. Unfortunately, some organisations do use selection methods which have very dubious validity, such as graphology – the analysis of a person's handwriting.

We do not have the space to explore these issues more fully.

Perhaps the most important implication for communication is the possible ambiguity and uncertainty which can creep into the interview room. If the job description and person specification are poorly prepared, then the interviewer might not have a very clear idea of what they are looking for. If there is a panel interview, then there might be confusion or even clear disagreement between interviewers. The candidate might also have developed a misleading picture of the job depending on how the advertising material was prepared.

BOX 11.3 SELECTION PRACTICES VARY

Various studies have shown that there are significant variations both within and between countries in terms of the methods they use to select employees. For example:

- an early study by Hodgkinson and Payne (1998) reviewed how British, Dutch, and French organisations selected university graduates. Among the significant differences were that traditional interviews were always used by nearly all organisations in the UK and Netherlands to select university graduates (89% and 85% respectively). Only 45% of French organisations always used them; criterion-referenced interviews were used much more in France than in the UK. Nearly half the UK organisations never used them; graphology was used much more in France than in the Netherlands. A total of 82% of French organisations sometimes used it.

- Zibarras and Woods (2010) found that organisations from their UK sample were more likely to use "informal methods" (e.g. unstructured interviews) than "formal methods" (e.g., assessment centres). There were differences across sectors – public and voluntary sectors were more likely to use formal methods.

Research on selection interviews has identified many potential problems and pitfalls in the interview process. For example, Mike Smith (1982) suggested five main sources of unreliability which still apply:

- different interviewers may look for different characteristics in the interviewees.
- the setting of the interview may influence the interviewee in ways which are unrelated to their skills for the job. For example, a candidate recently told us how he had failed his last interview after being "overwhelmed" by the surroundings. Instead of the expected formal panel interview, he was taken to a lounge with low comfy chairs.
- poor structure. The same candidate can give a very different impression depending on which sequence of questions they receive.
- interactive problems. Even interviewers with clear plans and objectives may make unreliable decisions unless they recognise that their behaviour in the interview can influence the way it progresses.
- interviewers may use the information they have gained from candidates in different ways. One bias that may be especially important in interviews is the finding that interviewers can place too much emphasis on negative or unusual information.

BOX 11.4 FAIR TREATMENT OR INCOMPETENT PRACTICE?

How would you have responded as a candidate to the following three interview situations?

Straight out of college, this was one of my first interviews, for a copy-writing trainee in an advertising agency. I was shown into the manager's room and sat on the low, comfy chair facing his desk. He looked up and leaned back in his chair, looked me straight in the eye, and said 'Hello, Tony.' I said 'hello' and paused. I was expecting the first question. Nothing happened – he continued to look me straight in the eye. After an awkward pause where I started to panic, I realised he was not going to say anything, so I started – 'I suppose you'd like to hear something about me.' He nodded slightly but still did not say anything. So, I started to talk about myself. I wasn't prepared for this and so I didn't feel I was giving a very coherent presentation. After about ten minutes (it seemed a lot longer), I said: 'and I'd really like to work for an organisation which has exciting development plans. What are your plans?'He leaned back again –'That's a very interesting question – what do you think we should be doing? After a few more minutes of desperate improvisation, I was told the interview was over. I crawled out of the office, feeling completely dispirited, angry, and frustrated. I did not get the job. In retrospect, I'm glad I wasn't offered it.

I was pleased to be offered an interview for this post in local government as it meant more responsibility, better career prospects, and a useful promotion from my present post. I also wanted to move to that part of the country. I was asked to attend for interview at the local college. When I arrived, I was asked to wait as apparently the 'interviews are running a few minutes late.' Eventually, I was escorted to Lecture Room 6. When I walked in, I was shown to a chair in the position where the lecturer would usually be. I looked up and discovered I was in a banked lecture hall and there must have been about 70 people sat looking at me. I was asked six questions by different members of the audience – who introduced themselves before their question. None of my answers received any follow-ups or probing questions. If I had known this was going to happen, I would have given fuller answers. After my six questions I was thanked and asked to leave. Afterwards, I discovered that these six questions were a standard procedure. The job was controversial because of local politics so the large audience was because all the interested parties had exercised their formal right to see the candidate.

I walked into the interview room. The interviewer was standing behind the desk, clutching a stopwatch. He didn't say anything, so I sat down in what was obviously the interviewee's chair. He leaned over towards me and said, 'Right, you've got ten minutes to sell yourself to me. Go!' He clicked the stopwatch to start the time and sat down with arms folded.

In all three situations, the candidate expected to receive a conventional interview: a series of relevant questions, some probes and follow-ups, the chance to add their own comments, and the chance to ask questions.

Table 11.1 The interview as planned communication

Stage	Content	Points to watch	Example
Decide the general goal	What do you want to achieve overall?		You have been asked to carry out the first round of Interviews on the candidates for the supervisor position. You have to Interview eight candidates, all external, and recommend three for a second Interview
Consider the context	What has happened In the past?	Are there any hidden agendas because of the history?	As all the candidates are external, there should not be any problems because of "internal politics". Will the candidates know what this first Interview Is for? What sort of Interview will they expect?
	Who are the participants? What Is the setting?	What does the other person need or expect to happen?	What setting will be the best place to Interview them to give a professional Impression of the organisation (not a corner of a busy office with phones ringing all the time)
Plan	Decide on the objectives Decide on the structure	Make your objectives realistic and achievable Make sure your structure leads up to your objective	Your objectives are to: 1 Find which three candidates match the job and person spec. 2 Give them the best chance to show what they can offer. 3 Show them that the organisation Is a good place to work.
			You must make sure that you have done your homework: read all the applications; research the Job and person spec.
			You must have an Interview plan which Is well-structured (and check your questions before the event)
			Give the Interview a clear, confident Introduction
			Make sure you listen to each candidate

(Continued)

Table 11.1 (Continued)

Stage	Content	Points to watch	Example
			Make sure you probe the answers to uncover 'the evidence'
Act	Use the relevant skills	What are the most important skills In this situation e.g. listening,- questioning, etc.?	Give the candidate the chance to ask questions
			Complete the documentation
Follow-up			Make sure that all candidates are told of the outcome

In all three situations, the organisation ignored these expectations and presented the candidate with a very different challenge (although situation 2 is closest to the expected format, the setting is totally unexpected). In each case, was the organisation behaving legitimately? Does it have a rationale for the specific tactics? How will candidates feel about this "induction" to the organisation? Why weren't candidates told what to expect?

There is no real evidence to suggest that "shock tactics" help an interviewer arrive at a better opinion of the interviewee's competence and potential. The evidence points the other way. All these three organisations are failing to communicate clear expectations to their candidates. If they make bad selection decisions, they should not be surprised!

Despite continuing concerns about the reliability of interviewer judgements, the interview remains one of the most popular selection methods. Research suggests that its reliability can be improved in several ways, notably by training interviewers to avoid the problems we listed above. If interviewers are sufficiently trained, if they know what characteristics they are looking for, and if they follow a clear (but not over-rigid) interview plan, then they can perform well. They must also have the specific social skills we highlighted in the last chapter.

The general issues we have identified are summarised in Figure 11.1 which applies the model developed in Chapter 10 to the selection interview. This also shows that the specific skills covered in Chapter 10 are all relevant to interview practice. The example of opening and closing will illustrate this.

OPENING AND CLOSING

The choice of opening can be very important in formal situations such as an interview where the opening can establish either a positive or negative atmosphere. Which of the following opening techniques would you prefer in a selection interview:

- the interviewer gives you a positive welcome and spends some time in social conversation – breaking the ice – before getting down to business.
- the interviewer starts by describing important features about the company, and the job and then goes straight into critical questions, like: "What are the most important attributes you have for this job?"

The first strategy is designed to make you feel relaxed so you can put on the best performance you can. The second is much "colder" and more official. If it is repeated to every candidate, then you can wonder whether this opening is the best use of interview time – why not have a general briefing to all candidates?

There is also a variety of tactics available to close or conclude the interview. The good interviewer will make sure that the interviewee has a chance to clear up any points they have not understood and will make sure that they know what is going to happen as a result of the interview. We know from our own experience that this does not always happen!

When cultural differences make the difference

As we argued in the previous chapter, it is not sufficient just to "know the techniques" to become a skilled interviewer. The skilled communicator must also be looking for the different meanings which might affect different participants. Many advice books on interview performance are written from a perspective which favours candidates from particular cultural backgrounds (often reflecting middle-class white American values!) Candidates from different cultural backgrounds may not recognise or adapt to the "hidden rules" as the following examples illustrate (from Hargie, 1997):

- the question "why have you applied for this position?" may be recognised as an opportunity to show how your skills and background fit you for the position. From a different cultural expectation, it may be seen as too obvious to warrant a detailed answer.
- the question "do you have any questions to ask us?" offers an opportunity to impress by asking intelligent questions about prospects and development.

It may be ignored by candidates who have the cultural norm of showing respect to the person of high status. From this perspective, asking would be disrespectful.

Organisation and structure in the selection interview

Another characteristic which is emphasised in interviewer training is the importance of a clear structure in the interview. Structure can be discussed at two levels: the overall structure of the interview, and the way that questions can be organised in a sensible sequence.

Overall structure

The simplest way of summarising the likely structure of a selection interview is to say it will have a beginning, middle and end.

There are several models of the selection interview which are more elaborated versions of this. Problems occur when interviewers "change the rules" without giving a clear idea of what to expect, as Box 11.4 illustrates.

Question sequences

In the last chapter, we introduced the difference between open and closed questions. Open questions invite the candidate to answer in any way they see fit; closed questions ask for a yes/no or specific answer. Hargie (2022) suggests that other types of questions are important, including:

- leading questions. These are "assumption laden. By the way they are worded they lead the respondent towards an expected response" (Hargie, 2022, page

Table 11.2 Stages in the selection interview

Section	What they might contain
Beginning	Candidate is welcomed
	Interviewer(s) introduce themselves and explain how the interview will be conducted
	Opening questions are designed to make the candidate feel at ease
Middle	Interviewer asks main questions and follow-ups
Ending	Interviewer invites candidate to ask any questions
	Interviewer explains what will happen next

138), and which could give a misleading impression in a selection interview if the candidate feels obliged to give the "expected answer".

- multiple questions, where two or more separate questions are bundled together as one. This confuses candidates – which question should I answer first?

Of course, there is no guarantee that a specific type of question will elicit the intended response, as the following examples illustrate:

Q: "How long did you spend in the Sales Department?"
(closed question anticipating short, factual answer)
A: "Well, I don't think that I really spent long enough as I felt that I should have been able to..."
(extended answer)
And the other way round:
Q: "What do you think about expanding international links?"
(open question anticipating a long answer)
A: "Very good idea".
(restricted answer)

Interviewers may need to ask a series of open or closed questions to get the response they want from candidates, and this is where *sequences* of questions and the use of probes become important.

Probes are designed to "probe" the previous answer in order to get a more detailed picture. For example, suppose you were interviewing a young graduate and wanted to check their IT competence. You might start with a general question: "How much IT did you use at college?" Suppose the candidate simply said, "We used it quite a bit". This answer could be probed in a number of ways – one sequence could be:

- which software packages have you used?
- what did you use them for?
- what is the most complex task you've done with those packages?

This sequence and further probes should establish both the breadth and depth of the candidate's expertise. Good interviewers will also probe to establish the evidence behind the candidate's answers. For example, does using IT "quite a bit" mean "word-processing one essay a month" or "using the internet and computerised databases every day"?

Popular sequences of questions include:

- funnel sequence, which starts with open questions and then narrows down, using closed questions and probes.

- inverted funnel, which starts with closed questions and then opens out.
- tunnel sequence where all the questions are at the same level. They are usually closed. (Hargie, 2022, page 131ff)

Communication and feedback in the appraisal interview

Many organisations have an appraisal system with the following characteristics:

- a formal meeting takes place between a boss (appraiser)and subordinate (appraisee) which takes place at least once per annum and which reviews how the appraisee has performed over the previous period.
- the appraiser gives feedback to the appraisee, and the meeting discusses this feedback.
- the meeting is based in some documentation which both parties have to consider before the meeting.
- the outcomes of the meeting are a formal assessment (usually written and kept) of how the appraisee has progressed and what this means for future performance (e.g., future targets agreed) and staff development (e.g. agreed training or development plan).
- these procedures are usually established and monitored by the human resources function within the organisation.

You can analyse the appraisal interview in the same way that we analysed the selection interview – as planned communication; as an interaction with expected structures; as an opportunity for interviewers to make systematic errors, and so on. In this chapter, we shall focus on the process of feedback which is a key component of many interactions.

Do the appraisers have the necessary skills to give productive and supportive feedback?

If the appraiser does not have the necessary social skills, then the system can easily collapse. Is there training to make sure that everyone is adopting a consistent approach?

Factors which strongly influence the quality of appraisal interviews include:

- *The amount of critical feedback.* Where managers can spend up to one quarter of the interview criticising or attacking the appraisee, it is not surprising if the appraisees adopt a defensive attitude!
- *The balance in the performance review.* The balance between positive and negative feedback is very important.

- *The content of the feedback.* For example, is it clear and unambiguous? Is it relevant to what the person *does*, or does it focus on more personal characteristics?
- *The use of a range of measures.* If there is a wide range of evidence on how well the person is doing and if this evidence is available before the meeting, then this will support the discussion.
- *The way the interview is organised and conducted.* Perhaps the critical factor here is how well and how much the appraisee is able to participate in the discussion.
- *The relationship between the appraiser and appraisee.* If there is already a good relationship, then this will make the appraisal much easier.

The problems with many appraisal schemes has led to new variations emerging. For example, some organisations have put much more emphasis on self-appraisal as a device for encouraging staff to reflect on their performance and suggest ways they can improve. Another way is to increase the variety of feedback available, as in 360-degree feedback which we describe in Box 11.5.

Even with expert appraisers and a carefully prepared meeting, there are important weaknesses of the annual appraisal system. For example, it offers a good opportunity to "game the system" from both the employer's and employee's perspective and can fail to recognise the importance of collaboration and teamworking. As a result, many organisations have abandoned this system.

BOX 11.5 360-DEGREE FEEDBACK

Peter Ward, a consultant who used this method in a number of British organisations, defined the method as:

> *The systematic collection and feedback of performance data on an individual or group, derived from a number of stakeholders in their performance.*
>
> *(Ward, 1997, page 4)*

Susan Heathfield is more specific:

> *360-degree feedback is a method of employee review that provides each employee the opportunity to receive performance feedback from their supervisor or manager and four to eight peers, reporting staff members, co-workers, and, in some cases, customers.*
>
> *(Heathfield, 2022)*

For example, suppose you are a junior manager in a retail company. Data on your performance would be collected from relevant stakeholders such as your staff, your boss, other managers you have to deal with, and your main customers.

The data would be collected systematically using questionnaires or interviews or perhaps both. You receive a written report which summarises the results and you have a chance to reflect on this report before you discuss it with your appraiser. This discussion will cover four areas:

- your strengths – those behaviours where you see yourself as strong and where others also rate you as strong.
- your development areas – those behaviours where you think you need to improve and so do others.
- discrepancies – those behaviours where you see yourself as strong and but where others do not. In other words, there is a discrepancy between how you see yourself and how others see you.
- hidden strengths – those behaviours where others you see you as strong but where you have not rated yourself highly.

As this brief summary implies, a comprehensive 360-degree system is both complex and time-consuming. If it is implemented carefully then it can make a significant impact on the culture of a company over time. If it is treated as a "quick fix" then it will probably do more harm than good.

Beqiri provides a useful overview of the potential strengths of the system (e.g., increased awareness of personal skills) and limitations (e.g., feedback may conflict; over-concentration on weaknesses; lack of support/commitment from senior management), alongside other useful articles on organisational communication (https://virtualspeech.com). As with all these schemes, the quality of communication is critical to its success.

Defining the skills of feedback

Feedback is obviously a critical component of the appraisal interview but there are a number of less formal situations where someone might need to receive feedback on their performance. So, is there a "correct" way of delivering feedback so that the person accepts it without becoming antagonistic or defensive?

There are a number of guidelines available. Most of them focus on issues identified by Harry Levinson who offers the following advice, especially when giving negative feedback (quoted in Goleman, 1996, pages 153/4):

- *Be specific.* Feedback should highlight specific events or examples rather than just general advice. It should also be specific about what the person did.
- *Offer a solution.* Feedback should suggest ways of resolving any problems. There is little or no point in offering negative feedback where there is no way the person can improve.

- Deliver the feedback face-to-face.
- *Be sensitive.* This is simply a reminder that feedback, even negative feedback, should be delivered in a positive way rather than simply attacking the other person.

Douglas Stone and Sheila Heen (2014) offer useful advice on how to "receive feedback well". They identify three "triggers" which can get in the way:

- truth triggers, where we feel that the feedback is wrong or unhelpful
- relationship triggers, where we are inappropriately influenced by the relationship we have with the other person.
- identity triggers, where the feedback makes us question our sense of who we are, and we feel "threatened and off balance".

These triggers "are obstacles because they keep us from engaging skilfully in the conversation" and they offer advice on how to recognise and overcome them.

SUMMARY OF KEY POINTS

- the skills and techniques which were explained in Chapter 10 can be applied in common face-to-face situations in organisations, both the more casual, conversations and discussions, and more formal interactions, such as selection and appraisal interviews.
- one important issue is the way that participants understand or "make sense" of the events which unfold. We can easily jump to misleading or unwarranted assumptions and base our communication on these. This can very easily lead to confusion and conflict.
- supportive communication is important, especially in encounters where there is a status difference.
- organisations which train employees to use standard, inflexible scripts are adopting a very limited view of human communication.
- in formal situations like interviews, the person in control, the interviewer, has special responsibilities to manage the interaction so that communication is open and focused on the specific objectives.
- a range of communication problems can affect formal interviews like the selection interview and interviewers should be trained to avoid these.
- feedback is a particularly important and difficult process which needs careful attention.

References

Andrews, P.H. and Herschel, R.T. (1996) *Organisational Communication: Empowerment in a Technological Society*. Boston, MA: Houghton Mifflin.

Cameron, D. (2000) *Good to Talk*. London: Sage

Ellinor, L. and Gerrard, G. (1998) *Dialogue: Rediscover the Transforming Power of Conversation*. New York: John Wiley.

Goleman, D. (1996) *Emotional Intelligence*. London: Bloomsbury.

Heathfield, S.M. (2022) What is 360-degree feedback? https://www.thebalancemoney.com/360-degree-feedback-information-1917537.

Heen, S. and Stone, D. (2014) *Thanks for the Feedback: The Science and Art of Receiving Feedback Well*. London: Portfolio Penguin/Viking.

Hodgkinson, G. and Payne, R.L. (1998) Graduate selection in three European countries. *Journal of Occupational and Organizational Psychology* 71(4): 359–365.

Guirdham, M. (1995) *Interpersonal Skills at Work* (2nd eedition) Hemel Hempstead: Prentice Hall.

Smith, M. (1982) Selection interviewing: a four step approach. In Breakwell, G., Foot, H. and Gilmore, R. eds. *Social Psychology: a practical manual*. London: McMillan, pages 19–37

Stone, D., Patton, B. and Heen, S. (2020) *Difficult Conversations: How to Discuss What Matters Most*. London: Penguin.

Ward, P. (1997) *360-Degree Feedback*. London: IPD.

Zibarras, L.D. and Woods, S.A. (2010) A survey of UK selection practices across different organization sizes and industry sectors. *Journal of Occupational and Organizational Psychology* 83(2): 499–511. https://openaccess.city.ac.uk/id/eprint/2213/1/UK%20selection%20practices_JOOP914_revision%20-%20final.pdf.

CHAPTER 12

How can we organise effective meetings?

Introduction

It is depressingly easy to find complaints about the sorts of meetings which are such a regular part of life in organisations. If presentations make us nervous, then meetings seem to make us disappointed and cynical:

> *a meeting brings together a group of the unfit, appointed by the unwilling, to do the unnecessary.*
>
> (many texts, e.g., Stanton, 1996)

> *My research suggests that only around 50% of meeting time is effective, well used, and engaging — and these effectiveness numbers drop even lower when it comes to remote meetings.*
>
> (Rogelberg, 2019)

> *70% of meetings keep employees from doing productive work.*
>
> (Larsen, 2022)

Various surveys reinforce these negative impressions as we see later in this chapter. Meetings are also a regular target for comedians and satirists, as you will see in Box 12.1.

Some management experts have suggested we "do away" with meetings altogether but we agree with Steven Rogelberg that

> *the elimination of meetings in and of themselves is a false goal – the goal should actually be to eliminate ineffective and bloated meetings.*
>
> (Rogelberg, 2019, page 8)

This chapter concentrates on principles and techniques which can overcome these issues and criticisms. We focus on methods and structure, but we also highlight

DOI: 10.4324/9781003297550-16

group dynamic issues which can affect meetings. Issues of group dynamics are covered more fully in Chapter 13.

We start by looking at important differences between professional and business meetings and then review various ways to improve their effectiveness. Applying the ideas and principles in this chapter should enable you to run the sorts of meetings which John Tropman describes as "excellent", where:

- decisions are made and agreed.
- the group does not have to revisit or rework "old" decisions.
- the decisions are good – well worked out and successful.
- members enjoy the meeting and feel that it has been productive. (Tropman, 2003)

In the next few years, organisations will continue to adjust in different ways to their post-pandemic ways of operation. This will involve some use of teleconferencing and so we need to consider how general principles apply to virtual interactions and also specific concerns which only apply online, such as "Zoom fatigue".

Finally, we highlight different ways of reviewing discussions and decisions and visual presentation techniques such as concept mapping.

OBJECTIVES

This chapter will:

- analyse main differences between different types of meetings.
- identify principles which have been associated with effective meetings, highlight potential pitfalls and problems, and identify important skills for meeting chairs.
- review different procedures and practical steps which have been proposed to improve meetings.
- identify general principles and particular techniques which can help us make meetings more effective using new technology.

What sort of meetings are these?

Consider the following two extracts (based on real business meetings) and identify what you think are the most important differences.

Meeting A

Speaker 1: "OK, well we need to consider John's concerns about the store in Smallville".

Speaker 2: "It's just not doing enough business for a store that size. You can see from the figures in Table 3 in the report sent out last week".

Speaker 3: "So how can we bump up business? Any ideas, Paul?" (everyone looks at the large screen monitor for a contribution from Paul – Speaker 4 – who is joining the meeting through a videoconferencing link).

Speaker 4: "The only way is to put up a Slow Down sign and lay a series of small sharp spikes across the road just outside the store".

Speaker 5: "Pardon?"

Speaker 4: 'It's obvious. People will slow down, get a puncture, and stop. While they're waiting for the breakdown services to arrive, they will have no choice but to go in the store and spend some money".

Speaker 5: "You're not serious?"

Speaker 4: "Of course not. But can you see my point?" (pause: some other members of the meeting groan at the very tortured pun). "We do need to get more people in that store. Look at the figures in Table 4 which compares different stores across the region – have you all got the figures? They are in the email I sent you this morning. (everyone agrees) You can see from column 5 that the customers who go in to Smallville spend more on average than customers who visit some of our other stores. We just need to get more people through the door".

Speaker 1: "So are we agreed that the best strategy is to work out how to attract more customers to visit the store? OK, so how can we do that?"

Meeting B

Speaker 1: "We are quorate so we can now move to the first item in the agenda - the proposal that we close the South Street office in Smallville. You will all have received the paper on this, reference 99/8/2, and I will ask the writer, John Smith, to summarise the main points for us".

Speaker 2: "The critical point here is that if we combined the Smallville offices on our main street site then we could offer a much better service to the local community. Apart from some savings due to greater efficiency, we would be more competitive. We could offer a wider range of services by putting the two offices together. We also have no evidence that the existing customers at South Street would be disadvantaged. In fact, we feel that many of them, if not most of them, would find it more convenient to come to Main Street".

Speaker 1: "So the proposal is that we merge the two offices on the main street site. Have we any comments or further proposals?"

Speaker 3: "I have to say that my staff are very concerned about this proposal, in terms of the messages it sends to loyal and hard-working staff. You have glossed over the fact that the South Street office is extremely profitable and has won awards for the quality of its service and management".

Speaker 1: "John, can you respond to that?"
Speaker 2: "We have considered these points. I can assure you that there will be no redundancies and all staff will be accommodated at Main Street".
Speaker 1: "Any other comments?" (pause) "So if there are no further points then we can move to a vote?"
Speaker 4: "Point of order, please, chair. According to our terms of reference, I do not believe that we can make this decision without further consultation."
Speaker 1: "Thank you, John. We don't want to go viral. I was going to say we need to check that. Rather than hold up this meeting, I shall ask the Secretary to check that during the coffee break and we shall return to this item of business at the end of the meeting. Moving on to item two on the agenda..."

So, what were the main differences between these two meetings?

You may want to pause here and note your answer to this question before you read our analysis. Have we missed anything important?

Our analysis

There are obvious similarities. Both aimed to reach a decision on an important issue. There was an exchange of opinions and the discussion moved towards the final decision.

The differences are more striking. For example:

- more members spoke in meeting A.
- in B, every comment was directed through the chair (Speaker 1).
- the style of conversation was more light-hearted in A (as in the rather feeble joke from Speaker 4).
  There is one reference in meeting B which could be construed as a joke – "we don't want to go viral" – and is based on shared understanding in the UK of the English Parish Council meeting over Zoom in 2021 which became famous after an angry dispute in the meeting. Clips from the meeting were seen by "millions" online and the chair of the meeting became something of a celebrity through media appearances, including a cameo role in The Archers – the longstanding UK radio soap opera.
  You can also interpret Speaker 1's response in different ways depending on the intonation. Is Speaker 1 trying to reassert their authority here – "I was going to say that...?" Depending on tone of voice, this could be a very clear attempt to "put John in his place".
- there were several references to formal rules and regulations in B (again the debate over the terms of reference, and the check on whether the meeting was quorate).
- the behaviour of the chair was very different (Speaker 1 in both cases).

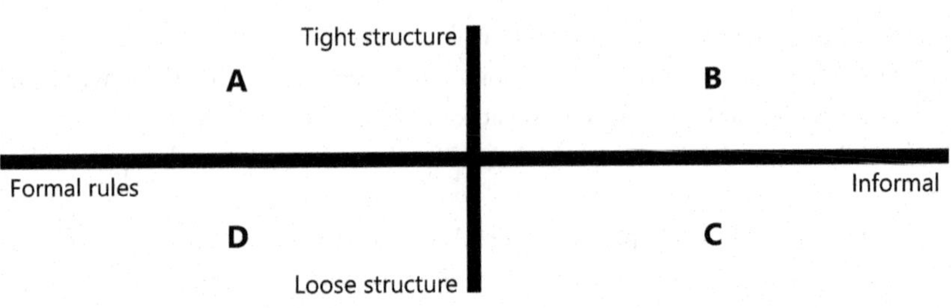

Figure 12.1 Dimensions of meetings

- the procedures were different (e.g., the automatic move to a vote to close the decision in B)
- the use of videoconferencing technology in A.

These examples illustrate two of the main dimensions along which meetings can vary:

- the use of formal rules and regulations by the members.
- the degree of formal structure in the meeting.

You can represent these dimensions as follows – Figure 12.1 – and you can imagine meetings which fall in different sections of the diagram. At position A, a meeting is very tightly structured and follows formal rules and regulations. An example here would be the annual general meeting of a company or the monthly meeting of a local government committee. At position B, the meeting is tightly structured but not subject to very formal rules. An example here might be a project group or management team meeting.

One obvious implication is that each meeting should be at the appropriate spot on this diagram. For example, suppose you wished to run a meeting to introduce new people to one another and to generate some fresh ideas for new projects. Organising in style A would be counter-productive, and you would probably use style C. On the other hand, the meeting of a very large official committee might have to follow format A to satisfy legal requirements.

BOX 12.1 MEETINGS CAN BE FUNNY

Sarah Cooper created and produces the satirical blog – TheCooperReview.com – where you can find "10 tricks to appear smart in meetings" (https://thecooper-review.com/10-tricks-appear-smart-meetings/) which has had over three million viewings. The "tricks" are almost too true to be funny, if our experience of meetings in educational, commercial, and professional organisations is in any way typical. If you read this blog, we think you will immediately look for her book (*100 tricks to appear smart in meetings* – Cooper, 2020). Of course, we do not recommend performing any of these tricks – they are all designed to disorient or impress colleagues and make you appear more of a "high-performing team-player" than you actually are. For example, she suggests "21 meaningless diagrams" – they look "smart" but do not actually mean much, if anything.

Online meetings have also seen their fair share of parodies.

Tripp and Tyler produced a series of short clips which managed to satirise ways we communicate in both face-to-face and online interactions. This one is a good starter:

https://www.youtube.com/watch?v=PpTTDfg4KLs&list=RDCMUC310aJFjr6Gn9mGZjMZ2VTQ&index=2

We have not identified the use of technology as a separate dimension as it can be used in any of the four main types. One obvious use is to set up the meeting so that some or all participants can attend online, e.g., using Zoom or Teams. You need to have both working practices and technology which enable virtual participants to contribute when they need to. And you need a skilled chair to ensure that everyone is engaged – and we return to this later. In a meeting which is totally or partly online, you also have the advantage of a text chat box so that participants can post comments and suggest links without interrupting the discussion.

There is also the problem that individuals may be coming to the meeting with specific hidden agendas – see Box 12.2.

BOX 12.2 WHEN MACHIAVELLI COMES TO THE MEETING

Political issues and hidden agendas may influence meetings even when most participants are trying to arrive at the most "rational" decisions. Buchanan and Badham (2008) highlighted some of the consequences of "power games" which can affect events like meetings:

> *"Agendas are restricted to 'safe' issues; controversial issues are excluded from informal conversations and from formal decision-making processes".*
> (page 55)

Martin (2000) describes bargaining tactics which can be used in meetings to gain an advantage, such as describing a worse situation than actually exists and then backtracking to the position which you wanted in the first place. For example, "we have to increase prices by 10%" after discussion becomes "we agree to increase prices by 5%" where 5% was the original hidden objective. The problem with all devious tactics like this is that they can rebound on you if they are discovered. And you may *never* achieve trust if others suspect you of these tactics.

What makes meetings effective?

Every textbook on business communication includes some advice on how to run effective meetings. But much of this advice seems to be based upon the author's personal experience rather than more comprehensive research.

Research studies comparing meetings in different organisations and contexts are relatively thin on the ground. Notable exceptions are two bodies of work which we summarise below by John Tropman and by Steven G. Fogelberg. You can also find useful resources from Fogelberg on his website – https://www.stevenrogelberg.com

Meeting Masters

Tropman reports the conclusions of the Meeting Masters Research Project which aimed to identify individuals who ran excellent meetings and decide how they did it (Tropman, 2014). The research suggested that "Meeting Masters" followed seven main principles – we list these below and highlight additional points from Rogelberg's research.

1. The orchestra principle

This emphasises the strong co-operation necessary to complete the task, as in a symphony orchestra. The meeting chair is analogous to the conductor – making sure that everyone delivers their best performance, and that everything fits together.

2. The three characters principle

Tropman suggests you can only do three things in a meeting:

- announce something.
- decide something.
- discuss something.

Tropman also suggests that each agenda *item* can only do one of these three things. The meeting should be organised so that members clearly know which item is which. Items should be dealt with in that order:

- first, all announcements, then...
- all items where you need decisions, and then...
- items which just need to be discussed.

3. The role principle

The person in the chair should act as role model to encourage other members of the group to contribute openly and positively.

4. No new business

The meeting should only cover items which have been placed on the agenda and which the members have had some chance to think about. Otherwise, members will not be prepared for the discussion.

5. No more reports

Members are never asked simply to "report from their department", as individuals may concentrate on topics which show them up in the best light and fail to identify important issues.

6. The imperative of proactivity

Meetings should *always* include some items which deal with future plans or problems. Early discussion can enable members to have an impact on future events.

7. High-quality decisions

Not only are decisions made, but those decisions show "evidence of quality".

Can you apply these principles to your organisation?

Rules to follow?

Tropman suggests rules which can help you apply these principles. Among the most interesting are:

The rule of six

Tropman suggests that

- about one sixth of the items on an agenda should be from the past. These are items which have not been completed or perhaps been deliberately held over.

- about four sixths of the items should come from the present. These are important issues that need to be dealt with immediately.
- about one sixth of the items should come from the future. These are issues which are likely to be important in the future and which need discussing before they become urgent.

This way of structuring a meeting also allows Tropman to introduce a subrule: the two-meeting rule – that controversial items should be discussed first at one meeting without any decision being taken. They should then be *decided* at the next meeting. This allows members to discuss the item freely and possibly disagree quite strongly and then leave some time to reflect upon the issues so that the final decision is not made in the heat of an argument.

The role of the chair

Tropman emphasises the importance of pre-meeting preparation and the influence of the chair's behaviour. We agree with this emphasis. Longstanding British research complements Tropman's analysis of what effective chairs usually do. For example, based on a series of very detailed meeting observations, Rackham and Morgan (1977) showed that effective chairs behaved very differently from the average member of the meetings – they did much more summarising and testing understanding.

Rogelberg highlights the importance of the chair's self-awareness:

> *There is compelling evidence suggesting we are poor judges of our own leadership skills when it comes to meeting.*
>
> (Rogelberg, 2019)

He sees this as a particular example of the "Lake Woebegon Effect" where "most people believe they are well above average" and suggests that all meeting chairs should search out feedback on their performance. They should also demonstrate all the positive behaviours on his 'Good Meetings Facilitation Checklist' (available on his website) which covers:

- time management.
- active listening.
- conflict management.
- ensuring active participation.
- pushing for consensus.

Developing and reporting the agenda

One of the most important devices for structuring a meeting is the agenda.

Table 12.1 Tropman's 7 categories of agenda items (Adapted from Tropman, 1996, page 24–27)

Category	Item	Type	Time(minutes)
1	Minutes		10
2	Announcements		15
3	Decision	Easy	15
4	Decision	Moderately difficult	15
5	Decision	Hardest item	25–40
6	Discussion		15–30
7	Discussion	Easiest item	10

Tropman proposes seven categories of agenda items which should be organised as follows in a two-hour meeting:

This distribution of time gives a bell-curve and so Tropman talks of the "Agenda Bell" (Tropman, 2014, pages 40ff). His argument for placing the "most difficult" item in the middle of the meeting, starting about one third of the way through, is to

> *take advantage of peak attendance, high energy, and the momentum that usually comes from handling less difficult items successfully.*
>
> (op cit, page 43)

Whether meetings follow this exact distribution or not, it is critical that members know the status and priority of each item on the agenda:

- "are we just discussing this, or do we have to make a decision?"
- "do we have to make a decision today?"

The agenda should communicate this information to members. Unfortunately, many agendas do not. This may be just a matter of adding a subheading to the title of the item. For example, consider the difference between these two agenda items:

4. Report from J. Smith on the Eureka Project.
5. Report from G. Smith on the Alumni Project:
    - review progress.
    - allocate resources for the next financial period.
    - decide whether to extend the project to the central site.

Item 4 gives no indication of what should be discussed or decided; item 5 gives very clear information on what needs to be done.

Rogelberg offers similar advice and suggests that the agenda should enable the meeting to "flow" in a way that engages all the participants. You can find examples of the way he expands agenda descriptions and his Agenda Template in his book (op cit, 2019, pages 65 and 161/2).

Minutes and follow-up

The minutes of a meeting can be very different in style and detail. At one end of the scale, we have decisions or action points recorded as a list with no explanation or elaboration of the discussion. This is appropriate for some meetings, say a small project group. At the other end, we have a complete record of what everyone said. This verbatim report is far too time-consuming and unnecessary for most if not all business meetings. A useful compromise is to prepare what Tropman calls "content minutes" – for each item on the agenda, a minute is written as two separate paragraphs which:

- summarise the main points in the discussion.
- summarise the decision taken, or the action agreed, naming whoever has to carry it out, and giving the timescale or deadline.

From this we can suggest that effective minutes must convey all the information set out in Table 12.2

There is also the problem of deciding the style and layout of minutes. For example, should the minutes identify who said what? Baguley (1994, page 94) gives an example of minute structure which includes the following item:

> *4. Joan Harris reported that software development was on target and still had an anticipated beta version completion date of end of March. There were, however, still problems with Ron Stanning's lack of co-operation over graphics programming availability.*

Table 12.2 Contents of minutes

Details of the meeting itself	Details of the outcomes
Who was present and who did not attend. When and where it took place. When and where the next meeting will take place.	What was agreed. Who has to take actions as a result, and by when.

Action agreed: Valerie Williams to set up meeting with Ron Stanning and Joan Harris to resolve problems.

Completion by: 21 Nov 1994.

This example does meet many of the suggestions given above. But there is one important issue – the minutes record that Ron Stanning *is* being "uncooperative". You might like to answer these questions for yourself before you read our comments:

- should this have been recorded?
- if you were asked to rephrase that minute, what would you recommend?

We would not be happy with this minute – especially if we happened to be Ron. How did the meeting establish Ron's "lack of co-operation"? Is it "fact" or is it simply Joan Harris' opinion? If you were Ron and felt there were good reasons not to supply a graphics programmer, how would you respond to this judgement in the minutes? Would it be fair to record that "Ron Stanning had not supplied a graphics programmer to the project"? Or is a more fundamental change of style required?

As minutes remain as a formal record of what has happened then you need to be very careful that they are accurate and that they do not record as "fact" anything which could be contested later.

Given that minutes are an important issue, it is worth thinking about different ways of producing them. One strategy which we have used is to create minutes in the meeting itself using a collaborative document format like Google Docs. At the end of each major item the chair reviews the minute onscreen and ensures that everyone agrees before moving on. There are also a number of apps available to make other parts of the meeting process easier to manage – see Box 12.3.

BOX 12.3 AND THERE'S AN APP FOR IT

A range of apps for tablets, laptops, and mobile phones now exists to help with aspects of the meeting process, offering suggestions for structuring different types of discussion, taking notes, taking minutes, and so on. One main advantage of many of these apps is their ability to sync with or send to other software like your calendar and email and you can find structures for different types of meeting. See the website for our current examples. If you have regular meetings with a specific team, then it is worth discussing possibilities with the team members as the use of a common app can often be very productive and increase collaboration and sharing.

Planning more effective meetings: procedures and techniques to consider

Several techniques have been recommended to improve particular aspects of meetings, either by changing the whole approach to the meeting or by including a specific technique at a certain point within a meeting. If you are planning a meeting, you should at the very least consider the following approaches:

- flexible meeting techniques to encourage more dialogue and discussion.
- brainstorming, to produce more creative ideas.
- structured problem-solving.
- Nominal Group Technique, also designed to help problem-solving and decision-making.
- Delphi technique, for a group which cannot physically meet.
- techniques for encouraging group innovation.
- techniques for clarifying decision-making.

Flexible meeting techniques

If you are organising a meeting which might attract a large attendance then it is worth considering some of the techniques which have been shown to work with large groups, such as Open Space and World Café. These techniques can also be applied with small groups where you can use approaches with specific supporting toolkits such as Ketso. These approaches share the aim of giving the participants as much opportunity as possible to shape the meeting agenda and outcomes, and encouraging dialogue across all the group members, regardless of their status.

Open Space

This term and approach was originated by Harrison Owen in the 1980s and its key features include the opening session where, after a short introduction to the theme of the meeting, participants propose the key issues which then form the detailed agenda. Participants work on these in a flexible way over the course of the meeting and can move around different issues as they see fit, so you will usually find a number of discussions going on at the same time. The role of the meeting facilitator is to support this process and to ensure that the outcomes and proposals are suitably recorded. There is a very useful summary on Wikipedia and you can find details of recent developments at: http://www.openspaceworld.org

World Café

The World Café approach is described on their web site as follows:

"seven World Café design principles are an integrated set of ideas and practices that form the basis of the pattern embodied in the World Café process"
https://theworldcafe.com/key-concepts-resources/design-principles/

The principles include: "clarify the context"; "explore questions that matter"; and "connect diverse perspectives". World Café can be modified to meet a wide variety of needs. Specifics of context, numbers, purpose, location, and other circumstances are factored into each event's unique invitation, design, and question choice, but the following five components comprise the basic model:

1) *Setting*: Create a "special" environment, most often modelled after a café.
2) *Welcome and Introduction*: The host begins with a warm welcome and an introduction to the World Café process, setting the context, sharing the Café Etiquette, and putting participants at ease.
3) *Small Group Rounds*: The process begins with the first of three or more twenty-minute rounds of conversation for the small group seated around a table. At the end of the 20 minutes, each member of the group moves to a different new table...
4) *Questions*: each round is prefaced with a **question** designed for the specific context and desired purpose of the session.
5) *Harvest*: After the small groups (and/or in between rounds, as desired) individuals are invited to share insights or other results from their conversations with the rest of the large group.

The website provides a more detailed discussion of these steps and the design principles and links to the toolkit and book which gives a full insight to the method.

Ketso

As their website explains (http://www.ketso.com):

> *Ketso offers a structured way to run a workshop, using re-useable coloured shapes to capture everyone's ideas. Ketso is unique in that each part is designed to act as a prompt for effective engagement. ... Ketso is not just a re-usable 'workshop in a bag'. It comes with a growing range of free, open-source support resources, including workshop plans that you can customise to suit your needs.*

The practical kit to support a Ketso workshop includes re-usable cards of different types, on which participants write their ideas and comments, and large felt sheets, on which participants can stick the cards to build a concept map which everyone can view and amend. There is also an Action Planner resource.

After the meeting, the maps can be photographed or typed up to inform future actions.

During the pandemic, a new version was developed for online sessions – Ketso Connect – which also uses Padlet to support the discussion.

Which flexible meeting to use?

There is no easy answer to this question, and we are not aware of research which directly compares all the different formats. And there are other formats available – see the website for further examples and discussion.

We have used/experienced all three of these techniques and found them valuable in terms of generating useful ideas and stimulating more discussion than would have been possible in traditional meeting formats. We think that they are especially useful in encouraging open discussion in situations where the team or group is relatively new and/or seem to be a bit "stuck" and not making the progress they would like. However, not everyone feels initially comfortable in these more open-ended formats, and you do need a skilled organiser to set the meeting going and keep everyone involved. For example, the Ketso website does recommend that a meeting organiser should pilot/practise the method before running it "for real".

As well as running a complete meeting in one of these formats, you can of course also consider using some specific techniques from the different approaches to match your own context.

Brainstorming

Brainstorming is a technique which has received a good deal of publicity and generates very mixed reactions. There have been some objections to the terminology and some organisations have used "thought showers" as an alternative term.

Opinions about its value are also divided:

- "brainstorming provides a free and open environment that encourages everyone to participate. Quirky ideas are welcomed and built upon, and all participants are encouraged to contribute fully, helping them develop a rich array of creative solutions".
  (from http://www.mindtools.com/brainstm.html).
- "there is a problem with brainstorming. It doesn't work".
  (This quote from 2012 in *The New Yorker* has been widely discussed. You can find a good example and a number of links to useful studies from Torres, 2012.)

There are two general principles behind brainstorming: that problem-solving is best done in stages and that each stage should obey certain rules. The first stage is generating of ideas. *All* the ideas generated during this stage are recorded for later consideration. Brainstorming sessions usually have someone to lead the session who can enforce the rules and act as scribe. This first stage should also have a definite time limit, say ten minutes. During this time, everyone in the group must obey the following rules:

- no evaluation, no-one is allowed to criticise or evaluate any of the ideas being expressed.
- no censorship, so all ideas are accepted and recorded.
- you are encouraged to produce as many ideas as possible in the given time.
- you are encouraged to hitch-hike, i.e., to build upon the ideas that have been suggested by others in the group.

After the time limit is up, each idea is looked at in turn to see if it is worth pursuing.

But does brainstorming "work"?

This is difficult to answer and demonstrates some of the problems of undertaking social research. Current research and recent summaries often do not support the original claims of more productive and creative ideas. But some of the research studies have not been very 'realistic' tests of the method. Our conclusion is that we do not have definitive evidence either way.

Perhaps the best conclusion is to argue that brainstorming is worth considering as a technique but should be used carefully:

> *I will continue to use brainstorming groups because they can have important social effects - they can act as an 'ice-breaker' to help a group develop more of a co-operative spirit. They can also produce good ideas, especially when a group has tried other ways and is getting 'stuck' on a particular issue. But they are not a magic solution which will guarantee success.*
>
> (Hartley, 1997, page 16)

Structured problem-solving

This is the philosophy on which techniques like brainstorming are based - break down the problem-solving process into discrete stages and then deal with each stage in turn, as in:

- study/discuss/analyse the situation.
- define the problem.
- set your objective.

- generate alternative solutions.
- establish evaluation criteria.
- evaluate alternatives.
- choose among alternatives.

There are many slight variations on this theme. For example, you can argue that deciding the evaluation criteria – on which you judge the possible solutions or decisions – should be done earlier.

Nominal group technique

Nominal group technique (NGT) also tries to organise decision-making to give everyone in the group equal status. NGT mixes group discussion with independent generation of ideas and independent judgement.

It has been used by a wide range of groups in organisations.

Usually supported by an external facilitator, the specific steps are:

- the problem is fully explained to the group.
- individuals work independently to write down ideas and possible solutions.
- each individual presents one idea to the group in turn until all the ideas are recorded (on a flipchart or whiteboard or using Post-It notes on the wall).
- each idea is discussed, clarified, and evaluated by the group.
- individuals privately rank the ideas.
- the group decision is the idea which achieves the highest average ranking.

Delphi

This does not involve a face-to-face meeting. It uses the same steps as NGT and has been used in many different types of organisations since its early development in the 1950s. The group never meets and comments are usually collected electronically. The main stages are:

- enlisting the group of experts.
- distributing the statement of the problem to the group members and inviting them to respond.
- compiling the responses.
- sending out the compiled responses for further comment.

These last two phases are then repeated until a consensus is reached. We have used this technique successfully on research projects which demanded that we convene a panel of experts who were unable to physically meet.

Encouraging group innovation

Michael West and colleagues have carried out a number of studies which suggest four factors encourage team innovation:

- vision.
- participative safety.
- climate for excellence.
- support for innovation.

Research suggests that these factors accurately predict whether a team will be able to produce innovative ideas and solutions (West, 2012).

Changing decision-making

A group or committee should consider its present strategy for making decisions – what are its advantages and disadvantages? There are numerous alternatives. Table 12.3 below lists many of these and identifies one major advantage and disadvantage of each (from Hartley, 1997):

Table 12.3 Decision-making methods

Method	Advantage	Disadvantage
Decision by authority without discussion	Speed	Does not use members' expertise
Decision by authority after discussion	Allows everyone to express opinion	Members may not be committed to the decision
Decision by expert member	Good decision if expert	May be difficult to identify the most exert member
Average members' opinions	Speed	Members may not be committed to the decision
Majority control	Speed	Minority can be alienated
Minority control	Can be useful if not everyone can attend	Members may not be committed to the decision
Consensus	Members will be committed to the decision	Can take a great deal of time, skill, and energy

There are of course additional advantages and disadvantages to each. And we cannot decide on the "best" unless we know the context and the demands of the situation.

Comparing group methods

It is difficult to offer a definitive opinion on which of these methods to use as there is insufficient research on their everyday applications. The research to date does suggest a number of general conclusions:

- groups using systematic procedures probably do make better decisions.
- members of groups using these procedures seem both more satisfied and more committed.
- groups which regularly review their own procedures are usually more effective than those who do not. So, we should also apply this to committees and working groups in terms of their meetings.

This analysis of meetings has assumed that the members are co-operating and are genuinely interested in problem-solving. We must not forget that many real meetings are constrained or influenced by political factors, as illustrated in Box 12.1.

Virtual meetings

Technology has given us several options to improve the process of face-to-face discussion as we have already suggested, e.g., the use of online documents, the use of mind or concept mapping to suggest and record ideas etc.

As we are now familiar with online participation through lockdown, new technology gives us two major possibilities:

- enabling remote participants to join a face-to-face meeting.
  There is no excuse nowadays for even the smallest organisation to exclude a remote member from participating in a face-to-face meeting, unless you have very challenging network issues. The combination of a room equipped with pc/laptop and projector (or a very large TV monitor), wi-fi connectivity, appropriate audio-visual hardware, and software like Zoom or Teams enables remote participants both to attend and join in. The meeting chair needs to conduct the meeting so that they can bring in the remote attender at the right time.
- running a complete meeting online.
  Depending on the size of group, you need to check that your meeting software has the widest range of facilities, as we suggest in Box 12.4.

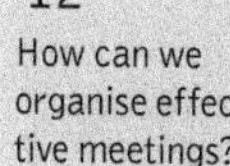

BOX 12.4 SOFTWARE FOR VIRTUAL MEETINGS

A wide range of software can now support virtual meetings. Depending on budget and networking facilities available, you can choose software which has the particular functions you need. From our experience, we suggest that you particularly think about:

- support for presentations.
  You should be able to display PowerPoint and other types of presentation, but certain features may not be supported (e.g., animations may not work on the slides).
  Always check for compatibility.
  Over 2022, we experienced several unexpected glitches (e.g. being unable to see the chat box as a presenter).
- application sharing.
  You may want to show a screenshot or some other software during the meeting and you need to be confident that you can share this application through the meeting software.
- chat box.
  This enables anyone without a mic on their setup to participate as well as encouraging additional comments from everyone. But you need to have a process to bring these comments into the meeting.
- polling and feedback.
  You can ask for reactions from members of the meeting and most software now has icons which allow participants to "show a smiley face" or other signal of agreement or disagreement. Some software offers more sophisticated polling options which can be especially useful in large meetings.
- use of webcams.
  It can be really useful to be able to see other participants as you can pick up on communications clues from e.g., facial expressions, though video signals require good quality telecommunications, and this is not always available.

How different are virtual meetings?

We are often asked how different online or virtual meetings are from their face-to-face counterpart. This is a difficult question to answer as we suggest that you should use face-to-face and virtual meetings in different ways. Table 12.3 below summarises some of the key issues. See the website for more extended discussion and examples.

We must recognise that virtual meetings demand different levels of concentration and attention in comparison to face-to-face settings. Research is now emerging about the nature of these different demands – as we describe in Box 12.4 below.

BOX 12.5 IS ZOOM FATIGUE "REAL"?

The short answer is "yes".

Research has identified four causes for "Zoom fatigue" (Bailenson, 2021):

- the "highly intense" nature of Zoom calls.
- seeing yourself all the time is fatiguing.
- lack of mobility.
- higher "cognitive load" because you need to concentrate more.

Bailenson offers several suggestions to resolve the problems. For example, you can hide or minimise the view of yourself, or include audio-only breaks.

Other recent research suggests positive value in switching off your webcam when you are doing particular tasks. Maria Tomprou and colleagues observed people working in pairs on problem-solving tasks using either audio or video calls. The audio pairs were more successful at collaboration, probably because of fewer distractions (Tomprou et al., 2021). It is dangerous to generalise from just one study, but this does suggest that experimenting with different formats during online meetings could pay dividends

Table 12.4 Comparing face-to-face and virtual meetings

Issue/question	Face-to-face meeting	Virtual meetings
Especially good for?	Establishing relationships Extended open discussion	Saving time and expenses when team is distributed. Progress meetings – keeping everyone up to date.
Not so good for?	Quick short meetings (especially given the time to set up/organise)	Establishing relationships. Extended open discussion. Resolving conflicts.
Ideal timing	Not more than two hours	As long as the main business takes (and no more) 1–1.5 hours as maximum.
Role of chair?	Keeping everyone engaged Working through the agenda on time Ensuring that decisions are clear and accepted	As for face-to-face but special attention on keeping all the participants engaged and able to contribute.
Need for training	Chairs should receive training as discussed in this chapter re agendas and meeting management	As for face-to-face plus necessary training on the technology to be employed.

If you are using software which allows both audio and video links, then you need to think about how you present yourself on screen. We say more on this in the next chapter. You need to consider such issues as how you "respond to silence" given that you normally receive little or no immediate feedback from the audience for your presentation (Koegel, 2010).

SUMMARY OF KEY POINTS

- meetings differ in terms of the level of formality (rules and regulations) and the structure. We need to ensure effective organisation and communication in all the different types.
- there are several compilations of research which have generated useful practical suggestions such as the American Meeting Masters Research Project. This identified individuals who ran excellent meetings and summarised what they did in 7 key principles.
- agendas and minutes are important documents which can support effective meetings. Both need careful attention to style and approach.
- various innovative meeting formats and techniques have been suggested to improve different aspects of meetings, e.g., Open Space, brainstorming, Nominal Group Technique etc. But we have limited evidence on actual organisational practice to offer solid recommendations on which are the most effective. Meetings should regularly review their own approaches and procedures and find the most appropriate solutions.
- following the pandemic, you can use the technology which is now commonplace such as Zoom and Teams to support and enhance your meetings. As well as the obvious use of desktop videoconferencing to allow everyone to contribute regardless of where they are, there are also new methods of transcribing and summarising meeting discussions.

References

Bailenson, J.N. (2021) Nonverbal overload: A theoretical argument for the causes of Zoom fatigue. *Technology, Mind, and Behavior* 2(1). https://doi.org/10.1037/ tmb0000030.

Buchanan, D.A. and Badham, R.J. (2008) *Power, Politics and Organizational Change: Winning the Turf Game*, 2nd edition. London: Sage.

Cooper, S. (2020) *100 Tricks to Appear Smart in Meetings*.

Koegel, T.J. (2010) *The Exceptional Presenter Goes Virtual*. Austin: Greenleaf Book Group Press.

Larsen, E.G. (2022) *70% of Meetings Keep Employees from Doing Productive Work*. https://erikgahner.dk/2022/70-of-meetings-keep-employees-from-doing-productive-work/.

Martin, D. (2000) *Manipulating Meetings: How to Get What You Want, When You Want It*. London: Prentice Hall.

Rackham, M. and Morgan, T. (1977) *Behaviour Analysis and Training*. London: McGraw-Hill.

Rogelberg, S.G. (2019) *The Surprising Science of Meetings: How You Can Lead Your Team to Peak Performance*. Oxford: Oxford University Press.

Stanton, N. (1996) *Mastering Communication*. London: Macmillan.

Tomprou, M., Kim, Y.J., Chikersal, P., Woolley, A.W. and Dabbish, L.A. (2021) Speaking out of turn: How video conferencing reduces vocal synchrony and collective intelligence. *PLoS ONE* 16(3): e0247655. https://doi.org/10.1371/journal.pone.0247655.

Torres, T. (2012) *Brainstorming: More Questions than Answers*. https://www.producttalk.org/2012/07/brainstorming-more-questions-than-answers/.

Tropman, J.E. (2014) *Effective Meetings: Improving Group Decision Making*, 3rd edition. London: Sage.

Tropman, J.E. (2003) *Making Meetings Work: Achieving High Quality Group Decisions*, 2nd edition. Thousand Oaks, CA: Sage.

West, M.A. (2012) *Effective Teamwork: Practical lessons from organisational research*. (3rd edition). Oxford: BPS Blackwell.

CHAPTER 13

Effective presentations

Introduction

Not so long ago, the common image of "presenting" in organisations was someone standing in front of an audience usually sitting in rows in lecture-hall format. This someone (typically male) delivered information, usually hoping that the audience would be engaged and learn from it. The presentation technology in this image changed over the years from the ubiquitous overhead projector to the current standard of data projector, computer/laptop, and PowerPoint. But this did not eliminate a common issue: audience complaints that they were being *talked at* – with the visuals adding neither interest nor learning.

"Death by PowerPoint" summarised this complaint. It became the shorthand description for a "boring presentation". It features in many popular cartoons and in numerous guides to combat it. It even has its own page on Wikipedia.

In recent years, and obviously influenced by the move online during the pandemic, presenting has become much more varied. As a result, you may be called on to present in any of the following situations:

- face-to-face presentations to different-sized groups and in different contexts (with or without slides).
- online presentations to either a group of colleagues or a broader audience.
- hybrid events where there is both a physical and an online audience.
- live and/or recorded vlogs and podcasts.

This demands an expanded skillset from us all, but with increased anxiety for many individuals, another longstanding issue which we need to resolve.

Concerns about presentation skills seem universal and longstanding. For example, Kakepoto et al. (2012) identified "poor oral communication skills" as an important barrier for engineers in Pakistan. These engineers were not fully prepared by their previous technical education for the demands for oral presentation in the workplace.

DOI: 10.4324/9781003297550-17

This chapter concentrates on principles and techniques which can deal with all the above contexts and issues and overcome these criticisms. We also introduce some possibilities offered by new technology to make a presentation part of a systematic communications campaign or process rather than just a "one-off" event.

As with all other forms of communication, you need to find a personal style which plays to your strengths and so we suggest alternative approaches and strategies.

OBJECTIVES

This chapter will:

- explain why oral presentations are still important in modern organisations.
- summarise main techniques which speakers can use to improve their performance and decrease anxiety.
- offer alternative approaches to "the presentation" which you can use in specific situations.
- describe how to ensure presentations are accessible to all members of an audience.
- review developments in technology which you can consider for your future presentations, e.g., vlogs and podcasts.

Why are oral presentations important?

They are now very common and becoming more important. Some organisations now use presentations in meetings where previously they received lengthy written reports. While this can speed up decision-making, a poor presentation might not do justice to the ideas presented and could have catastrophic consequences. So, organisations want staff who can present convincingly and will not confuse, irritate, or mislead an audience.

Presentations are also widely used in recruitment, especially for managerial and supervisory positions. Organisations will select staff who deliver convincing presentations as well as demonstrate other skills and capabilities. This does not necessarily mean people who can "perform" in a theatrical sense although this skill can come in handy if you are addressing large audiences. In keeping with the general theme of this book, we are looking for "effective"' communicators, i.e., those who engage an audience and enable the audience to respond appropriately.

YouTube, vlogs, and podcasts have allowed audiences to access presentations in a much wider context than in the past and this has heightened the need to be able to present in a range of different ways.

Effective communicators will make sure the presentation "flows" by clearly organising the material. They deliver confidently. A speaker lacking in confidence may well distract an audience from the main topic. A really poor presentation can linger in the audience's mind for a very long time. One of our most painful and long-lasting memories was the anxious conference speaker who tried to conquer his nerves by preparing far too many slides for his 20 minutes (in the days when presenters used acetate slides on overhead projector). As time went on, he went faster and faster in a desperate attempt to use all the slides. The audience's attention turned to whether he would finish the race in time (and he failed – delivering a fumbling and embarrassing ending). We have since met several colleagues who attended that presentation – they all remembered the "battle with the slides" but so far none have actually remembered what his talk was about.

Having said that there are certain critical features, you also need to develop your own style to suit your personality. Guidebooks and training texts offer different approaches, as we illustrate in Box 13.1.

Why are people so worried about giving presentations?

The previous paragraphs provide part of the answer to this question. One reason is the "fear of disaster". We have probably all attended at least one disastrous presentation. And we remember how embarrassing and uncomfortable these experiences were. So, we mentally anticipate the possibility that we could be responsible for a similar disaster.

There are two ways to resolve these anxieties:

1. make yourself *feel* less nervous both before and during the presentation, accepting that it is perfectly normal to feel some nerves.
2. *behave* in ways which are likely to conceal your nerves. If you behave confidently, this creates confidence in the audience.

Several techniques can help you to achieve (1) including:

- being really well-prepared.
- relaxation exercises such as deep-breathing.

Following the advice from this chapter will make sure you are well-prepared.

Techniques which help to achieve (2) include:

- starting the presentation in a very deliberate way.
  Make eye contact with the audience in a face-to-face environment. Remember that you are being observed by the audience from the moment you enter the room (or switch on the webcam connection in a virtual presentation).

- rehearse not just the presentation itself but also how you will set out your notes, slides etc.

  Where possible, you should check the venue or technology in advance. We remember the stress of a colleague who was delayed and turned up at the conference room just in time to find that there was no space on the lectern for both his laptop and notes. From our seats at the back, we could only empathise with his increasing anxiety level.
- deliver the presentation in a way which does not attract attention to your level of anxiety.

  For example, if you know your hand might shake a bit then do not use cue cards which you have to hold in front of you. Or hold cue cards but use your other hand to keep your arm steady.

BOX 13.1 DO THE TRAINERS AGREE?

As already discussed, advice on "effective written communication" can be confused or even contradictory. Internet search on 'delivering effective presentations' offers similar variety – different elements to the presentation and different numbers of steps to be taken. For example:

- 12 elements of successful presentation (Indeed Editorial Team, 2021).
- 16 elements of a powerful presentation (Lile, 2021).
- 3 elements of a powerful presentation (Anderson, 2013).
- 7 steps to create a powerful presentation (Campion, 2017).
- 5 strategies to give an effective presentation (Alvernia University, 2015).

Given all the evidence that communication depends on context, it is unwise to rely on absolute "golden rules". You need to find a process that suits you, after you have considered all the alternatives. And this is an area where you might be able to make some "small experiments" and receive feedback on your performance. You should be able to find opportunities to deliver presentations which will not matter too much in terms of your career development or reputation and where you can try out new approaches.

Planning the presentation

The most popular advice to presenters is to plan what you are doing in terms of key stages or key areas. You can find significant common ground between the guidance that experts have offered over the years:

- Raspberry and Lemoine (1986) suggested a four-step process: organisation, construction, practice, and delivery.

- Gallagher, McLelland, and Swales (1998) suggest an eight-step approach, starting by setting the objective. They suggest a simple, one-sentence objective is a good way of clarifying your purpose, as in their example – "As a result of my presentation, my audience will understand and be impressed by the new Customer Services system in Central Branch" (page 130).

There is considerable overlap and common ground between these and other common recipes. Table 13.1 uses the structure we introduced in Chapter 12 to identify main stages and important issues.

it is worth emphasising a few notes of caution:

- the danger with any series of stages is that they can be interpreted too rigidly. As we said earlier in this book when we reviewed strategies for preparing written documents, you need to be flexible and constantly revisit your objectives.
- as we suggested in Table 13.1, you need to find a system for preparation and delivery that suits *you* rather than follow a rigid recipe from the guidebooks. For example, we tend to use concept maps or mind maps to work out structures, but some people find this an unnatural way of organising notes. Some prefer a more structured or hierarchical method like the Pyramid Principle introduced in Chapter 5. The important thing is to find a method which you can work with – then make sure that it delivers a plan which ensures clear structure in your talk.

Presentation as process or event?

A further complication you should consider is one which seems to be neglected in many of the other handbooks and guidelines. Most advice on presentations still treats a presentation as a single "event". For example, Harvard Business School suggests that you need to "tailor your presentation" to these factors:

- Size of the audience.
- Formality of the situation.
- Regularity of the meeting (one-time, occasional, frequent)
- Time of day and other particulars of the occasion. (Morgan, 2007, page 5)

Another common piece of advice which we think is now outdated is to adopt a cautious approach about allowing questions during a presentation in order to avoid losing control when delivering. As a result of Covid and the growing use of the chat function, attitudes towards this have become more flexible. If you are very concerned about "losing control" then you need a strategy to manage this. One useful approach is to plan those points in the presentation where you will encourage questions or discussion and then make a point of pausing there – "can we see what has been raised in the chat...?"

Table 13.1 Planning a presentation

Stage	Content	Points to watch	Example
Decide the general goal	What do you want to achieve overall?	What amount of research are you expected to do? How far can you offer your personal opinion?	You have been working for the last six months in a sales team, promoting a new product which has only been distributed in your region. You achieved the most sales. You have been asked to deliver a ten-minute presentation to the regional sales management team on the likely prospects if they promote and distribute the product nationally.
Consider the context	What's happened in the past? Who are the participants? What is the setting?	Are there any hidden agendas because of the history? What do your audience need or expect to happen?	What do you know about the history of the sales management team in terms of their reaction to proposals? Is it usual to ask someone at your level to make a presentation of this type? You need to check whether you might be "being tested". You need to find out what criteria have been used to decide on a product's future after test marketing. And you need to know what level of detail the managers expect.
Plan	Decide on the objectives. Decide on the structure.	Make your objectives realistic and achievable. Make sure your structure leads up to your objective	Your objectives are to deliver a presentation which: Argues that the product should (or should not) be developed more widely on the basis of sensible evidence. Shows that you can present effectively to a given brief. Your structure should reflect the criteria which the managers will use to judge the product.
Act	Use the relevant skills	What are the most important skills in this situation? e.g., listening, questioning etc.	Explaining and presenting are obviously critical. You will also need to respond to questions and show evidence of research and preparation. And you *must* keep to time.
Follow-up	What can make sure the communication has been effective?	What can you do to reinforce what you have done?	Ask for feedback on the quality of the presentation as soon as possible after the event. This could give useful tips for next time as well as showing you are willing to learn.

We offer further comments on "control" later. The main assumption which you need to question is how far the presentation is a "standalone event" which you need to prepare for. Superficially, this is true, but could also be misleading if it forces you to think *only* about what happens in the presentation itself. It is worth stepping back and considering where your presentation fits into the broader history and context of your organisation. This suggests additional questions which can help you in your planning and preparation:

- what opportunity do you have to make contact with the audience beforehand and perhaps discover some of their issues and concerns?
- what opportunity do you have for dialogue with your audience before, during, and after the presentation?

Various forms of new technology give us options to extend our communication beyond the traditional boundaries. We shall discuss some of these options later in this chapter, including:

- surveying your audience beforehand or at key points to uncover their existing positions and expectations.
- making some content available beforehand (usually online).
- offering a "backchannel" such as a chat function – a dialogue which can go on in the background during a presentation (again usually online) which allows members of the audience to post and exchange comments and/or questions (e.g., inviting specific comments or answers to questions).
- setting up some online discussion either before, during, or after the event.

All of these options can now be realised with simple and accessible software. For example:

- a short survey (say, up to ten questions) can be constructed at little or no cost using tools such as Kahoot, SurveyMonkey, or Google Forms etc. Some software such as Vevox can be embedded into a PowerPoint presentation.
- part or all of a presentation can be made available through SlideShare, SharePoint, Teams, etc. either before the presentation, or afterwards, or both.
- We can provide a "backchannel" through the "chat" feature in software like Zoom or Teams, or by using software such as Twitter which can run in parallel with the presentation.

The importance of structure in presentations

As we say many times in this book, knowing your audience and structure are critical. Choosing the most appropriate will depend on the audience and context.

For example, suppose you have to deliver a presentation which advocates that the company adopts a new procedure for handling customer enquiries. Would the following outline be appropriate?

- confirm the Vision Statement (e.g., "we are leaders in customer care").
- state the Goal and Objective (e.g., "we need to handle customer enquiries more effectively than our competitors").
- summarise Today's Situation (e.g., "we deal with x enquiries at the moment/ we have seen increasing complaints from customers that we do not provide very good support").
- explain how we got to this position (e.g., "we have not reviewed the staffing or the methods since the year x").
- summarise available options (e.g., "there are new answering systems and techniques on the market and our competitors are doing this").
- make a recommendation (e.g. "we need to move to a new system and ensure that our staff are properly trained").

This is based on an outline offered as one of the templates within Microsoft PowerPoint. It is similar to a longstanding outline suggested by Wilder and Fine, 1996:

- Present situation.
- Situation Problems.
- Possible solutions.
- Recommendations.
- Requirements.
- Overcoming obstacles.
- Next steps.

This second outline goes further into the implementation of the recommended solution – overcoming obstacles and so on. The exact outline is probably not as important as making sure the audience knows where you are heading. There are various ways of achieving this and this highlights the importance of the first few minutes of any talk. Consider the strategies for opening and closing listed in Box 13.2.

Alternative structures and styles

Perhaps partly as a reaction to the misery of "Death by PowerPoint", several recent guides suggest moving away from conventional presentation styles to make presentations feel less like a "performance" and more like a conversation. Core to this is the use of storytelling to enhance the presentation. We need to develop and adapt the art of storytelling into the sphere of creating and delivering presentations.

A leader in the field, Garr Reynolds (2014), explains in his TEDx talk that

> *a good presentation is a mix of logic, data, emotion, and inspiration. We are usually OK with the logic and data part but fail on the emotional and inspirational end. Certainly, leaders and educators need to infuse a bit of wonder into their talks that inspire people to make a change. A good presentation should not end when the speaker sits down, or the class comes to an end.*

The use of storytelling was raised earlier in Chapter 7 when considering the way in which data can be presented (in written documents) so that not only is the information delivered clearly, but in a way that enables the readers/ listeners to respond in an appropriate way.

To understand how storytelling works, Reynolds recommends that would-be presenters view the unit on storytelling offered by the Khan Academy.

As well as promoting the significance of storytelling in the development of a good presentation, Garr Reynolds also promotes the importance of looking and sounding comfortable and natural:

> *Naturalness in delivery, then, should not be a formal, one-way didactic lecture. Rather, imagine the delivery of your presentation as a conversation between friends or coworkers, teacher and student, a master and apprentice, or scientist to scientist. They all involve personal connection by way of natural expression.*
>
> (Reynolds, 2011, page 13)

This does not mean that you just "let the presentation happen" but that you reflect very carefully on your style and approach. And you can use a combination of techniques to create your own style. For example, one of our colleagues has successfully used voting/polling to ask the audience what areas they would like to further explore, using a pyramid-style mind map for the overall structure.

BOX 13.2 STRATEGIES FOR OPENING AND CLOSING

The purpose of all of these is to make a connection with the audience so that they want to listen to what you say.

The following suggestions do tend to assume that you are offering a "standalone" presentation. In many if not most situations in organisations, you are delivering presentations to audiences you know to some extent and there will be a history to the event. The presentation may also be recorded and stored and used again in future: referred back to, used for decision-making, used within a series, shared with colleagues who were not at the event, and made available online etc. These all have an impact on the best start and finish for the presentation.

Lewis (1996) suggests six "classic openings":

- Provide a 'startling fact' which relates to your main theme.
- Tell a "strong and relevant anecdote".
- Give a "striking example" which illustrates one of your themes.
- Pay your audience a compliment.
- Raise a "challenging question".
- Tell a joke.

(pages 133–138)

For all these openings, his advice is that they should clearly relate to the main topic that you are presenting. This can be a particular problem for opening 6. The presenter who starts with an irrelevant joke will be seen by the audience as patronising or unprofessional.

He also suggests six "classic closes":

- The "surprise ending", where you make a comment which offers an original twist on your main argument.
- The summary.
- A joke.
- An "upbeat or uplifting exhortation".
- A "call to action".
- A final compliment to the audience.

(pages 139–152)

Of course, there are other alternatives. But do not forget these important principles when you choose your opening and closing:

- the opening comments establish the tone of what you are going to say and also establish your credibility. It can be very difficult to rescue a presentation from a poor or indecisive opening.
- in most presentations, the opening few minutes should provide clear signposts so the audience knows where you are going, what you are trying to cover, and what you want to happen as a consequence of this presentation. Otherwise, the audience will place their own interpretation on what you are trying to do.
- the closing remarks will leave your audience with a particular impression. You need to make sure that this confirms and reinforces the main argument you have offered.

Psychological research suggests that we often remember the opening and closing parts of a presentation and tend to forget the details in the middle.

Critical issues and skills in presentations

Bringing out the common points in the approaches listed above, we suggest that the most critical questions to raise are as follows:

- do you have clear objectives?
- do you know your audience? (What are they expecting? What views do they already have on the topic?)
- do you have a clear structure?
- is your style of expression right?
- can you operate effectively in the setting? (What technology are you using? How confident are you with it?)

Critical skills

Baguley suggests five "core" skills:

- Clarity
- Emphasis
- Using examples
- Organisation
- Feedback

(Baguley, 1994, page 107)

We have already stressed the importance of organisation so it is worth making comments on the other four skills. As a cautionary tale, we offer an embarrassing example of how not to do it in Box 13.3.

Clarity

As the size of the audience increases, so your chances decrease of simply defining what your audience will understand. You need to be especially careful with technical terms and jargon. Consider the jargon surrounding many descriptions of computer systems and see which of the following speakers from Table 13.2 you would prefer. This example illustrates the point that you can explain in a way that most levels of user will follow, especially if you can use everyday analogies to illustrate key ideas.

Emphasis

Good presenters usually give you a very clear sense of their main points. In other words, they emphasise what they think are the most important parts of what they say. There are various ways of doing this, including:

- using NVC to emphasise the verbal message, such as gestures.

Table 13.2 Demystifying jargon

Speaker A	Speaker B
"I want to explicate and demonstrate the additional functionality"	"This package can do things we can't do on our present system. I want to explain what the package can do, show you how it does it, and highlight the advantages over what we do now".
"We've redesigned the user environment for improved ease-of-use".	"We've redesigned how it looks on the screen to make it easier to use".

- pausing before key points.
- stressing key parts of the sentence.
- using rhetorical devices to emphasise – as in the recent British political party slogan – "we have three priorities: education, education and education," or by saying "and if there is one thing, I would like you to remember from this talk, it is..."
- signposting that a main point is coming: "and this highlights one of the most important things I have to say"; "and so my three main concerns are...".

Of course, visual aids can be a major vehicle to convey the emphasis. One final point is the value of a brief handout to summarise main points.

Using examples

Baguley suggests that examples on their own are "not sufficient" (page 108), suggesting that examples should be used to illustrate general rules in a particular sequence, depending on the audience:

- if the audience is familiar with the topic but need to review or be reminded of the rule then you can use either the rule–example or the example–rule sequence.
- if the audience is not familiar with the topic, then you should use the rule–example–rule sequence. In other words, you tell them the rule, give them an example, and then remind them of the rule.

Another important point about examples is that they must clearly highlight the rule and not be open to very different interpretations or contain too much irrelevant detail.

BOX 13.3 HOW TO SHOOT YOUR PRESENTATION IN THE FOOT IN THE FIRST FEW MINUTES

You can "lose" your audience within the first few minutes!

The following example illustrate this:

I (PH) recently attended a seminar where an experienced speaker from industry opened the afternoon session (using PowerPoint). He included *all* the following statements in his opening few minutes:

- "this is the graveyard slot, just after lunch".
- "the previous speakers have said much of what I'm going to say".
- "some of you will have seen these slides before".
- "you can go to sleep now".
- "this is not the most exciting theme of the day".

No prizes for guessing how much interest and enthusiasm this presentation generated in the audience!

Presentation technology

Only a few years ago, the *only* presentation technology mentioned in many guidebooks was Microsoft PowerPoint. PowerPoint is now the "conventional method" but has been criticised for the restricted way it is often used. For example, one senior manager advises us to

> *constantly question to get beneath the platitudes of PowerPoint presentations*
>
> (Woodford, 2012, page 31)

The reliance on standard techniques such as bulleted lists and stock visual aids does not guarantee interest or enthusiasm (as in "Death by PowerPoint") which can be made even worse by the presenter simply reading what is on the screen.

BOX 13.4 BULLET POINTS CAN KILL?

The unthinking use of PowerPoint has been blamed for some serious misrepresentations and distorted arguments. One of the most serious examples is the work by Edward Tufte on the engineering presentations used by NASA where the standard method was PowerPoint (Tufte, undated; Avyukta, 2020; Harris, 2010).

Tufte analyses the PowerPoint slides used in 2003/2005 and it well worth looking at his detailed analysis of particular slides to see how technical data should *not* be reported. His analysis reinforces the conclusions of the Columbia Accident Investigation Board that:

> *distinctive cognitive style of PowerPoint reinforced the hierarchical filtering and biases of the NASA bureaucracy.*

Important technical issues were effectively buried in the detailed bulleted lists of PowerPoint presentations such that the important safety messages were not revealed or highlighted. He concludes that:

> *for nearly all engineering and scientific communication, instead of PowerPoint, the presentation software should be a word-processing program, capable of capturing, editing, and publishing text, data, tables, data, graphics, images, and scientific notation.*

As a result, you need to consider very carefully the nature of the information and messages you wish to present. Looking at the examples in Tufte's article above, we would say that the problem lay not just in the default structures of PowerPoint but also in the way it was used by the NASA scientists and engineers. They could have used the software in a much more flexible way, and they could have supplemented the presentations with detailed technical notes in different formats. But they did not, and this led to tragic and avoidable accidents.

Reflecting on your use of software like PowerPoint

Whatever type of information you are presenting, you need to avoid the "mindless" application of PowerPoint and develop a broader range of skills. Consider a range of alternatives, such as:

Using PowerPoint in a more flexible and varied style, especially if that is the standard organisational system. For example:

- one of our colleagues is a very enthusiastic user of PowerPoint on the grounds that it offers a lot of control over the space on the screen. But he *never* uses any of the standard templates and designs his own from scratch. You may not be able to do this if you have to conform to an institutional template, but you can use the variety of slide styles to ensure that you are not burying or obscuring important information.

Using other software such as Keynote from Apple to take advantage of different styles and templates

- there are now other presentation packages such as Apple's Keynote which offer a similar broad range of facilities to PowerPoint.
- there is an increasing range of presentation packages which enable quick construction of simple messages with libraries of images and icons to help you. See the website for further details and discussion.

Using software with a very different style of navigation such as Prezi

- Prezi treats your presentation as a giant canvas and zooms in and out on the particular slides which you move to. We think this should be used very carefully as the "roller-coaster" transition between slides can be disorienting.

Using embedded presentation tools

- the presentation builder in our preferred concept mapping software (Cmap) allows you to show how a map develops. Alternatives are available in many mind map applications.

Whatever software you choose you should make sure that you are thoroughly familiar with:

- the navigation controls and options.
- The computer setup in the location. Screen resolution on the data projector can still be a particular problem if you are using your own laptop or tablet.

Alternative presentation strategies

There are also some important alternatives to the conventional presentation strategy of "delivery plus questions/comments":

Using pre-presentation surveys

The availability of free or inexpensive survey tools like Survey Monkey or Google Forms means that we can all prepare simple surveys to test opinions.

Polling the audience during the presentation

There are various ways of doing this, including a number of ways of integrating polls into standard PowerPoint presentations.

Incorporating the back-channel for discussion and comment

This can place additional pressure on the presenter to keep up with the chat. There are ways of dealing with this which we suggest below.

Flipping the presentation

The idea of the "flipped classroom" has received considerable publicity in education over the last few years although the method has a longer history than some current accounts give credit for. In its simplest form, the method reverses the conventional lecture and seminar structure that has been a main feature of further and higher education. The presentation, which was the traditional lecture, is made available online in advance so that students work through basic content before the face-to-face class session and are therefore ready to engage in workshop and/or discussion activity. This has a number of advantages, including the fact that students can work through the content at their own pace and at a time which suits their own lifestyle.

This format can be very successful. There is no reason why it cannot be used in contexts other than education or training, as long as you make sure that your audience "knows the rules" and are prepared to put effort in before the meeting.

Using visual slides which engage the audience

An important aspect of any presentation is to use visual images and style to support the argument you are making. Robin Williams (2010) suggests that we apply four general principles of "conceptual presentation design" as we develop and plan the presentation:

- Clarity: making sure that your presentation is "clear and understandable and that viewers can easily assimilate your information".
- Relevance: eliminating all irrelevant material and making everything relevant to the specific audience.
- Animation: using animations to clarify your argument.
- Plot: making sure that you "tell the story".

You can then apply a further four principles of "visual presentation design" to deliver a professional impression through your slides:

- Contrast: using contrast help organise information on your slides.

- Repetition: keeping some constant elements on the slides to give a coherent impression.
- Alignment: keeping items aligned.
- Proximity: using spacing to show the audience which information goes together.

Virtual presentations

One consequence of the pandemic was the explosive growth of online meetings and presentations. As well as exponential growth in numbers, Zoom and other platforms saw new types of online activity across education, business, and in our social and family lives, as well as new forms of negative behaviour such as "Zoom-bombing".

Increasing pressures on time and resources have led to the increasing use of virtual presentations – webinars – using desktop conferencing software, in both the commercial and educational worlds. The software is easy to use and will run effectively on any modern desktop or laptop PC and more recently tablets. This form of presentation will continue to grow, and you should be prepared and able to use it. These presentations are often recorded so you have an additional incentive to make a good impression.

All of the suggestions made earlier in this chapter about face-to-face presentations (importance of objectives, structure etc) also apply to virtual presentations. There are some additional things to worry about and prepare for:

Your on-screen presence

You are presenting to an audience you probably cannot see. Even the best large screen systems can only give you a partial view of the audience and you will not be able to focus on individuals in the same way that you can in a face-to-face presentation. So, you have to be able to include "digital body language" techniques as we discussed in Chapter 5.

Making good use of chat

Webinar software typically allows the audience to interact with you in different ways – voting on a question, asking questions by signaling for access to the microphone, and the ongoing chat box allows anyone to type a comment or message.

How do you manage all these?

You can adopt a team approach to avoid the overload of multi-tasking. In a team approach, the presenter focuses on his/her arguments and engaging the audience

Table 13.3 Practical suggestions for online presentation (based on Reynolds)

Tips from Garr Reynolds	Our comments and further suggestions
Simplify your message	As it can be more difficult to spot when your audience is confused, then you need to keep your message as simple and "sharp" as possible.
Keep it short and mix things up	
Use a variety of visuals	Make sure that you do not use "too many" and confuse your audience.
Make visual elements large	Your audience may be watching you on a smartphone!
Place yourself well in the frame	Record yourself so that you can adjust your position if necessary.
Look at the camera	There are various stands/tripods you can use to adjust the camera position.
Remove clutter behind you	Decide on the best background to avoid distracting viewers.
Get comfortable with the technology	Rehearse and practice – "overlearn" the setup so you will not panic if anything goes wrong.
Upgrade your microphone	It is worth investing in the best mic you can afford.
Upgrade your camera	It is worth investing in the best camera you can afford, or you can take advantage of recent developments like using the iPhone as your webcam.
Improve your lighting	Another area where you can make a big different with a bit of experimentation.
Use direct ethernet connections	Especially if your wi-fi connection is poor or irregular.

while a colleague or colleagues manage the technical process and channel the questions/comments (e.g. Koegel, 2010).

We have used this process effectively in large conference sessions which brought together an audience in the room and virtual delegates from across the country (and in some cases across the world).

For smaller session and audiences, we think that an experienced presenter can effectively manage the whole process, especially if you build in deliberate and regular pauses in the presentation to "catch up on the chat". This is a skill which you can develop with practice.

Podcasts and vlogs

Podcasts and vlogs have grown exponentially since the early 2000s with the increased capability of telephones for recording both audio and video as well as platforms such as Spotify, YouTube, and Instagram to publish recordings. Whilst superficially attractive, offering opportunities to enhance your professional presence within online spheres, you need to consider carefully both the costs and benefits of choosing to participate. As with all professional communication, planning is a necessity – you need to develop skills as well as considering the multiple audiences that can access the outputs. These audiences include unintended viewers or listeners, such as future employers, as well as the audiences that have been planned for.

There is now an enormous number of guides to podcasting, both in books and online. This volume of sources reflects the place of the podcast in developing an online presence. If you are completely new to this area then look for a source which is run by seasoned podcasters and which offers a general overview, such as: https://www.thepodcasthost.com/planning/how-to-start-a-podcast/. The technology has developed rapidly so you also need to follow current practice (see more suggestions on the website).

Podcasting is a useful professional skill to develop and, like other aspects of online presence, can straddle your professional and personal space. You may feel that this is "not your thing", but it is a skill that can be learned, like any other. Also, you may feel that this is something that you may be a natural at, but we can all improve what we do with practice and wider reading.

If you decide to get involved, you will need to develop basic technical skills and understanding. Your choice of platform to host a podcast will influence the level of possible engagement with an audience (García-Marín, 2020).

In preparing to develop podcasts there are some key elements to identify before hitting "record", including:

- why you want to develop a podcast.
- what the key theme(s) of the podcasts will be.
- who the audience will be.
- the level of competition.

To maintain your own commitment to the production of a podcast series and the level of quality required to keep your listeners interested, you need to identify something that you are genuinely enthusiastic about (Kretz, 2018; Wolpaw and Harvey, 2019, Podcast Insights, 2021). If you feel that this is something that you may struggle with, then having a co-creator is something to consider.

At this point you would need to consider the format of the podcast, the level of scripting that might be involved, as well as what avenues you will use to promote the podcast series in order to get listeners. Whilst scripting may seem to be in contrast to the impression that you want to create of a free-flowing delivery or interview, thorough preparation in terms of the content and direction of the podcast are required. This preparation will enable you to produce a podcast that presents you as a professional, i.e., knowledgeable of your subject and in command of your delivery.

Where your podcasts include interviews, knowing the background and area of expertise of the interviewee will enable you to generate interesting and insightful questions to support the delivery. In some ways, this aspect reflects the development of a semi-structured interview that would be used for a research project. In both cases, it is important to let the interviewee speak at length while you and keep your own contributions to a minimum.

The world of vlogs is currently more limited in the range of subject matter compared to podcasts, despite the size of YouTube and Instagram. At the time of writing, the most popular themes for vlogs are: beauty, gaming, travel, technology, health and fitness, cooking, do-it-yourself, and lifestyle (adobe.com, 2022). This presents a list of areas where there are already substantial audiences but also significant competition. Moreover, despite the apparent authenticity of vloggers in terms of presenting themselves as being spontaneous and genuine, the reality is that the most popular are professionally edited and curated and supported with brand sponsorship. Engaging in the world of vlogging may only be really beneficial if you are committed to developing a career in vlogging. But we hesitate to make detailed predictions as technology is advancing so fast.

SUMMARY OF KEY POINTS

- presentations are increasingly common in organisations. You should be prepared to confidently deliver presentations where the presentation flows and is clearly organised.
- there are two main ways to resolve anxieties about presentations. First, you can make yourself feel less nervous by using relaxation techniques and being well-prepared. Secondly, you can behave in ways which conceal your nerves.
- characteristics of effective presentations include a clear structure which is communicated to the audience. Other important issues are clear objectives, how far you know your audience, your style of expression, and whether you can operate effectively in the setting. All depend upon the audience and context.
- Microsoft PowerPoint is the industry-standard presentation software, so you need to be able to use it. But you also need to decide when and where to use different software or a different approach.
- there are some important alternatives to the conventional presentation strategy of "delivery plus questions/comments". Alternatives worth

considering include: the use of pre-presentation surveys; incorporating the back-channel; flipping the presentation.

- increasing pressures on time and resources have led to the increasing use of virtual presentations – webinars – using desktop conferencing software and you should be prepared and able to use this form of delivery.
- presenting online has its own challenges and you need to make sure are both well-prepared and suitably equipped with technology.
- podcasting offers opportunities to enhance your professional and personal presence online – again you need to do the necessary groundwork and preparation.

References

Alvernia University. (2015) *Speaking Up: 5 Strategies to Give an Effective Presentation*. https://online.alvernia.edu/articles/effective-presentation-skills/.

Anderson, G.Z. (2013) *The Three Essential Elements of a Great Presentation*. https://managementhelp.org/blogs/communications/2013/11/04/the-three-essential-elements-of-a-great-presentation/.

Avyukta. (2020) *Death by PowerPoint. The Slide that Killed*. https://medium.com/the-futuristic-co/death-by-powerpoint-the-slide-that-killed-f3265a8d284a.

Campion, S. (2017) *7 steps to create a powerful presentation* The Actuary. At: https://www.theactuary.com/features/2017/10/2017/10/10/7-steps-create-powerful-presentation

García-Marín, D. (2020). Mapping the factors that determine engagement in podcasting: design from the users and podcasters' experience. *Communication and Society*, 33 (2): 49–63.

Indeed Editorial Team. (2021) *12 Elements of Successful Presentation*. https://www.indeed.com/career-advice/career-development/elements-of-presentation.

Kakepoto, I., Said, H., Buriro, G.S. and Habil, H. (2012) Beyond the technical barriers: Oral communication barriers of engineering students of Pakistan for workplace environment: Preliminary results. *Research on Humanities and Social Sciences* 3(10): 2013.

Kretz, C. (2018) How To Start A Podcast. *Library Journal*, 143(9), pp. 18.

Lile, S.P. (2021) *What are the Elements of a Powerful Presentation?* https://www.beautiful.ai/blog/what-are-the-elements-of-a-powerful-presentation.

Morgan, N. (2007) *Giving Presentations*. Boston, Mass: HBP

Morgan, G. (1997) *Images of Organisa*tion, New Edition. London: Sage.

Podcast Insights (2023) *How to start a Podcast: A complete Step-by-Step Tutorial* How To Start A Podcast In 2023: A Step-By-Step Guide (podcastinsights.com)

Reynolds, G. (2011a) Blog at www.presentationzen.com.

Reynolds, G. (2011b) *The Naked Presenter: Delivering Powerful Presentations With or Without Slides*. Berkeley, CA: New Riders.

Reynolds, G. (2014) TEDx Talk "Why Storytelling Matters" https://youtu.be/YbV3b-l1sZs

Tufte, E. (undated) *PowerPoint Does Rocket Science – And Better Techniques for Technical Reports*. https://www.edwardtufte.com/bboard/q-and-a-fetch-msg?msg_id=0001yB&topic_id=1.

Wolpaw, J. T., and Harvey, J. (2020). How to podcast: a great learning tool made simple. *The Clinical Teacher*, 17(2), 131–135. https://doi.org/10.1111/tct.13040

CHAPTER 14

Effective teams

Introduction

Many organisational analysts emphasise the importance of teamwork to organisational success:

> *Pretty much all the most challenging work today is undertaken in groups for a simple reason: problems are too complex for any one person to tackle alone.*
>
> (Syed, 2020, page 14)

As a result, many companies worldwide have made significant investments in team training. For example, we will describe Belbin's model of team roles. According to their website, this

> *now operates in over 100 countries, has been translated into 25 languages and has more than 35 distributors worldwide*
>
> (https://www.Belbin.com; last accessed 9/10/22)

We need to know the essential characteristics of a successful team, define the most important processes for effective teamwork, and work out the best ways to develop effective teams. This chapter confronts all these questions and emphasises that the quality of communication, allied to the quality of the team members, makes the real difference.

We now have a range of new technologies which can either help or impede this communication and we are now all familiar with the mechanics of Zoom and/or Teams meetings. We summarise important findings from recent research which suggests the particular advantages and possible limitations of this technology.

DOI: 10.4324/9781003297550-18

BJECTIVES

This chapter will:

- define an "effective team".
- show how important effective teams are to modern organisations, and comment on moves to "empower" work teams.
- analyse important processes which can influence group and team working, including team roles, leadership, and problem-solving.
- suggest ways in which virtual and online teamwork are best supported.
- discuss how we can best develop teams in organisations.

We need a team!

Consider the following extract from a management meeting. Are their plans likely to be successful? Jim is the manager:

Hugo: "ABC are offering an upgrade on the network software for a special price".
Mo: "We'd better check that carefully before we commit ourselves."
Jan: "We'd better ask a team to investigate it and report back quickly".
Mo: "Needs Harry and Fran from my department – they've got the technical expertise."
Hugo: "Don't forget finance – Michael and Mika should be involved".
Sasha: 'Don't forget users – How about Helen from head office and Joe for the other sites?"
Pat: "That team will never work together – they are all too concerned with their own issues. Who is going to co-ordinate?"
Jim: "They'll be all right. All they need is a clear deadline. It won't take more than a couple of meetings".

What chance would you give this working group of working effectively as a team? What confidence would you have in their recommendations after a couple of meetings?

What makes a team?

Jim, senior manager, has no time for this question. In his opinion, all you need to do is assemble a group with necessary technical expertise, give them a deadline, and wait for the result. But will it be a "good" result?

In his book which aims to "revolutionise your thinking and make wiser decisions", David Robson summarises research demonstrating what he calls the "intelligence trap" – where "smart people" make bad decisions because of faulty thinking. This typically happens because of four factors:

- people may lack *necessary tacit knowledge* and *counter-factual thinking.*
- people may fail to recognise flaws in their own thinking. They rationalise and perpetuate mistakes due to *dysrationalia, motivated reasoning, and the bias blind spot.*
- people may be overconfident and failed to recognise their limitations because of *earned dogmatism.*
- people may employ *entrenched, automatic behaviours* that render us oblivious to the obvious warning signs that disaster is looming, and more susceptible to bias.

(Robson, 2019. Page 84)

Fortunately, he suggests ways to avoiding this "trap", reflecting points we have made in previous chapters, including:

- do not jump to premature conclusions.
- be aware of your own prejudices and typical assumptions and actively avoid them.

Differences between teams and groups

What are the most important differences?

Leading American experts, Katzenback and Smith, distinguish different types of team/group and argue that high-performance teams are much more effective than working groups. In "working groups", staff meet together to share information and to co-ordinate and make decisions. This is very different from what they call a "real team":

> *a small number of people with complementary skills who are committed to a common purpose, performance goals, and a working approach for which they hold themselves mutually accountable.*
>
> (Katzenbach and Smith, 1998, page 220)

The critical differences are the levels of commitment and the strong sense of mutual support and accountability.

Think of a working group that you have been involved in – what happened when something went wrong? Did *everyone* feel *equally* accountable? Did they *all* pull together to put it right? Or did the group search out and perhaps "punish" the member who had made the mistake? According to Katzenback and Smith, a real team will always do the former – they will always take collective decisions and they will always hold themselves mutually responsible.

They suggest six basic elements of a team. High-performance teams score highly on *all* these:

- size (is it large enough to do the job but small enough for easy communication?)
- skills (does the team have all the necessary skills?)
- purpose (is this "truly meaningful" – do all members understand it and see it as important?)
- goals (are they clear, realistic, specific, shared, and measurable?)
- working approach (is this also clear, shared, fair, and well understood?
- mutual accountability (is everyone clear on their individual and joint responsibilities? Do they feel mutually responsible?)

Katzenback and Smith accept that working groups can be effective and make sensible decisions. But "real teams" will be much more effective. They also define other varieties of group/team:

The pseudo-team

A working group may call itself a team when actually there is no real shared responsibility – the members act as individuals. Their failure to share and co-ordinate may make them perform worse than a working group which has fewer pretensions.

The potential team

The potential team is the group which is trying to move to full teamwork but still not clear on its goals/priorities and still struggling with issues of individual responsibilities and loyalties. Whether it make the transition will depend on the quality of the leadership/management and the commitment of the members. Box 14.1 gives an example of how *not* to manage this transition.

BOX 14.1 HOW NOT TO MOVE TO TEAMS.

Workers in the British factory of a large American corporation were called to a mass meeting on Friday afternoon. The management presentation explained the advantages of "self-managing teams" – work teams are responsible for setting targets and monitoring quality and left to get on with it, without continual management supervision. The factory was moving to this system the following Monday morning, and all the existing supervisors were reallocated to other work within the company. The presentation finished and everyone went home for the weekend.

What do you think happened on Monday morning? An immediate upturn in productivity and morale? Or confusion, chaos, and anxiety? And why were an intelligent management group surprised when it was the latter?

A major issue in any discussion about teams is the amount of control and power which they have over their operations and progress. Many organisations have not just been training workers to work together more co-operatively but also giving the teams more responsibility.

Group and team processes

Turning groups into teams is not quick or easy. It depends on understanding fundamental group dynamics, which we discuss below:

- group development.
- team roles.
- leadership.
- problem-solving and decision-making.
- inter-group relationships (relationships *between* groups).

Group development

Many business texts paint a very definite picture of how groups change over time – moving through four stages: forming, storming, norming and performing.

This account – four stages in a definite sequence – is probably the most well-known account of group development and you can find numerous accounts online and on YouTube. It is based on work by Tuckman (1965) who surveyed all the studies of small group development he could find at the time and suggested this was the common pattern. Groups start with a period of uncertainty. They then move into a phase of conflict – members argue about the task and more personally. Roles and relationships then get established. Only then is the group able to get on with the job at hand.

But is this the "natural" or typical sequence for *all* small groups? Tuckman himself was not so certain, pointing out some limitations in the studies he surveyed. Nonetheless, his account has become the dominant model, as summarised in Table 14.1 in terms of the content (how members approach the task) and the process (how members relate to one another).

Table 14.1 Tuckman's four-stage model of group development

Stage	Content	Process
Forming	Members try to identify the task and how they should tackle it. The group decides what information they need and how they are going to get it. Members try to work out the "groundrules".	Members try to work out what interpersonal behaviours are acceptable. Members will be very dependent on the leader and the reactions of other members.
Storming	Disagreement and argument over the task.	Members are hostile to the leader and other members.
Norming	The group agrees on the task and how to do it.	Group members start to accept each other. Group norms develop.
Performing	The group concentrate on completing the task.	Group members take on roles which enable them to complete the task.

In 1977, Tuckman decided this model could still account for all the studies he could identify, provided you added a final fifth stage – adjourning. In this final stage, group members know that the group is about to part or split up. They make efforts to complete the task and say their farewells.

We have certainly experienced these phases in *some* project groups and teams we have been involved in. But is this life cycle inevitable? In fact, several stage theories offer variations on the themes set out by Tuckman. And many of these suggest that stages can occur in various different sequences (e.g. Hartley, 1997, Chapter 4). For example, Susan Wheelan (1996) proposed five stages:

- "needs and inclusion", where members are anxious and dependent on the leader.
- "counterdependency and flight", characterised by conflict.
- "trust and structure", where norms develop.
- "work".
- "termination" – the group finishes and disbands.

But she also pointed out exceptions: groups can get "stuck" or "regress" to a previous stage; groups can get stuck in a conflict phase and self-destruct.

An important principle here is that members of groups should try to work out what stage of development they are in and act sensitively to "move the group along". Wheelan used her model to also offers practical advice to members and leaders, summarised in Table 14.2, highlighting that it is not just the leader who is responsible for helping the group develop.

Table 14.2 Working through Wheelan's stages of group development

Stage	What leaders need to do	What members need to do
Dependency and inclusion	Enable open discussion of values, goals, tasks, and leadership.	Request information about goals. Raise their personal concerns.
Counterdependency and flight	Make sure that the conflicting issues are dealt with constructively.	Work to resolve conflicts constructively.
Trust and structure	Organise in ways that make the group productive.	Organise in ways that make the group productive.
Work	Periodically assess how the group is going to ensure that the group can adjust to any changes.	Periodically assess how the group is going to ensure that the group can adjust to any changes.

The problem is that real work groups are not likely to follow the "textbook" sequence of stages in such an orderly and predictable way. There are several good reasons why we can expect more complex and more fluid development:

- membership may change, forcing the group to re-form in some way.
- the task facing the group may change.
- deadlines may change.

Other theories challenge the idea of groups progressing through a series of stages. For example, we have observed project groups which follow the theory of "punctuated equilibrium" where there is a very different pattern:

- starting into the task fairly quickly (not necessarily any "storming").
- hitting something of a crisis halfway through when the group is not making the progress it should.
- changing tactics (and sometimes the leadership) for the second half of the project.

Whether the group is successful or not depends on the effectiveness of the tactics they adopt at this halfway point.

How will your group develop?

We cannot offer a definitive answer, especially as we do not have sufficient research yet on changes in post-pandemic work practices. We can say that:

- it is important to regularly review your group development.
- you can use insights from theories, such as the value of a "halfway progress meeting" for project groups.

- you should investigate developments in group theory (e.g. Hurt and Trombley suggest an alternative model which integrates elements of Tuckman's work and ideas from punctuated equilibrium).
- you should investigate and implement practical strategies which suit your context.

Understanding leadership

An enormous range of books claim to unravel the mysteries of leadership: from social science research, through the literature from management and business studies, and on to the various leading personalities who want to tell us how to "do it right". You can also find interesting mixtures of fact and fiction, as we illustrate in Box 14.2. Although very diverse, many texts agree on a few fundamental points:

- leaders have special qualities which we can identify.
- leaders have an important effect on their organisations.
- we need leaders, and only one leader in each situation.

However, *all* of these views can be (and have been) disputed, at least in some contexts. Many researchers do not believe that we really understand enough about leadership and that we have ignored cultural factors.

One recent book by Jo Owen identifies 35 "myths" of leadership. He comments that "there is no definitive answer on leadership" (Owen, 2022, page 3) and discusses specific myths, including:

> "We know what leaders do".
> "Great leaders build great teams".
> "Male and female leaders are different".

Each of these generalisations can be questioned which means that "leadership is contextual" (Owen, op cit, page 59). For example, the claims of differences between male and female leaders are often based on stereotypes which are not borne out by systematic research.

BOX 14.2 DIVERSE VIEWS OF LEADERSHIP

Many management texts on leadership have wandered into fantasy and parable to make their points more entertaining. For example, Wess Roberts' *Make It So* (1995) contains leadership lessons supposedly written by Captain Jean-Luc

Picard – well-known across the world as a previous Captain of the Starship Enterprise and in his recent series on Amazon Prime.

But can we transplant the qualities required by a group of intrepid space travellers confronting the unknown on a regular weekly basis to the office or factory? You can ask the same question about Roberts' earlier best-seller – *The Leadership Secrets of Attila the Hun.*

Dominant views on leadership have changed over the years and some views have slipped out of favour. For example, the search for personality traits and characteristics to underpin leadership was very popular in the early 20th century. But researchers found different traits were important in different situations. Studies failed to show strong relationships between the leader's character and team performance. More recently, this line of research has been revived and some modern theorists emphasise the importance to the personality of the leader, and how this is perceived by followers.

One example of this interest is the study of a so-called charismatic leader, who

> *is regarded by his or her followers with a mixture of reverence, unflinching dedication and awe.*
>
> (Bryman, 1992, page 41)

Rather than see this form of leadership as just emerging from the leader's personality, this style of leadership is often conceptualised as a particular form of relationship between leader and followers.

Recommendations about leadership often have strong moral or ethical overtones as illustrated by this quote from Simon Sinek:

> *Leadership is about integrity, honesty and accountability…To be a true leader, to engender deep trust and loyalty, starts with telling the truth.*
>
> (Sinek, 2014, page 150)

The difficulty with many of these recipes for success and the underlying studies is that they often focus on the "movers and shapers" of corporations or on people who have responded heroically in emergencies. Do the same considerations apply when we think of more modest attempts to lead?

The search for leadership functions and style

Looking at what leaders do has taken a number of directions, one of which was to try to define the functions of leadership. For example, a series of American studies suggested that effective leaders should score highly on both the following dimensions:

- initiating structure, i.e. organising to complete the task.
- consideration, i.e. developing good relations with the members.

In the UK, the work of John Adair has been used for leadership training in a wide variety of organisations. He suggests that leaders fulfil three functions:

- achieving the task.
- building the team, maintaining good working relationships throughout the team.
- developing the individuals in the team, dealing with the members' needs as individuals.

(Adair, 1986)

If we know what leaders "do" then perhaps we can also define an ideal leader style. Many texts still quote the classic study from the 1930s by Lewin, Lippitt and White to suggest that democratic leadership is unequivocally the "best". But this is not a full picture of their results. Democratic groups reported the highest morale and satisfaction, kept working even when the leader was absent, and produced the highest quality models. Autocratic groups produced the most models – but only when the leader was present. When the autocratic leader was absent, groups quickly turned to misbehaviour. Later studies produced mixed results, especially when comparing groups from different cultural backgrounds.

Despite mixed research findings, the notion of an ideal style of leadership which blends concern for the task and support for the members is still popular.

Contingency approaches

Given that research on style and functions did not always deliver consistent results, some researchers turned to more complex models, suggesting that effective leadership depends on (is contingent upon) several factors.

Fiedler's Contingency Theory

Fiedler started from the idea that there were two fundamental types of leader – task and socio-emotional – and that these were taken on by different types of people. He developed a measure of these leadership styles and investigated which style was effective in which situation. Two important conclusions were:

- leadership style should match the situation to get best results.
- if the match is poor then leaders could alter the situation to improve it

Evaluating Fiedler

Although Fiedler cited an impressive range of supporting studies, there are important criticisms of his approach, e.g. is leadership style as fixed as he maintains? Other contingency theories incorporate the level of maturity of the group members and the cultural context. Unfortunately, the message from this and other research is that any simple model of leadership behaviour is almost certainly mistaken.

Leadership and management

Another important issue is the difference between leadership and management – often differentiated as in Table 14.3.

The general distinction is between the notions of "direction" and "vision" associated with leadership and notions of "competence" and "efficient operations" associated with management. This is often summarised in the catchphrase "leaders are people who do the right things and managers are people who do things right" (this last quote is attributed to Warren Bennis and dismissed as part of yet another myth by Jo Owen (op cit, page 11).

We agree with Owen that this very clear distinction does not hold true in many context – he prefers the definition of leader offered by Henry Kissinger:

> *someone who takes people where they would not have got by themselves.*
>
> (Owen, op cit, page 12)

Another way of approaching this distinction is to say that leadership is simply *one* of the many roles which managers may play. One influential proponent of this approach was Henry Mintzberg (1973), suggesting that managers can occupy ten roles:

- three interpersonal roles, including leader.
- three informational roles, including monitor and disseminator of information.
- four decisional roles, including negotiator and entrepreneur.

Table 14.3 Comparing leadership and management

The leader	The manager
Creates and communicates the vision	Controls
Develops power base	Is appointed
Initiates and leads change	Maintains status quo
Sets objectives	Concentrates on results

This concern with the roles associated with leadership is just one recent trend in leadership research which we now turn to.

Recent developments in leadership research

We are still searching for a definitive account of leadership. Barbara Kellerman has spent a good deal of her professional life "making a living from leadership" through writing, teaching, and research. So we need to take her very seriously when she castigated what she calls the "leadership industry" (all the training, books, courses etc.) for failing to deliver:

> *while the leadership industry has been thriving...leaders by and large are performing poorly, worse in many ways than before.*
>
> (Kellerman, 2012, page xiii)

She argued that times have changed but our leadership practices have not responded and cites multiple examples of failure, including the finding that (in the USA)

> *only a dismally low 7 per cent of employees trust their employer.*
>
> (op cit, page 170)

Given this level of scepticism with conventional wisdom, how can we respond?

Kellerman reported a growing level of support for her views in her later book. She suggested that things had not improved and that:

> *leadership has stayed stuck – remained an occupation, as opposed to becoming a profession.*
>
> (Kellerman, 2018, page 9)

She offers a way forward based on the need to treat leadership "more soberly and seriously, like a profession" (op cit, page 9).

If you are preparing for a leadership position, our recommendation is that you should investigate proposals for leadership style which specifically respond to the world of digital connections – such as the concept of the "network leader", represented as three overlapping areas (Hall and Janman, 2010, page 91ff):

- Cognitive flexibility – being able to face new and unanticipated challenges.
- Strategic resilience – with strong perseverance and focus on outcomes.
- Network excellence – the quality of our connection to others.

The importance of networking is paramount:

> *everything that leaders think, do or aspire to is mediated through the thoughts and actions of others with whom they interact.*
>
> (op cit, page 109)

Another approach which ties in with much of the thinking in this book is the work by Clampitt and DeKoch (2011) based on the idea that effective leadership leads to progress:

> *Leaders who are willing to embrace certain strategies and tactics can become progress makers.*
>
> (Clampitt and DeKoch, page 6)

We also suggest that you keep a watchful eye on other important themes which have emerged from recent research including:

- vision, communication, and networking – emphasising the leader's need to communicate a clear vision for the group or organisation.
- culture and values – emphasising the leader's role in building and maintaining an appropriate culture for the group to work in and for the leader to be concerned with values and goals.
- leadership as "situated action" – trying to provide a more sophisticated analysis of the situations that leaders find themselves in than you find in earlier contingency theories.
- leadership as skilled behaviour, making a more detailed analysis of the skills and behaviour which "good" leaders use.
- cultural differences, recognising that there may be some common qualities required of leaders in many cultures but that these will be expressed differently.
- power and authority structures, looking at the different forms of power which leaders may use and how followers see their power and authority.
- "service or servant leadership", where "the entire organisation is focused on supporting customer-facing teams, and so the customer" (Laker, 2020). This "upends" the typical organisational pyramid – "instead of employees serving the leader, the leader serves the employees" (Indeed Editorial Team, 2022).

BOX 14.3 THE LEADER AS COMMUNICATOR

Georgiades and Macdonell suggest that leaders carry out four "explicit imperatives":

- scrutinise the external environment.

- develop a vision and communicate its strategic implications.
- develop the organisation culture so that can deliver this vision and its strategy.
- specify what management has to do to "drive the desired culture".(1998, page 21)

The search for group roles

Until recently, the typical description of roles in small groups borrowed the three-way distinction originally set out by Benne and Sheats:

- group task roles, such as initiating ideas, requesting or giving information.
- group maintenance roles, such as supporting or encouraging others, or resolving tension.
- individual roles, such as blocker or recognition-seeker.

But this is purely descriptive – it does not tell you which combination of roles is most effective. An important example of work which tries to answer this question comes from Meredith Belbin (2010).

Belbin's Team Roles

Over a period of around ten years, Belbin and colleagues observed several hundred teams of managers on management games and exercises and found that:

- team members' behaviours were organised in a limited number of team roles.
- these team roles were independent of members' technical expertise or formal status.
- managers consistently adopted one or two of these team roles.
- preferred team roles were linked to personality characteristics.
- the effectiveness of the team depended upon the combination of team roles.

Originally, Belbin identified eight team roles. He later added the role of "specialist" who brings specialist expertise to the group. Their main contribution to the group is summarised in Table 14.4 with our comments on practical implications. Belbin's own recipe for success is summarised in Box 14.4. You can find the latest development in their thinking at the website https://www.belbin.com..

Table 14.4 Belbin's team roles

Role	Main contribution to the group	Our suggestions re practical implications
Chair	Organizes and co-ordinates. Keeps team focused on main objectives. Keeps other members involved.	You need to ensure that the chair has the appropriate personality and skills.
Team leader (shaper)	Initiates and leads from the front. Challenges complacency or ineffectiveness. Pushes and drives towards the goal.	Who is the actual leader – the chair or the shaper? There may be interpersonal conflict here if both try to be "the leader". This needs managing.
Innovator (plant)	Provides new and creative ideas.	At least one person needs to be creative in relation to the task.
Monitor–evaluator	Provides dispassionate criticism.	This can be an "uncomfortable" role so needs to be appreciated.
Team worker	Promotes good team spirit.	A really important role if progress is slower than expected.
Completer	Checks things are completed. Monitors progress against deadlines.	Another role that can be "uncomfortable" if other members do not appreciate its value.
Implementer (company worker)	Practical and hard-working. Focuses on the practical nitty-gritty.	This role can be seen as a "bit boring" – another one that should be appreciated by other members.
Resource investigator	Makes contacts outside the group.	Networking skills can be critical in some projects.

(Titles in brackets are the original labels used in Belbin's earlier book, 1981.)

BOX 14.4 BELBIN'S RECIPE FOR SUCCESS

Once you know which roles are strongly represented in the group, then you can check whether your group has all the recommended ingredients:

The right person in the chair

Make sure that the person who is carrying out the functions of chairing the group meetings has the appropriate personality and skills.

One strong plant in the group

Do you have at least one person who is both creative and clever in terms of the job at hand?

Fair spread in mental abilities

What is needed is a spread of abilities, including the clever plant and competent chair.

Wide team-role coverage

As many of the roles should be there as possible.

Good match between attributes and responsibilities

This is where members are given roles and jobs which fit their abilities and personal characteristics.

Adjustment to imbalance

If the group can recognise any gaps in its make-up, can it adopt strategies to make good these problems?

Some implications of Belbin's work

We suggest three very important implications:

- all the roles are valuable (some other approaches include destructive or negative roles).
- groups can develop strategies to cope with any imbalance.
- the third is best expressed as a question – using Belbin's role.
- descriptions, who is the leader? Is it the chair or the shaper? Belbin says it depends on the situation.

We still do not have enough independent research evidence to assume that Belbin offers a definitive account of group roles. There are both critical and supportive studies, especially concerning his self-report questionnaire.

To reflect on how you relate to these team roles, you can find early copies of his questionnaire (Belbin, 1981). You should also consider his recommendations that people should seek feedback from others (his system uses observer ratings as well as the questionnaire data) before accepting any classification. We are not necessarily accurate judges of our own behaviour.

Other systems of classifying roles are available which have some similarities to Belbin including the Team Management Wheel from Margerison McCann at http://www.tmsdi.com. You can also find free inventories on the web often based on the Myers Briggs model of personality, e.g. at http://www.teamtechnology.co.uk.

With any/all self-test systems, we repeat Belbin's warning that you should supplement any results with reliable feedback from others.

Problem-solving and decision-making

Many studies show that groups can fail to solve problems or make ineffective decisions if they ignore some of the following:

- determining the type of task.
  For example, can the task be divided into subtasks (divisible) or not (unitary)? Does the group need to produce as much as possible (maximising) or are they trying to achieve some predetermined standard (optimising)?
- problem-solving barriers, biases, and traps.
  For example, we may perceive selectively. We may have subconscious biases. We are very sensitive to contextual influences. We sometimes use inappropriate heuristics (a heuristic is a general rule of thumb). We use misleading frames of reference. We can fall into problem traps, such as overconfidence, which is usually inversely related to accuracy. The more confident people are, the more likely they are wrong!

Communication and decision-making

On the positive side, the quality of communication is critical on both simple and complex tasks. What is still not clear is some of the relationships between communication, interaction and other components of the decision-making-process.

Group goals are important, e.g. groups working towards specific, difficult goals perform better than those without specific goals. Research suggests the following practical strategies:

- setting goals which cover all aspects of the performance.
- providing regular feedback on progress.
- encouraging communication between members.
- encouraging and supporting planning activities.
- helping group members manage failure.

Groups can fail to recognise that they are not considering all the alternatives needed to arrive at a balanced decision. For example, in 1961, James Stoner suggested that groups tend to move towards more "risky" decisions than those initially expressed by individual members - the "risky shift". Later work concluded that the actual group process was "group polarisation" – if the individual average is on the cautious side, then the group decision will be *more cautious*. If the individual average is towards the risky side, then the group decision will be riskier than the average of the individual opinions.

But will this group make effective decisions?

How much trust would you place in decisions from a group which had the following characteristics?

- they are very cohesive.
- they seem to be insulated from information from outside sources.
- as decision-makers, they rarely make systematic search through alternative decision possibilities.
- they feel under stress to make quick decisions.
- they are dominated by a directive leader.

This group suffers from "groupthink", a concept suggested by Irving Janis, after investigating historical accounts of poor group decisions. These group characteristics lead to "concurrence-seeking tendencies" which then lead to faulty decisions. If you have a cohesive group with all these characteristics, then they will likely fall victim to groupthink.

The good news is that groups can work out strategies to avoid these problems. For example, Janis cited the Kennedy administration as victims of groupthink after the Bay of Pigs crisis in the 1960s which nearly escalated into World War 3. A year later, they successfully managed an even more serious crisis – they had implemented strategies to avoid groupthink. For example, they appointed one member of the group to play "devil's advocate" at each meeting, rotating this role round the group so it did not become one person's responsibility. This made sure that every decision was scrutinised with a critical eye.

How widespread is "groupthink"?

Other investigators query some of Janis' conclusions, questioning whether his historical analysis is so clear-cut, and arguing he might have underestimated political forces. Other researchers have questioned the role of cohesiveness. Some studies suggest the opposite relationship – low cohesiveness associated with groupthink – or no strong relationship between the two. The style of the leader comes out as very important in many studies.

Some commentators have used the concept of groupthink in a way that seems to overgeneralise Janis' original ideas. For example, Christopher Booker uses the concept in case studies ranging from political correctness to global warming (Booker, 2020).

Further research looking at the detailed impact of group communication and interaction processes on decision-making identified five critical functions:

- is the problem thoroughly discussed?
- are the criteria for a successful solution thoroughly examined?
- are all realistic alternative solutions proposed?
- are the positive aspects of each proposal fully assessed?
- are the negative aspects of each proposal fully assessed? (Hirokawa and Poole, 1996)

Problem-solving groups which can honestly claim to achieve all these functions in open communication have the best chances of success.

Inter-group relationships

Question: When is "a" group not "one" group?
Answer: When it's an intergroup!

In other words, when we communicate with another person we may choose to communicate with them on the basis of the social categories which we occupy, as in the following examples:

- I am lecturer, you are student.
- I am manager, you are trade union representative.
- I am engineer, you are from sales and marketing.

In each case, we may be more aware of our "group responsibilities" than our individual characteristics. And this can have a very powerful influence on our behaviour. The easiest way to illustrate this is to briefly describe a classic study from social psychology and explore its implications for organisational behaviour.

The Sherifs (Muzafer and Carolyn) wanted to understand processes of conflict development and discrimination and wanted to use a 'natural' situation. They chose an American summer camp and did a series of naturalistic experiments where they manipulated events in the camp without the boys knowing about it. For example: they let boys make friends and then split them into two different groups to see if that affected subsequent competition; they set up "frustrations" effecting both groups in camp to see how they would react.

They were surprised how easy it was to create discrimination as opposed to "healthy competition", and noticed how the groups changed to focus on this conflict:

- both groups developed biased perceptions ("we're ok but they are rubbish!").
- groups became more cohesive.
- leadership became task-centred and authoritarian.

They were also surprised how difficult it was to resolve the conflict and to restore open communication between the groups: only a *series* of what they called "superordinate goals" made any real difference. Superordinate goals are goals where both groups have to co-operate to achieve something which is equally important to both.

The Sherifs suggested that this conflict and the breakdown in communication was a product of the conflict of interests – groups attempted to build their self-esteem by winning the conflict. Later research suggested that intergroup conflict could be much more deep-rooted – we build our sense of self-identity by comparing ourselves with other groups (e.g. Hartley, 1997, Chapter 9).

We cannot resolve theoretical issues here but we can highlight important implications for organisational life.

An organisational team containing members from different areas or functions may fail because members have negative stereotypes of other members and may use the team to foster their own group interests. In other words, the team becomes an arena for intergroup conflict. For example, Putnam and Stohl (1996) describe several studies of cross-functional teams. One team was characterised by "win-lose" negotiation, strong allegiance to the home department, and continuing "power plays". The members took every opportunity to highlight departmental differences, including sarcastic wisecracks about ordering and paying for lunch. This continuous conflict "stifled decision making and led to delays in product introduction" (Putnam and Stohl, 1996, page 160) It is difficult to see how practical techniques for improving meetings suggested in Chapter 13 would make much difference to this situation until the more deep-rooted conflict had been confronted.

In contrast, groups which were sensitive to these problems managed much better, for example, where different department representatives worked very hard to create "win-win" negotiations (creating superordinate goals which everyone could commit to). And this highlights the importance of negotiation and communication processes, recognising there are likely to be different views of reality, as in Box 14.5.

BOX 14.5 MULTIPLE VIEWS OF REALITY

One consequence of intergroup difficulties is the multiple perceptions of reality. Different groups have views of reality which reflect their own experience and interests and this can have very serious consequences.

An example is the accident which befell the NASA space shuttle Challenger which we discussed in Chapter 13 and which exploded just after take-off. Subsequent investigations showed that the potential for this disaster had been recognised and investigated by NASA engineers.

So why was the launch given the go-ahead? Could one problem have been the different perceptions held by different groups in the organisation? Yiannis Gabriel contrasts claims by management that communication was "open and free" with testimony that engineers "agonised over flaws in their equipment" but "did not feel that they could voice their concerns" (Gabriel, 1999, pages 2–5). For further comment on Challenger, see Hartley, 1997.

So how can we develop more effective teams and working groups?

We well as the work of Katzenback and Smith on high-performing teams (already discussed), we suggest you consider the following ideas and approaches.

Michael West (2012) offers one of the most comprehensive reviews of effective teamwork in organisations and suggest five main components which we have turned into questions as below;

- does the team meet its task objectives?
- do the team members develop in terms of well-being?
- is the team viable over time?
- does the team innovate effectively?
- does the team co-operate effectively with other teams?

Similar problems are identified by Joiner Associates (Scholtes, 2003), American management consultants, including clarity in team goals, clearly defined roles, and clear communication. They offer downloadable checklists and emphasise the scientific approach – insisting that opinions are supported by data and that groups avoid jumping to conclusions and/or unwarranted assumptions.

Another example based on observation of a real "world-class" team in action is from Hilarie Owen (1996). Once again the team is characterised by expectations and striving for outstanding performance. Strategies and skills required to create such teams include open communication, negotiating the success criteria, planning both the goals and the process, and effective leadership.

Based on research into "eight of the world's most successful groups", Daniel Coyle proposes three fundamental skills:

Skill 1 – Build Safety – explores how signals of connection generate bonds of belonging and identity. Skill two – Share Vulnerability – explains how habits of

> *mutual risk drive trusting cooperation. Skill 3 – Establish Purpose – tells how narratives create shared goals and values.*
>
> (Coyle, 2018, pages xvi/xvii)

He suggests that these skills:

> *work together from the bottom up, first building group connexion and then channelling it into action*
>
> (Coyle, op cit, page xvii)

How do these skills operate in your organisation?

Does your management focus on building the connections between team members, ensuring that everyone feels psychologically safe and secure and free to contribute? Do team members trust one another, and are they prepared to discuss issues and mistakes openly? Is there a clear shared purpose?

Different ways of mending teamwork

One approach is to simply identify all the process problems which might be impeding group progress and try to resolve each one in turn. For example, Robbins and Finley (1997) list 14 major problems, including confused goals, bad leadership, lack of team trust, and unresolved roles. For each problem, they identify the main symptom to observe and a possible solution. For example, consider the problem of unresolved roles. The main symptom is that "team members are uncertain what their job is" and the solution is to "inform team members what is expected of them" (1997, page 14).

Specific interventions

West (2012) suggests main types of team-building interventions. These have different aims and scope and will satisfy different needs and different situations:

Team start-up

A newly-formed team may need work on clarifying the team objectives, deciding the member's roles and co-ordination, and other forming issues.

Regular formal reviews

This may involve "away-days" where the team takes a day out of the usual routine and environment to reflect on how things are going and being done.

Addressing known task-related problems

This also involves some time out but perhaps not so much as an away-day to focus on a very specific problem.

Identifying problems

This is where the focus of the team review is on identifying task-related problems, where a team feels that it is not functioning as effectively as it could but is not sure why. This may involve discussion or some questionnaire analysis or use of an external facilitator.

Social process interventions

Here the focus is very much on the social climate and member relationships.

Role clarification and negotiation

West describes a useful exercise for this (op cit, page 100).

The Culture Playbook

During his research mentioned above, Daniel Coyle collected examples of team development activities, now published as *60 Highly effective actions to help your group succeed* (Coyle, 2022). These are organised under the three skills mentioned above, and Table 14.5 gives an example of each.

New technologies and team behaviour

Before the pandemic, David Sibbert described a number of ways in which teams could incorporate new technologies into their group process (Sibbert, 2011, page 219ff), including:

- Web conferencing with documents distributed beforehand.
- Web conferencing with documents onscreen plus audio links and web chat.
- Use of graphics tablets and shared document access to develop collaborative documents.

Table 14.5 Examples of team development activities (based on Coyle, 2022)

Skill	Example of activity to encourage positive team development
Build Safety	"Make a habit of over-thanking people". (Tip 6)
Share Vulnerability	"Build the AAR habit". (Tip 28) AAR means "after action review". This process is used "not just to figure out what happened but also to build a shared mental model that helps the group navigate future problems". (op cit, page 10)
Establish Purpose	"Build the habit of a post-meeting reflection". (Tip 53)

All of these are now available (and largely commonplace) in organisations of any size, depending on their location and the quality of internet connections.

These methods certainly add value to a team that has already developed effective team dynamics. Planting new technology on an already dysfunctional group is likely to simply speed up or further complicate the mess.

Best practice in virtual and hybrid teams

In his Culture Playbook mentioned above, Daniel Coyle includes several tips relating to hybrid working. We would emphasise Tip 4 – "To actively avoid Cool-Kid bias" which is

> *"the misperception that working in the physical office possesses more value, leverage, and impact than remote work".*
>
> (Coyle, op cit, page 32ff)

He suggests four specific "antidotes" to this bias which are also reflected in other expert recommendations for good hybrid practice:

- "overcommunicate office happenings".
  This is the notion that remote work remote members should receive as much information as possible so that they don't feel isolated.
- "spotlight the benefits of working remotely".
  Management and team leaders have a particular role to play here.
- "seek gender equity".
  Women can often feel disadvantaged and isolated by hybrid working and it is important to ensure that this does not happen.
- "use in-person interactions like a booster shot" (Coyle, op cit, page 34)
  Recognising the importance and value of in-person interactions, there should be opportunities for team members to meet face-to-face at regular intervals to build relationships.

Managing those online meetings

> *"Video meetings are a source of fatigue and anxiety due to one or all of the following, easily mitigated factors: notice given, length, intensity, frequency and format".*
>
> (O'Meara and Cooper, 2022, page 165)

The other side of the coin is that well-managed and carefully-run meetings can make a significant contribution to team morale and productivity. As well as the factors you need to manage from the above quote, you can incorporate a range of specific behaviours into your practice, including:

- avoiding "Zoom fatigue" through effective timing and agenda planning.
- using the chat box positively to elicit comments and suggestions.
- organising your setting so that you appear professional on screen.

Final words on self-managed teams

The debate on how far organisations can or should implement these is longstanding. For example, Ulich and Weber (1996) emphasised that teams must tackle "whole tasks", where they can set goals, plan what needs to be done, decide how the work should be done, and receive clear feedback on their performance.

Richard Hackman argued that their success depends on three factors:

- the group task is "well designed"– members are motivated by a task which is "meaningful" and receive clear feedback.
- the group is "well composed"– members have the necessary range of skills.
- the group's authority and accountability is clearly specified.

(Hackman, 1990)

These recommendations reflect points we made at the beginning of the chapter when we looked at the differences between groups and teams. The important implication is that organisations cannot just expect these teams to happen overnight:

> *the spread of 'self-managing teams' will be a slow process…it involves very complex organisational interventions, which must be consistent both with the values of an organization and its technology.*
>
> (Ulich and Weber, 1996, page 273)

There are some well-established examples of success. For example, Stewart et al. (1999) reviewed examples of self-managed team interventions in organisations. They highlight some major organisational benefits, such as the Texas Instruments Malaysia (TIM) move to an organisational design based on self-managing work teams in the 1990s. This delivered major savings, quality improvements, low absenteeism etc. Important lessons can be drawn from this and other cases. Team practices must:

- be compatible with overall company philosophy and values, and with the revised organisational structure.
- be supported by senior management.
- ensure that team members have developed necessary new social and technical skills.

Effective implementation is a long and careful process. It took TIM 12 years.

Alongside the changes in flexible and virtual working we discussed in Chapter 5, we see a renewed interest in the possibilities and practicalities of self-managed teams (Waters, 2021).

SUMMARY OF KEY POINTS

- truly effective teams differ from working groups. Critical differences are the level of commitment and the strong sense of mutual support and accountability.
- to create effective teams, we must understand the most important processes which can influence group and team working, including group development, team roles, leadership, problem-solving, and intergroup behaviour.
- there are several models of group development. None are inevitable if the members make an open attempt to review their processes.
- the role of leader may be critical. Modern views of leadership place particular emphasis on aspects of communication.
- models of team roles (e.g. Belbin) suggest we all have consistent preferences. The effectiveness of the team depends upon the combination of team roles. The outcome is not predetermined – the effective group adjusts to any imbalance in roles.
- group communication and interaction processes have an important impact on decision-making.
- teams who are sensitive to intergroup issues tend to be more effective as they can communicate and negotiate in ways which can minimise these problems.
- we can develop teams through improved communication, either by conscious reflection on their major processes and adopting strategies for effective working or by using specific team-building interventions.
- it is important to choose the right team-building intervention to suit the situation: different types have different aims and scope and will satisfy different needs.
- many organisations now use self-managed teams. They are not a "quick fix" and involve complex organisational interventions.

References

Adair, J. (1986) *Effective Leadership: A Modern Guide to Developing Leadership Skills*. London: Pan Books.

Belbin, R.M. (1981) *Management Teams: Why They Succeed or Fail*. Oxford: Butterworth-Heinemann.

Belbin, R.M. (2010) *Team Roles at Work*. Oxford: Butterworth-Heinemann.

Booker, C. (2020) *Groupthink: A study in self-delusion*. London: Bloomsbury.
Bryman, A. (1992) *Charisma and Leadership in Organisations*. London: Sage.
Clampitt, P. and DeKoch, R.J. (2011) *Transforming Leaders into Progress Makers: Leadership for the 21st Century*. London: Sage.
Coyle, D. (2018) *The Culture Code: The Secrets of Highly Successful Groups*. London: Penguin.
Coyle, D. (2022) *The Culture Playbook: 60 Highly Effective Actions to Help Your Group Succeed*. London: Cornerstone.
Gabriel, Y. (1999) *Organizations in Depth: The Psychoanalysis of Organizations*. London: Sage.
Georgiades, M. and Macdonell, R. (1998) *Leadership in Competitive Advantage*. Chichester: Wiley.
Hackman, R. (1990) *Groups that Work (and those that don't]: creating conditions for effective teamwork*. San Francisco, CA: Jossey Bass.
Hall, T. and Janman, K. (2010) *The Leadership Illusion: The Importance of Context and Connections*. Basingstoke: Palgrave Macmillan.
Hartley, P. (1997) *Group Communication*. London: Routledge.
Hartley, P. (1999) *Interpersonal Communication*, 2nd edition. London: Routledge.
Indeed Editorial Team (2022) *10 Principles of Servant Leadership (With Examples)* at: https://www.indeed.com/career-advice/career-development/servant-leadership
Katzenbach, J.R. and Smith, D.K. (1998) *The Wisdom of Teams: Creating a High-Performance Organisation*. London: McGraw-Hill.
Kellerman, B. (2012) *The End of Leadership*. New York: HarperCollins.
Kellerman, B. (2018) *Professionalizing Leadership*. New York: HarperCollins.
Laker, B. (2020) *How Service Leadership Is Changing The World*. At: https://www.forbes.com/sites/benjaminlaker/2020/03/09/service-leadership-is-the-new-servant-leadership/
Mintzberg, H. (1973) *The Nature of Managerial Work*. New York: Harper and Row.
O'Meara, S. and Cooper, C. (2022) *Remote Workplace Culture: How to Bring Energy and Focus to Remote Teams*. London: Kogan Page.
Owen, J. (2020) *The Leadership Skills Handbook: 100 Essential Skills You Need to be a Leader*. London: Kogan Page.
Putnam, L.L. and Stohl, C. (1996) Bona fide groups: An alternative perspective for communication and small group decision making. In Hirokawa, R.Y. and Poole, M.S. (eds) *Communication and Group Decision Making*. Sage Publications, Inc, 147–178. https://doi.org/10.4135/9781452243764.n6.
Robbins, H. and Finley, M. (1997) *Why Teams Don't Work: What Went Wrong and How To Make It Right*. London: Orion.
Roberts, W. (1995) *Make It So: Leadership Lessons from Star Trek: The Next Generation*. New York: Gallery Books.
Robson, D. (2019) *The Intelligence Trap: Revolutionise Your Thinking and Make Wiser Decisions*. Hachette UK.
Scholtes, P.R., Joiner, B.L. and Streibel, B.J. (2003) *The Team Handbook*. Madison, USA: Oriel Incorporated.
Sibbert, D. (2011) *Visual Teams: Graphic tools for commitment, innovation and high performance*. Hoboken, New Jersey: John Wiley.
Sinek, S. (2014) *Leaders Eat Last: Why Some Teams Pull Together and Others Don't*. New York: Portfolio Penguin.
Syed, M. *Rebel Ideas: The Power of Diverse Thinking*. London: John Murray.
Tuckman, B.W. (1965) Developmental sequences in small groups. *Psychological Bulletin* 63: 384–389.
Ulich, E. and Weber, W.G. (1996) Dimensions, criteria and evaluation of work group autonomy. In West, M.A. (ed) *Handbook of Work Group Psychology*. Chichester: John Wiley, 247–282.

Waters, S. (2021) What are self-managed teams (and how can you create them)? *Betterup.com*. https://www.betterup.com/blog/self-managed-teams.
West, M.A. (2012) *Effective Teamwork: Practical Lessons from Organisational Research*, 3rd edition. Oxford: BPS Blackwell.
Wheelan, S.A. (1996) *Group Processes: A Developmental Perspective*. Boston: Allyn and Bacon.

PART 4

Future-gazing

CHAPTER 15

Change and future-gazing

Introduction

The rate of change is ever-increasing. Can we predict what changes are most likely? And what implications do these changes have for our professional practice and development?

Writing predictions, particularly those involving technology, is fraught with pitfalls. Consider these predictions made by "experts" (more examples on the website):

- the chairman of IBM predicting "a world market for maybe five computers" (1943).
- the computing company head – "there is no reason anyone would want a computer in their home" (1977).

This chapter tries to avoid placing "feet in mouth" by suggesting general trends to look out for rather than trying to predict specific detail. In the next and final chapter, we suggest ways we can best manage our professional development in future.

OBJECTIVES

This chapter will:

- show how communication is an essential feature in both the acceptance and implementation of different types of organisational change.
- identify key social, cultural, technological, and economic trends and scenarios.
- (hopefully) stimulate you to continually reflect on these trends and scenarios.

DOI: 10.4324/9781003297550-20

What are the different types of change?

Different definitions of the organisational environment suggest different types and "triggers" of change.

The organisational environment

There are several ways of categorising factors in the organisation's environment. One popular mnemonic – PEST – identifies four factors:

- political/legal (including Government legislation and ideology; employment law; taxation policy; trade regulations etc.).
- economic (including business cycles, inflation, interest rates etc.).
- socio-cultural (including social mobility, lifestyle changes, attitudes to work and leisure, education levels, consumerism etc.).
- technological (including new discoveries, speed of technology transfer, rates of obsolescence etc.).

Some writers turn this into PESTLE – adding Legal and Environmental issues.

These factors combine in particular ways to trigger certain changes. Senior et al suggest that organisations operate in at least three types of environment (Senior, Swailes and Carnall, 2020):

- temporal: historical development over time.
- external: the sum-total of the factors identified above in PEST/PESTLE.
- internal: "first-line responses to changes in the external and temporal environments" (Senior, Swailes and Carnall, 2020, page 22), such as appointing new management after poor economic performance, or installing new computer software to meet legal requirements.

Triggers and sense-making

Change can be "triggered" in several ways, depending on the organisation noticing or anticipating relevant change. And this depends on communication.

History is full of examples of organisations failing to appreciate key changes in their environment. For example, the British motorcycle industry refused to believe that new (cheaper) Japanese machines would affect them, arguing that customers would pay more for "traditional" quality. By the time they recognised the threat, their industry was in terminal decline. See Box 15.1 for further examples.

Many organisations place increasing emphasis on "sense-making" – trying to ensure that their managers and staff continually scan the environment and competitors' behaviour to look for impending change. Management may use particular strategies to ensure this is done, e.g. setting up special groups or task forces.

These strategies will only succeed if results are quickly and accurately communicated to decision-makers within the organisation. If decision-makers do not accept the need for change then the organisation may be in trouble. This highlights the need for an organisational culture which allows "bad news" to reach senior management.

One issue which might prevent bad news "surfacing" is the possible isolation of senior managers. This is a longstanding issue. Chaudry-Lawton and Lawton (1992) found senior executives suffering from "feedback starvation" –

> *subordinates may constantly try to provide their leader with a flow of support and good news.*
>
> (page 7)

If this happens, executives receive distorted pictures of the organisation's performance. This problem can be exacerbated by poor management – Box 15.1 again – or alleviated by good management and sensible use of technology.

BOX 15.1 WHO DO YOU CONSULT ABOUT CHANGE?

Many on-screen features we take for granted nowadays started as developments by Xerox – e.g. desktop icons. So why didn't Xerox become the early market leader? Why was it left for Apple, who came along several years after?

One factor was the way that Xerox demonstrated their prototype incorporating these features (the Alto). Alto was presented to male Xerox executives and their wives. Many wives had secretarial/administrative experience and were immediately impressed with Alto's ease of use. But the men did not understand the benefits, as one Alto inventor admitted – they "had no background, really, to grasp the significance of it" (Shapiro, 1996, page 127)

You may not be surprised to learn that the male viewpoint prevailed!

Another example of male arrogance and insensitivity leading to economic decline and failure is the British computer industry after World War 2, as summarised by Marie Hicks (2017):

> *In the 1940s, computer operation and programming was viewed as women's work - but by the 1960s, as computing gained prominence and influence, men displaced the thousands of women who had been pioneers in a feminised field of endeavour, and the field acquired a distinctly masculine image.*
>
> (page 1)

From the position where "Britain led the world in cutting-edge computing technology" (page 4), its computing industry failed to capitalise on the expertise built up by their female workforce. The UK government played a central role in shaping the industry and it "neglected most of its trained technical workforce" (page 15).

It would be nice to think that modern organisations had left behind these sexist attitudes but there is plenty of evidence that such practices are still prevalent.

Type and rate of change

We must also consider the rate and scale of change. Dunphy and Stace (1993) suggested four different types:

- "fine tuning" (small change in department(s)).
- "incremental adjustment" (gradual changes).
- "modular transformation" (radical change in one area).
- "corporate transformation" (radical change right across the organisation; major changes to organisational structures and procedures).

Unfortunately, this (and similar models) contains a dangerous assumption – that everyone in the organisation shares the same definition or understanding of the change. What senior management sees as "incremental" is often perceived as a fundamental shift by the employees involved.

This raises issues of communication: how is change communicated to staff?

How is change described? For example, consider the organisation which decided to move all salaried staff to a new "more flexible" contract. Senior management extolled the virtues of the "new, professional contract" in meetings and the company newsletter. They saw this as one step towards a more "flexible" organisation. Staff saw the new contract as a fundamental shift in their relationship with management – they resented the implication that their previous contract (and behaviour) was somehow "unprofessional".

There are also questions about the pace of change. Many models of change in the literature were written before the pandemic, i.e. before *every* organisation had to change "overnight".

The organisational life cycle

Conventional organisation theory suggests that organisations grow through at least four stages:

- entrepreneurial: a small number of people form the organisation. If it grows, it confronts a crisis of leadership – it must decide its future strategy.

- collective: the organisation has grown. Appropriate division of labour becomes critical. Departments or other subdivisions need managing and co-ordinating.
- formalisation: the organisation is big enough to need more formal systems and procedures. These could become over-bureaucratic – there may be a crisis of "red tape".
- elaboration: the company reaches a plateau and performance may even decline. Can it change to remain competitive? (Senior, Swailes and Carnall, 2020)

There are further complications. Organisations can experience "waves" of change. Change does not just happen and go away – it continually reappears in various forms. A period of relative calm involving incremental change may be followed by dramatic and turbulent change.

Strategies for change

If you are proposing and/or managing change, what strategy will you use?

Alternative strategies involve different approaches to communication, including:

- education.
- participation.
- intervention/manipulation.
- management direction.
- coercion.

"Nudge theory" uses a mix of these approaches (Thaler and Sunstein, 2021). This aims to influence people's behaviour by adjusting their environment so they make specific "decision choices" – they are "nudged" in the desired direction. It is "based on indirect encouragement and enablement. It avoids direct instruction or enforcement" (Businessballs, 2013/4).

Many organisations established "nudge units" to implement this approach, including the UK government. Their Behavioural Insights Team has since been privatised and you can find examples of their current work on their website (https://www.bi.team).

Each strategy has pros and cons. For example, participation can be time-consuming but increases the chances of acceptance. A very directive strategy may be quick but will often be resented and obstructed by staff.

Perhaps the most important conclusion is that there should be a strategy to manage change which is communicated and open to feedback.

Effective change messages

One useful review of research suggested that an effective change message incorporates five components (Armenakis and Bedeian, 1999):

- this organisation needs to change.
- we can change successfully.
- change is in our best interest.
- the people affected support the change.
- this change is right for this organisation.

But we cannot just rely on "messages" – we also need to consider the stages of change and the organisational context (see more examples on the website):

Stages of change

One of the most famous stage theories came from Kurt Lewin. He proposed three stages: (Lewin, 1947)

- unfreezing.
  People must see a reason to move from their existing attitudes or beliefs – their existing attitudes must be "unfrozen".
- changing.
- refreezing.
  New attitudes/behaviours are tested to see if they "work".
  They only become embedded if this refreezing process is successful.

A practical example of this often-neglected final process is the effectiveness of management training courses, e.g. courses designed to make supervisors adopt more democratic leadership. Suppose we find the course "works" when we measure supervisors' attitudes immediately after the course. What if we send these supervisors back to an autocratic environment *where nothing else has changed*? Research into situations like this suggests that, after a short while, supervisors are overwhelmed by the unchanging prevailing culture. Their attitudes and behaviour can become more autocratic than before! Refreezing is ignored.

Johnson et al (2014) offer an expanded three-step model:

- unfreezing – organisational anticipation.
  Management persuade staff of the need to change.
- organisational flux
  "competing views surface about the causes of, and remedies for, the problems" (page 453).

- information-building
  Managers find information to support their position. They need to manage this process (e.g. through strategy workshops and/or project groups) rather than leave it to political in-fighting.
- experimentation
  New ideas are tried out.
- refreezing
  Organisations must ensure new practices are embedded and staff are supported during the transition.

Learning organisations as the answer?

One solution to change issues (strongly advocated in the 1990s) is the "learning organisation" – an organisation actively embracing change as ongoing and inescapable, where all employees commit to continuous learning and self-improvement.

This approach challenges traditional practices. For example, research and development (R&D) is not a specific department/section. As everyone is responsible for contributing to development, R&D functions are integrated into production facilities.

Another important feature is the leader's role. Senge (1994) argued that learning organisations must abandon traditional views of leaders as "special people who set the direction, make the key decisions, and energise the troops" (page 5). Instead, leaders must focus on the "creative tension" created by the gap between where the organisation is now and where it wants to be in future. They need to ensure the organisation has a coherent vision of where it wants to be.

Evolving scenarios and the implications for communication

Scenarios introduced in earlier chapters will be particularly significant.

Globalisation

This can be defined in different ways. For example, views of how trading will evolve range from a "scattered" world – a future of monopolistic unregulated competition – to a more connected world where companies collaborate domestically and internationally with enlightened Governments regulating for the global good.

Underpinning such integration/collaboration is the internet. But increasing the interdependence of economies, communications and cultures depends on political systems. And there are disturbing examples of increasing control and censorship in countries like China. There are also consequences from tragedies such as the war in Ukraine which will take a long time to resolve. And there are long-term consequences of political turmoil such as UK government changes in the autumn of 2022.

Portfolio careers and job change

The notion of a "job for life" has been eroded in the private sector (less so in the public sector), leading to very different work arrangements, from full-time, to part-time, to "zero hours", with different employment status.

For individuals, this probably means "portfolio careers", with less upward promotion and more horizontal career development.

One key impact of this jobs market is the need for individuals to take control of their careers as early as possible – careers may well include several major changes of direction.

Flexible and virtual working

Flexible and virtual working is now commonplace. As well as providing more efficient support systems, IT departments face increasing challenges around security as well as compliance with internal protocols and Government regulations e.g. data protection.

Blurring of professional and private lives

Changes described above increasingly blur our professional and private lives.

Work-life balance

During/following the pandemic, many of us became more aware of limitations in our current balance. This has affected the job market – individuals seek out jobs offering more flexible working conditions.

The nature of offices

Increases in flexible and mobile working beg the question – what will offices become?

Collaboration, collaboration, collaboration

Effective collaboration is a core capability for all professional staff – not just with local colleagues, but with partners, suppliers, associates and clients – locally, nationally, and internationally.

Digital capability and integration

Further software and hardware advances will support the plans announced by Microsoft and Google in 2023 to integrate AI into *all* forms of everyday and professional communication supported by computers.

Digital literacy/fluency is critical

One thread running through all these scenarios is the need for IT systems to support flexible and mobile working and provide access to different communications channels, networks, systems, data and information.

Digital literacy becomes ever more important, requiring more sophisticated capabilities – we need to become more proactive in identifying, choosing, and implementing appropriate technology.

Open innovation and new product development

Open innovation can be realised in different ways. For example, consider how the mountain bike evolved (Charles Leadbeater, TED, 2007). A group of Californian kids, frustrated by the inadequacies of normal bikes over rough terrain, cobbled together parts (e.g. from motorcycles) to construct the first "mountain bike" – an idea totally driven by consumer need.

Developments in the internet and social media now make open innovative practices both easier and more likely:

- companies use social media to create communities of interest and interact with customers, helping to identify new markets and new product ideas.
- open source products offer another model. Here, disparate individuals (sometimes companies) collaborate to develop products that are "open for use". Examples include open-source content management systems such as Joomla, Drupal, and Wordpress.
- companies diversify their products to build a community of customers.

Equality, Diversity and Inclusion v internationalisation

In the UK, we see moves to improving opportunities for all, increasing awareness of racism, gender stereotyping, LGBTQi rights, and the benefits of neurodiversity (with members of LinkedIn listing dyslexia as a skill) etc. These moves may clash with expectations and cultures in international markets. This can create tensions as well as present opportunities to influence the creation of a fairer world.

Increased individuality

The rise of the "social influencer" allows these individuals to have significant influence and earning power that sits outside of traditional business structures. Influencers are themselves subject to the influence of large corporations who buy access to their followers.

Internet ethos and control

All these open approaches require a more "social" and cooperative approach to innovation which does chime with the original ethos of the Internet.

And that takes us to our final chapter where we discuss how you can use ideas from this book to build your own professional development.

References

Armenakis, A.A. and Bedeian, A.G. (1999) Organisational change: A review of theory and research in the 1990s. *Journal of Management* 25(3): 293–315.

Chaudry-Lawton, R. and Lawton, R. (1992) *Ignition: Sparking Organisational Change*. London: BCA.

Dunphy, D. and Stace, D. (1993) The strategic management of corporate change. *Human Relations* 45(8): 917–918.

Hicks, M. (2017) *Programmed Inequality: How Britain Discarded Women Technologists and Lost its Edge in Computing*. London: MIT Press.

Johnson, G., Whittington, R., Scholes K., Regner, P. and Angwin, D. (2014) *Fundamentals of Strategy* [3rd edition) London: Pearson

Leadbetter, C. (2007) The era of open innovation [video]. TED Conferences. https://www.ted.com/speakers/charles_leadbeater.

Lewin, K. (1947) Group decision and social change. In Newcomb, T. and Hartley, F. (ed) *Readings in Social Psychology*. New York: Henry Holt and Company.

Mahase, E. (2022) Type 1 diabetes drug was withdrawn because of "commercial conflict of interest" charity argue. *BMJ* 375: 0373. https://doi.org/10.1136/bmj.o373.

Shapiro, E.C. (1996) *Fad Surfing in the Boardroom: Reclaiming the courage to manage in the age of instant answers*. Oxford: Capstone.

Senge, P.M. (1994) The leaders new work: Building learning organisations. In Mabey, C. and Iles, P. (eds) *Managing Learning*. London: Routledge.

Senior, B., Swailes, S. and Carnall, C.A. (2020) *Organizational Change*, 6th edition. Upper Saddle River: Pearson.

Thaler, R.H. and Sunstein, C.R. (2021) *Nudge: The Final Edition*. London: Allen Lane.

CHAPTER 16

Planning your future

Introduction

We keep returning to an image of the future – a world of change, uncertainty, and unpredictability as the pace of technological innovation increases and disrupts the way we work, learn, and live.

How can we cope with all this uncertainty and change?

We advocate an approach to your future career planning which uses two key themes:

Adapt basic principles of effective communication to your context

The principles in Chapter 2 will (hopefully) stand the test of time. Please use and *adapt* these to guide your communication (and your organisation's) irrespective of which media/technologies you adopt in future.

Adopt the review, plan, and improve approach

Chapter 1 introduced the "review, plan, and improve" approach – what we also call the "researcher approach". For example, you can use this approach towards emerging technologies and new media. It means spending time horizon-scanning and getting to grips with emerging technologies. You need to work out how you and your organisation can best use them. And you cannot simply rely on your computing or IT departments – unfortunately, these departments are often constrained by pressures which do not give them time or resources to come up with creative/innovative uses of technology.

Using these themes, we suggest you develop a plan covering all the areas in Figure 16.1. After a few words on main headings, the rest of this chapter focuses on the following as both priorities and good places to start:

- proactive professional development.

DOI: 10.4324/9781003297550-21

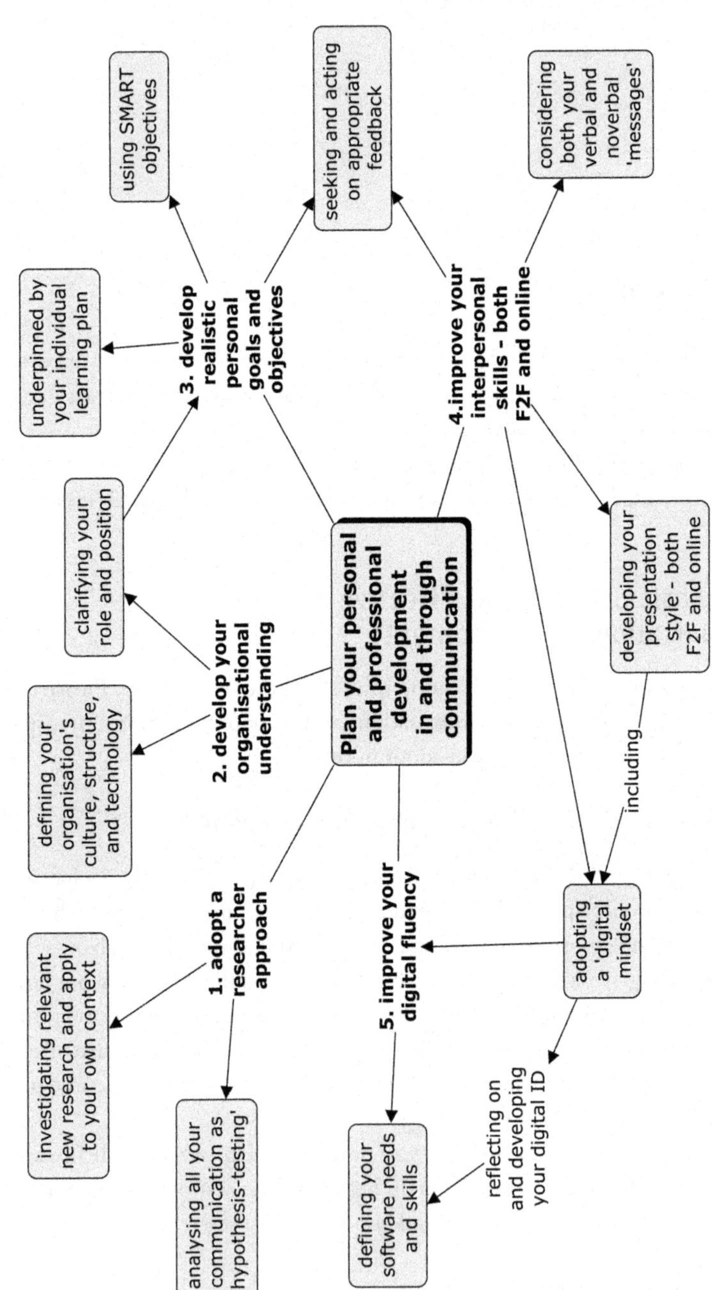

Figure 16.1 Mapping your professional future

- recognising boundaries and managing your digital identity (ID).
- collaboration and networking.

Organisational understanding

We offered several different models of organisational culture and structure. You need to decide which is most relevant in your context and consider how this affects your behaviour and communication. If you do happen to find yourself in a "toxic" culture then you should move on (quickly).

Personal goals

These should be both realistic and challenging. They should also be flexible as you respond to the uncertainties of change.

Interpersonal skills

The important principle here is to develop your skills to cope with *both* face-to-face and online situations – we cannot predict the balance of those in your working life over the next decades.

Digital fluency

The term "fluency" suggests that this is more than just acquiring a set of technical skills. As we suggest in previous chapters, this is an area we *all* need to further develop over the next decade.

Proactive professional development

Taking responsibility for your own learning is one overarching principle to follow in future – whether you or your employer are funding your learning programmes. The uncertainty of the jobs market, the growth of the gig economy (Kessler, 2018), the emergence of "portfolio" careers, and the likelihood of step-changes in careers means that employers are less likely to fund ongoing professional development. This leaves us as individuals to pick up the tab for our "lifelong learning".

We also predict further growth of "learn while you earn" approaches: part-time courses, distance learning courses, or participating in work-based learning programmes.

Smart universities and colleges work closely with employers to design learning programmes that serve the dual purpose of developing employees as well as helping the employer organisation to improve, aligning with the organisation's strategic goals. Even smarter universities and colleges help organisations to measure their impact. We see this happening in economies worldwide, e.g. recent initiatives in the USA to rebuild regional economies through local partnerships, including colleges and universities.

New online services are appearing to support ongoing learning, not just from traditional providers. Growing support for "open" approaches to education/training means more OERs (open educational resources). These typically comprise small chunks of digital learning materials which can be used standalone or by course developers to incorporate in modules or programmes.

One important development of the OER concept was the MOOC (massive open online course). The year 2012 was proclaimed "The Year of the MOOC" by *The New York Times* with assertions that this approach would "save higher education's crises and educate the world using Internet-based approaches" (Riel and Lawless, 2017). This "revolution" did not materialise but MOOCs have become a significant component in the educational landscape which are likely to develop further and which we should all explore.

Other learning concepts likely to increase in use include:

Personalisation of learning

Following the pandemic, worldwide student numbers continue to increase in higher education, and educators generally acknowledge the need to focus on 'personalisation' of learning, helping learners to plan their learning to align with their own needs and goals, and to help them monitor and assess their development.

Social, informal, peer, and work-based learning and assessment

Increasing recognition of the importance of learning that occurs in social and work-based environments (not just in the classroom) leads to more collaborative programmes, increasing accreditation of experiential learning – Accreditation of Prior Experiential Learning (APEL) – as well as designing learning programmes that are based around individual employee working practices and activities.

Core to making all of these developments work is the efficient and effective use of communications technologies and online learning techniques.

New and changing providers of education and training

Increasing availability of educational resources and learning tools on the internet raises questions for the future role of universities/colleges and training providers.

As well as many universities offering online education and training, either on their own or through agencies such as FutureLearn (https://www.futurelearn.com), we see more "non-traditional providers" entering the online market, such as courses offered by Linkedin, or the Multiverse, founded by Euan Blair in 2016, now with degree-awarding powers (https://www.multiverse.io).

Increasing coaching/mentoring

One crucial role for all providers is that of accreditation and "brands" are extremely important in the education sector. However, there is more to education than just downloading chunks of knowledge/learning. There are issues of broadening horizons, raising aspirations and motivation, stimulating creative and critical thinking and, overall, instilling a passion for learning. Coaching and mentoring can be very effective techniques here both face-to-face and remotely. The important general principle here is to:

- identify important gaps in your skills and/or understanding.
- find a way to plug that gap (see further suggestions on the website).

Recognising your own professional and personal boundaries, (public and private spheres) and managing your digital ID

Writing online typically blurs the boundaries between communicating with internal and external audiences. It can also blur the boundaries between the personal and professional parts of your individual identity. We all need to manage this (see Chapter 9 of O'Meara and Copper, 2022 for further discussion and useful personal examples).

The distinction between the professional and private spheres of life used to be much clearer. Such a distinction was, and is, exemplified in rules that limit or prohibit interactions outside of business interests within the working day, e.g. no personal phone calls during business hours. In contrast, in the online world, there are benefits in being able to engage with external audiences in a personal way in order to build professional identity and enhance the reputation of a business. However, not everyone is equally equipped or comfortable with managing communication in such a range of contexts. It can be useful to review how and when different media are used from your own perspective.

The following model provides a visual representation of public-private and personal-professional communication categories:

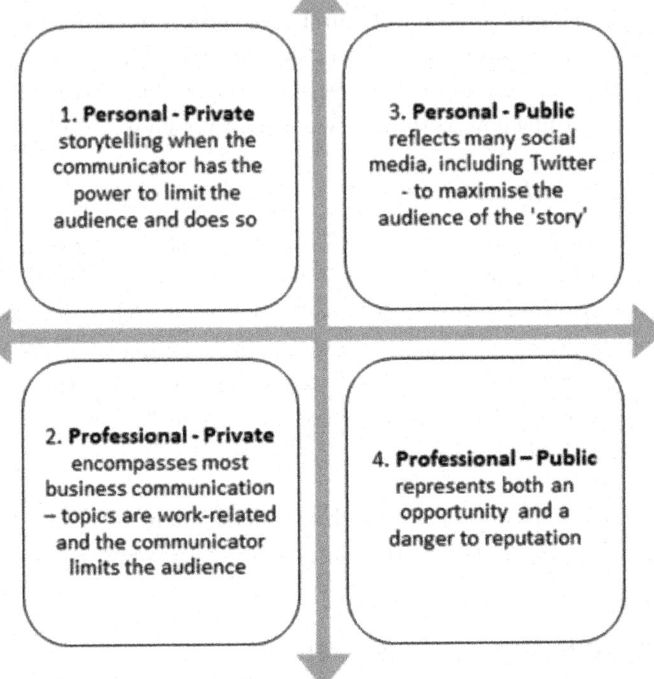

Figure 16.2 Reflective tool to analyse your own use of social media (adapted from Jameson, 2014)

BOX 16.1 CHOOSING TO MAKE BEST USE OF TECHNOLOGY AND SOCIAL MEDIA

In the spirit of "review, plan, and improve", we offer a couple of personal examples which (hopefully) demonstrate how we have taken to heart principles and techniques recommended in this book

From Helena

As someone who works for a large employer within a specific sphere, has a professional identity that overlaps with the business of my university employer, a small business owner, and having a religious affiliation, I have to think carefully about the different social media that I use and how I use them. The model described in Figure 16.1 was useful in identifying when to use which social media in a way that reflects my own sense of personal integrity. For me, it has been important to keep the various forms of social media that I use for specific parts of my professional identity separate, e.g. Facebook, Instagram, and Google, to support the reputation and branding of my small business, whereas Twitter and LinkedIn are linked to my professional, academic identity.

From Peter

As a lifetime educator, now part-time educational consultant, I am also selective in my use of web and social media. My suspicion of corporations' use of data influences my selection, e.g. DuckDuckGo for internet search. More positively, I could not have maintained professional practice over the last few years without technology, especially:

- Zoom, Teams, and Wonder.me (webinars and meetings). And YouTube for recordings of ones I missed!
- occasional Facebook/Instagram for family use.
- Twitter for professional messages and networking (although I suspect Twitter will lose me through Elon Musk's direction!).
- ChatGPT/Bing and the explosion in potential of AI (with some concerns about future directions and implications).

For example, my Twitter use includes the weekly educational Tweetchat, where we respond online to six questions (a new one every ten minutes) set by that week's facilitators (https://lthechat.com).

Concept mapping has also been very important, both personally/professionally (see Figure 16.3 below) and as trigger for research into notetaking (with Dawne Irving-Bell and colleagues). We are now planning to generate further resources for the National Teaching Repository. (See the website for further details of these initiatives.)

From Susie

In my professional life, I use LinkedIn regularly to network with colleagues, alumni, and also special interest groups. The Business School in which I work also has a dedicated area on LinkedIn to maintain contact with our current students and our alumni. This proves highly beneficial in creating links with employers and invitations for guest speakers to enrich and enhance student opportunities. The links with special interest groups helps to generate conversations around my research and informs my teaching both in Marketing and specialist study skills.

Box 16.1 shows that we use the web and social media in different ways – but we are all selective in the applications. Other people comfortably manage their personal and professional online presence within the same space. Where this is done well, there can be significant benefits both to the individual and to the business(es) that they represent.

A classic high-profile example of this is Fernando Aguirre - an early adopter of Twitter in the 2000s for personal communication, often tweeting about his love

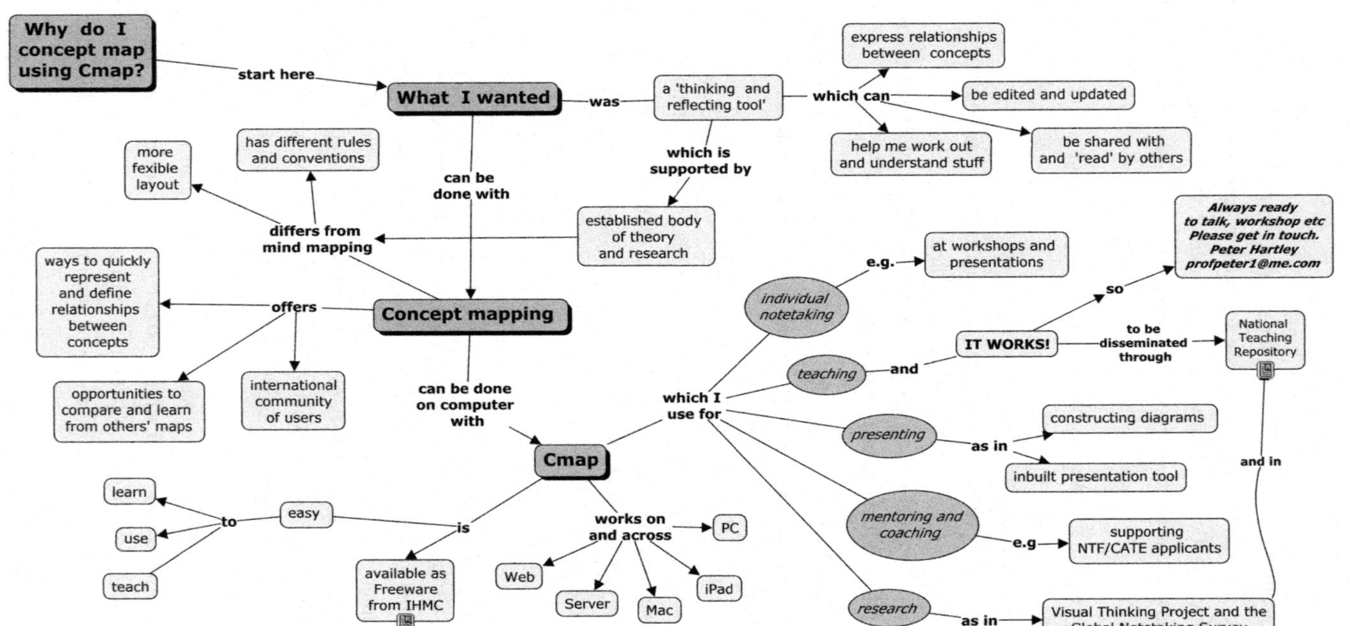

Figure 16.3 Why I concept map with Cmap

of baseball. In 2011, he was CEO of Chiquita Brands International considering relocating its headquarters to another state. Twitter provided a space to discuss this possibility in the public sphere in a way not possible before – and it was 24 hours a day, seven days a week. When Aguirre was asked about the public's level of engagement (in both cities and states) he tweeted:

> *2Pleasantly surprised. Positive for both cities. Direct contact consumers. Creative. Fun. Humbling and humanizing 4 CEO*
>
> (Darics, 2016, Jameson, 2014)

Pitfalls and cautionary tales

There are pitfalls to developing an online presence. Before entering a new professional sphere, you should complete a personal audit of your online presence, redacting or deleting past posts. Many if not most employers now check candidates' online presence – few of us would want an employer or client to access online versions of our teenage self. We have already mentioned case studies of "careless" tweets or other posts which destroyed careers by going viral (Ronson, 2015).

Collaboration, co-creation, and networking

During the pandemic, the availability of applications, such as Teams, and the awareness of opportunities to co-create documents online improved and, in many cases, led to better collaborations around documents. What has also happened is a realisation that personal style influences decision-making on how we can best collaborate online. To illustrate the point, Box 16.2 compares our own experience and preferences – we use very different techniques for personal note-taking and document development.

BOX 16.2 TECHNIQUES FOR DOCUMENT DEVELOPMENT

Our techniques reflect both personal differences and our commitment to collaboration.

From Peter: using concept maps as a collaboration tool

I use concept maps as an alternative to conventional notes. I explain my attachment to concept maps in the concept map which is Figure 16.3 (see the website for further explanation) and can highlight uses especially relevant to this book:

- as a tool in meetings, stimulating dialogue, and focusing attention on main points.
- summarising a discussion.
- constructing diagrams for publication.

From all of us: developing our collaboration

Up to the submission of the final draft of this book to Routledge, all three of us had *never* met face-to-face. Thanks to the pandemic, we had to prepare the book proposal through email. We then developed a collaboration based on remote working and weekly online meetings – not always straightforward – as the following changes illustrate:

- chapters were uploaded to a shared area in Teams to allow access and asynchronous review of individual chapters.
- initially, this worked well for Helena and Susie who were able to work together on a single chapter and see suggestions and changes that were being made. Working for the same institution meant access to the necessary online spaces/tools was straightforward.
- unfortunately, Peter had difficulties with remote access.
- Helena and Susie also found challenges due to different, well-established, styles of working, and competing work demands at different times of the year.
- after discussion (and with deadlines looming), we reverted to exchanging document files with comments and tracked changes. Helena continued to use documents within Teams.
- Susie found she needed to work away from the PC/laptop to review the structure/contents of chapters before reassembling them into single documents.
  Her approach reflects her research with neurodivergent students, emphasising the place and use of physical and visual resources (e.g. flipchart paper, Post-it notes and headings) in both individual and collaborative settings. Online contexts struggle to emulate this, even where programmes can mirror the processes.
- in contrast, Helena's cross-faculty and cross-university project work meant she was very used to working with colleagues, using shared technologies to develop documents within short timeframes (usually achieved more quickly than by using traditional email).

A few observations from our experience:

- pressures caused by the pandemic meant that we did not have enough time to fully map out our process at the start.
- some longer meetings (ideally face-to-face to help open discussion) at the start would have helped (especially as we did not know one another).
- we were able to adjust to our different styles as the writing developed.

This brief account of our experience highlights general principles for collaborative communication:

- make sure you spend sufficient time in the initial planning stages, especially with a newly formed group.
- if an approach is not working then discuss it and find an alternative that does.
- we have different styles of writing and preparing documents – it is important to find a way of collaborating which plays to everyone's strengths.

Using these reflections as a starting point, consider what approach to documents (and to communication more generally) has been adopted by your organisation and compare that with your own ideal approach.

Final words on the future

There is perhaps one final message about dealing with the unpredictability of emerging technologies – rather than focusing on predicting the future, instead focus on "inventing the future".

We cannot all be digital entrepreneurs, but we can all influence and shape the way we adopt and use new technologies for communications purposes and it is important to believe that we can "invent" (or at least influence) the future – this is after all, one of our basic principles of communication: the ability to influence has become a key communication skill in modern organisations, and we wish you good fortune in all your efforts.

References

Darics, E. (2016) *Writing Online: A Guide to Effective Digital Communication at Work*, 1st edition. New York: New York Business Expert Press (Corporate communication collection).

Jameson, D.A. (2014) Crossing public-private and personal-professional boundaries: How changes in technology may affect CEOs' communication. *Business and Professional Communication Quarterly* 77(1): 7–30.

Kessler, S. (2018) *Gigged: The Gig Economy, the End of the Job and the Future of Work*. London: Penguin Random House.

O'Meara, S. and Cooper, C. (2022) *Remote Workplace Culture: How to Bring Energy and Focus to Remote Teams*. London: Kogan Page.

Riel, J. and Lawless, K.A. (2017) Developments in MOOC technologies and participation since 2012: Changes since "The year of the MOOC." In Khosrow-Pour, M. (ed) *Encyclopedia of Information Science and Technology* (4th edition). Hershey, PA: IGI Global. Available at SSRN: https://ssrn.com/abstract=2827693.

INDEX

Page numbers in *italics* mark the location of figures, while page numbers in **bold** indicate tables.

Printed in the United States
by Baker & Taylor Publisher Services